HIS-Story
THROUGH
HIS-Bloodline

The Genesis Pre-Flood Prophecy of the Ages

Cindy Lyons

RoseDog 🐾 Books
PITTSBURGH, PENNSYLVANIA 15238

HIS-Story through HIS-Bloodline:
The Genesis Pre-flood Prophecy of the Ages

Printed in the United States of America.

First Edition.

RoseDog Books
585 Alpha Drive
Suite 103
Pittsburgh, PA 15238
Visit our website at www.rosedogbookstore.com

ISBN: 978-1-64957-894-5
eISBN: 978-1-64957-915-7

TO MY FAMILY AND FRIENDS, ESPECIALLY THOSE CLOSEST TO ME

Thank you for your continued support of this labor of love and all your tireless efforts that it took to help me complete this book. I stand in awe as to what the Lord hath done.

TABLE OF CONTENTS

CHAPTER 9 – METHUSELAH

CHAPTER 10 – LAMECH

CHAPTER 11 – NOAH

CHAPTER 12 – THE CONCLUSION

BIBLIOGRAPHY

TABLE OF CHARTS

INTRODUCTION

One Man, One Race, One Bloodline

We all know that every family's genealogy has a personal story to tell. It is the same within the family of Jesus Christ. If we believe the Bible is true, then Adam is the father of us all. By tracing Father Adam's family tree to Christ, Scripture instantly selects one family on the earth to represent all families from every nation and every kingdom. It is time we get the story straight because Christ's bloodline lives on to tell His story!

The title, *HIS-Story Through HIS-Bloodline*, understandably then, seeks to stress how the pre-flood family members of Christ have inside information to pass on to future generations. This is realized from the abridged character and literary devices employed by the Genesis narrative, which preserves their record. All that seems buried and dead suddenly springs to new life when "His story" is revealed through "His bloodline."

Divine DNA Delivers a Divine Story

DNA is said to be the blueprint of life and the Bible says that Christ is the sum of all life.[1] He is "the beginning and end, the first and the last," and "the sum of all things" through judgment.[2] As the Word, Christ is a "living letter" that creates an everlasting document.[3] Christ's birth into the Adamic family is the day eternity penetrated the earth. The only "skeletal remains" we have left of Him are His genealogy and the legacies left behind. His record is their record. Their record has become part of His eternal script and DNA.

Therefore, when we consider Christ's family tree and trace it back to Adam's third son, Seth, we suddenly realize that Cain and Abel are excluded from the record. Such a fatal omission is understood as being "blotted out" of the book of God.[4] Consequently, the omission of Adam's first two sons within the holy lineage forces us to view any omission as an eternal loss.

---

[1] Rom. 8:29; Eph. 1:10.

[2] **Rev. 22:12-13:** And, behold, I come quickly; and my reward *is* with me, to give every man according as his work shall be. I am Alpha and Omega, the beginning and the end, the first and the last.

[3] Jn. 1:1, 14; 2 Cor. 3:2-6.

[4] Ex. 32:32-33; Rev. 20:15.

More importantly, when we consider that out of Adam's three sons, Seth's line is the only line that survived the flood and finishes with Christ, who is eternal life itself. The Biblical framework is not only deliberate but immensely profound. We are to understand that Adam's two lost sons represent the two lost lines of the family, who in turn, represent all lost family lines of the earth. With that breathtaking thought, Christ's mission "to seek and to save" takes on a whole new dimension.

Could the summary theme of Christ and His line in the pre-flood world of the Genesis narrative be a clue that there is more to the bloodline's story? Could Christ's lineage in that same period reflect a summarized plan of the ages that end in judgment like the message of the Bible? The answer is yes, which explains the subtitle of this book—*The Genesis Pre-Flood Prophecy of the Ages*.

The Framing Chapters of HIS-Story

The first four chapters set the stage and will introduce the "first family" as the cast of characters for *HIS-Story*. They are Adam, Eve, and the family lines of their three sons[5] within the pre-flood period. As their personal contributions and figurative constructs are garnered, their collective efforts set the stage for the overarching story in terms of Christ and His eternal family.

Chapters 5-11 begin tracing *HIS-Story*, by evaluating the ten members of Christ's lineage in the pre-flood period in comparison with the summary statement that they produce from the meaning of their names. This process will amazingly take us on a journey of discovering the secrets of the family, their fate, as well as the fate of the world.

Chapter 12 concludes by charting the restoration of all things as disclosed in the final pages of the Bible's last book. Here, the epic story ends with an epic ending. The Divine purpose can finally be surveyed in all its splendor as one glorious undertaking. It is interwoven within the fabric of time, which moves into eternity as all things are reconciled in Christ, who is the sum of all things.

The Bloodline Challenge

Once we realize that the pre-flood period represents a prophetic plan of the ages, we cannot help but become enthralled with the wonder of how

---

[5] Scholars hold that Adam and Eve had many children after the fall, but the Genesis record is only concerned with three: Firstborn Cain, Abel, and Seth, the appointed replacement son. This assumes Abel's genealogy is omitted in the record because he died before he had children.

His line, saved by His blood, lives to tell *HIS-Story* to warn future generations. The challenge for the reader is to consider the bloodline messages
as powerful evidence of how the Bible is fully capable of interpreting itself. [6]
The purpose is to satisfy those who hunger and thirst for Truth.

This epic tale is not presented from what we think we know, but instead,
has been preserved in a record written in blood, that is, the very bloodline
of Christ. Are we ready for the bloodline challenge?

---

[6] **2 Pet. 1:20:** Knowing this first, that no prophecy of the scripture is of any private interpretation.

CHAPTER 1
Charting the Family Tree

With our introduction out of the way, the main takeaway is to remember that as far as Scripture is concerned, all genealogical records begin with fallen Adam. His family represents all the fallen families of the earth. Out of Adam's three sons of record, Seth is the only line that survived the flood to start life anew because his line ends with Christ, who gives new life. From that profound platform, we can now add the literary elements of the family tree.

Genesis Chapter 4 traces Adam's line through his firstborn, Cain. Adam's second son, Abel, was killed causing the line to skip to Adam's third son, Seth, in the next chapter. Seth's line is known as the "blessed line," while Cain and his line are typically viewed as the "cursed line." For our discussion, they will simply be known as the "Christ-line" and the "Cain-line."

Besides possessing a genealogical record that is preserved by Holy Writ, both lines share another interesting feature. Both can form a "summary statement," from the meaning of each member's name. To better illustrate, the genealogies of Adam's first and third sons will be displayed in vertical charts (Chart 1 and Chart 3) to review separately. Then the two lines will be compared together in a final chart (Chart 4) so that we can get a better understanding of what we are working with.

The Christ-Line Chart

Our review starts with the Christ-line. This chart reflects all ten members listed in Genesis 5:3-32. The grouping begins with Adam then traces through Seth to end with Noah. Like all official registers, the order of entry is governed by the eldest to the youngest, which correlates with a fixed "generational" time in history.

The Christ-line chart not only lists each member in their sequential order, but it also includes the corresponding meaning of each name. The summary statement that is produced is shown directly below the chart.

The Christ–Line Genealogy Chart
(Genesis 5:3-32)

No.	Name	Meaning[7]
1	Adam	Man
2	Seth	Appointed
3	Enosh (Enos)	Mortal
4	Kenan (Cainan)	Sorow
5	Mahaalaaleel	Praise, illumination/glory of God (the Blessed God)
6	Jared	Decent, coming down (shall come down)
7	Enoch	Taught, dedicated (teaching/discipline)
8	Methuselah	When he is dead it shall be sent (his death shall bring)
9	Lamech	Powerfully humbled, lowered (the despairing)
10	Noah	Rest

Chart 1 — The Christ-Line Genealogy Chart

---

[7] Collective, general, and/or contextual meaning key sources: *The Scripture Lexicon, or a Dictionary of Above Four Thousand Proper Names of Persons and Places* (1797); *Abarim Publications, Meaning and Etymology of the Names* (2011); *BDB Lexicon*, (1906); *Strong's Concordance* (1890); *The Complete Word Study Dictionary* (1992); and *Jones' Dictionary* (1990). However, the most publicly recognized rendering is used herein, being popularized by Chuck Missler and his ministry, Koinonia House, Inc., which generally follows the entries from *The Scripture Lexicon* (1797), except for Seth and Kenan, in which case Abarim Publications offers additional insight. Also note that the *Strong's Concordance* is not a lexicon, even though the 1890 version added a Hebrew, Chaldee, and a N. T. Greek Dictionary to its offerings. In his preface, Strong advised that the purpose for such additions was to serve those "who have not a wish or the ability to use more copious and elaborate Lexicon." By design, *Strong's Concordance* can only serve as a starting point in one's studies because it is limited to "gloss definitions" for its indexed and uniquely numbered entries. On the upside, the concordance provides a quick method to look up words to get a general sense of its meaning as well as to identify other occurrences and how it was translated elsewhere in the original language, at least in those manuscripts used by the *King James Bible*.

Christ-Line Summary Statement:
Man, appointed mortal sorrow, [but] the Blessed God shall
come down teaching, His death shall bring the despairing rest."

It is remarkable to think that from the meaning of these names, an actual summary statement emerges. The words shown in brackets make the sentence easier to understand, but those words can be easily left out. Without the aid of the words in the brackets, it would read more like: "Man, appointed mortal sorrow, the Blessed God shall come down teaching, His death shall bring the Despairing rest."

No matter how we choose to translate it, the message remains the same. Namely, Christ's death redeems mortal man. This is not just any message, but it is an evangelical proclamation addressed to the "Despairing." By using the term despairing, by definition, it immediately assumes there is a subset of humanity that is in despair and needs rest.

The Numbers Chart

While we are familiar with the idea that "a picture is worth a thousand words," we are not as familiar with the use of numbers in Scripture. In truth, the Bible has many literary devices at its disposal. It makes use of not only names, as we just mentioned, but also certain numbers, colors, materials, measurements, and even keywords or phrases.

The precise nature of Scripture naturally produces its own technical terminology, just as any other field of study would. Once identified, these terms function almost in the same way that hyperlinks do in today's digital world. To demonstrate how this works, this next chart shows the consistent reference or associations ascribed to the more commonly used numbers in Scripture.

Number Typology Chart

No.	Basic Meaning[8]
1	Singleness, uniqueness, and unification
2	Adequate witness, testimony
3	The number of the Godhead, completion, and unity
4	Relates to the earth and creation
5	Relates to grace and unmerited favor
6	The number of man and human weaknesses, the evils of Satan and manifestation of sin
7	The number of Divine perfection and/or completeness
8	Relates to new beginnings
9	Holy Spirit's completeness, fullness, and judgment
10	Signifies world system and complete global cycle
12	Relates to Divine government
13	Relates to rebellion, apostasy, defection, corruption, disintegration and revolution
14	Deliverance and double blessing
40	Relates to testing, judgment, and trials
50	The number of jubilee or deliverance
666	The number of the beast

Chart 2 – Number Typology Chart

As we can see from the numbers chart, each number has a specific association, which we can apply to the fuller story of *HIS-Story*. For example, the number ten on the chart indicates God working on a worldwide basis.

---

[8] Sources: *Numbers in Scripture* (1967); *Book of Bible Lists* (1987); *and Tyndale Bible Dictionary* (2008).

Because there are ten members listed in the Christ-line in the pre-flood generation, we should expect to see how *HIS-Story* has a global address to the world.

Note, too, how the number ten also signifies the completion or an end of a cycle. Thereby, because Scripture assigns such a reference to this number, we can apply it as it suits the context. In the case of Noah, the flood represents a global judgment cycle and foreshadows how the world is going to end like before only to begin anew.[9] We know this because Noah was born in the tenth generation of Adam. His placement explains why Jehovah (Yahweh[10]) judged Noah as "perfect in his generations." (Gen. 6:9). We will explain more, once we get to the chapter on Noah.

Consider what the flood represents in type. Without the great divide, Noah and his three sons would not be able to become the new progenitors of a new world. The flood is used in Scripture to separate "the old" from "the new." It is from this perspective that we can see how the flood places one generation on cleansed *new* ground that was purified by the waters of God's wrath. The new ground typology gives new opportunities and new hope, which is apart from all hope lost due to the cursed, *old* ground resulting from the fall.

The flood, then, serves as a deliberate partition between the old and new life, much like the Old and New Testaments do in the Bible. By this comparison, it is easy to see how the former, naturally born sons of Adam, are plagued by the curse of death. In the same way, the new, spiritually born sons of Adam are on a path to a new beginning, as represented by the remnant saved in Noah's Ark.

The flood is not only a purification method, but it is also a picture of baptism as typified by those saved in the Ark.[11] This same judgment cycle, as summarized by the first few chapters of the Bible's first book, will be repeated, once again, in the Bible's final chapters in its last book, which concerns Adam's last generation. Except in that future day, instead of judgment waters, the last "righteous remnant" will be saved from judgment fires. (2 Pet. 3:6-7). Fire is the ultimate purification method.

---

[9] Isa. 65:17; Rev. 21:1-2.

[10] Keeping to the traditional English spelling, we will continue to use "Jehovah" as God's name throughout this book. However, please keep in mind that modern scholarship supports "Yahweh" over "Jehovah." For example, see, *NIV Study Bible* (1998) and *The Living Bible* (1971) notes at Exodus 3:15.

[11] **1 Pet. 3:19-21:** So he went and preached to the spirits in prison those who disobeyed God long ago when God waited patiently while Noah was building his boat. Only eight people were saved from drowning in that terrible flood. And that water is a picture of baptism, which now saves you, not by removing dirt from your body, but as a response to God from a clean conscience. It is effective because of the resurrection of Jesus Christ. (NLT).

The Bible's "old and new" concept falls within two global judgment periods (2 Pet. 2:5), called "the first and the last." It is not by accident that Genesis uses the great divide and the pre-flood period as a summarized picture of the biblical puzzle. Nor can it be by accident the first generation of His bloodline is a mirror image of its last.

The Cain-Line Chart

However, we are getting ahead of *HIS-Story*. For now, we need to continue our review of the bloodline statements. Next, are Cain and his line, who represents the firstborn line of fallen Adam. As such, Chart 3 lists each member of the Cain-line in their sequential order as recorded in Genesis.

The Cain-Line Genealogy Chart
(Genesis 4:17–22)

No.	Name	Meaning[12]
1	Adam	Man
2	Cain	Acquired
3	Enoch	Taught, dedicated (teaching/discipline)
4	Irad	Fugitive, city of witness, fleet
5	Mehujael	Smitten by God
6	Methusael	Who is of God
7	Lamech	Powerfully humbled, lowered (the despairing)
8a	Jabal[13]	Leading/conducts, flowing stream
8b	Jubal	Joyous trumpet sounds of jubilee
8c	Tubal-Cain	Flowing forth from Cain to the world/earth

Chart 3 – The Cain-Line Genealogy Chart

---

[12] Collective, general, and/or contextual key sources: Abarim Publications, *Meaning and Etymology of the Names* (2011); *Jones' Dictionary* (1990); *BDB Lexicon* (1906); *The Complete Word Study Dictionary* (1992); *The Scripture Lexicon* (1797); *and Strong's Concordance* (1890).

[13] *Jones' Dictionary* (1990) lists "leading, flowing, and river" for Jabal; "joyful sound, music, and jubilee" for Jubal, and "flowing forth of Cain" for Tubal-Cain.

Cain-Line Summary Statement:
"Man, acquired [as a] dedicated teaching fleet of witnesses
[decline as] fugitives, smitten by God, who is of God, powerfully
humbled [as] the despairing, leads a joyous jubilee."

The Cain-Line Chart (Chart 3) concerns the firstborn of fallen man and demonstrates how the members of the Cain-line can also form a sentence. This second statement speaks of a teaching "fleet," which is the size of a city, who becomes a dedicated group of the Despairing. The Cain-line statement also suggests that the firstborn line of Adam is considered a collective body of witnesses, who declined to become "smitten by God," then "powerfully humbled to lead a joyous jubilee." Such a message appears to go against our current popular view of how Cain and his line are virtually irredeemable.

Notice on the chart that the three sons of Lamech in the eighth generation take on a collective interpretation because the three boys share the same Hebrew root. The meaning of Lamech's sons fits nicely with the meaning of Mehujael's name, who is the fifth member in the line. Together, they emphasize how this line becomes "declining fugitives" but later they are recognized as God's own as one united force who "flows forth as a stream" to "lead/conduct the world in a joyous jubilee."

Unlike the Christ-line statement, which addresses the world in a general sense, the Cain-line statement celebrates the destiny of Adam's firstborn, no matter how undeserving that line may seem to be to us. Again, such a conclusion appears to defy the traditional negative beliefs, which are associated with this so-called "cursed" line of Cain.

Comparing the Charts

For further illustration, this next chart compares both lines together. This view helps to show how the Cain-line stops at the eighth generation, yet it has ten members, while the Christ-line has ten members for all ten generations in the pre-flood period.

The Cain and Christ–Line Genealogy Chart
(Genesis 4:17-22; 5:3-32)

Generational Number	Cain-Line Members	Christ-Line Members
1st generation	Adam (1st member) "Man"	Adam (1st member) "Man"
2nd generation	Cain (2nd member) "Acquired"	Seth (2nd member) "Appointed"
3rd generation	Enoch (3rd member) "Teaching, dedicated"	Enosh (3rd member) "Mortal"
4th generation	Irad (4th member) "Fugitive, city of witness, fleet"	Kenan (4th member) "Sorrow"
5th generation	Mehujael (5th member) "Smitten by God"	Mahalaleel (5th member) "The Blessed God or Glory of God"
6th generation	Methusael (6th member) "Who is of God"	Jared (6th member) "Shall come down"
7th generation	Lamech (7th member) "Despairing or powerfully humbled/lowered"	Enoch (7th member) "Teaching, dedicated"
8th generation	Jabal (8th member) "Leading/conducts, flowing stream" Jubal (9th member) "Joyous trumpet sounds of jubilee" Tubal-Cain (10th member) "Flowing forth from Cain"	Methuselah (8th member) "His death shall bring"
9th generation		Lamech (9th member) "Despairing or powerfully humbled/lowered"
10th generation		Noah (10th member) "Rest or comfort"

Chart 4 – The Cain-Line and Christ-Line Genealogy Comparison Chart

As we continue to compare the two genealogies side by side, there are other surprising factors to note about the eighth generation of the Cain-line. The first aspect relates to the names of Lamech's three sons. Notice how the three sons reflect a one-character difference in the spelling of their names. Due to such intriguing connections, Jewish scholarship tends to view the three brothers as an extension of the other. Many compare the three brothers to three hands of a clock, in hours, minutes, and seconds, to illustrate how their collective contributions work together as one unit in time. This clock imagery puts the three sons of Lamech in the context of the function of the whole.[14]

In effect, Lamech's three sons extend the Cain-line's reach to an international level by increasing the number of descendants to ten—the number that relates to the world. Just as the Christ-line with its ten members will have a global impact on the world in some way, so we should expect to see how the Cain-line will also.

But the Cain-line has a ten-to-eight structure due to its ten members stopping at the eighth generation. As we glance back at the number chart, eight means a new beginning, while ten means the end of a cycle, in addition to having a global reference. These associations indicate that the Christ-line's summary statement addresses the world at large, while the Cain-line statement speaks only of Cain and his line to impact the world and to begin anew.

Note too, how both lines have three names in common: Adam, Enoch, and Lamech. Adam is first because he fathered both lines in "mortal sorrow." Enoch means "teaching," and represents when the Despairing on each line (Cain and the Christ-line) receives the teaching about the "Blessed God." Lastly, Lamech means "despairing." The use of his name represents a subgroup that both lines share, who become despairing in their own way and time, which requires Divine intervention.

According to the Cain-line summary statement, his line will have a new beginning to "lead a joyous jubilee." Before then, his line declines and will be known as "smitten of God," but later seen "as of God." Could this "smitten of God" status be the reason why the Cain-line has received such undue hate and prejudice by both Jews and Christians alike? Is it possible that society has misunderstood the plan of God for this line, which has caused a gross misinterpretation of Scripture by the world? The secrets of the family are about to unfold.

---

[14] Sources: *Jones' Dictionary* (1990), *The New Open Bible Study Edition (NOBSE)*, Topical Index (KJV), and Abarim Publications, *Meaning and Etymology of the Names* (2011).

CHAPTER 2
The Father and His Lost Family

By default, the Cain and the Christ-line naturally create two main branches of the Adamic family tree. Oddly, the prophet Jeremiah also speaks of two lines of one family when he prophesied, "I [Jehovah] will take you one of a city, and two of a family, and I will bring you to Zion" (Jer. 3:14b). Many commentators[15] suggest the broader interpretation of this verse refers to the Jews and Gentiles as the two-family lines, who are united by one city, Zion. Keep this in mind as we begin our excavational quest with the one man who started it all—Adam.

The Genesis record tells us Adam begat his firstborn son, Cain, as well as a younger son, Abel. Sadly, most never realize the genealogical record of Christ excludes Adam's first two sons. From a Christian perspective, this appears trivial, especially since *HIS-Story* is the Good News or Gospel Message to humanity. So, why should we care? We care because when we realize how the blessed-bloodline has excluded the first two sons of the first family, biblical typology explodes with immense implications.

If we consider Adam, Eve, and their two lost sons, Cain and Abel, as the first family, then, in type, they become the quintessential representation of all families of the earth in every age. As we saw earlier, the number four in biblical typology relates to the earth in its present condition while the number ten relates to the world and its secular system.

In terms of the first family's number type, the number four also highlights their sinful nature. In the words of the Christ-line summary statement, all are born[16] in mortal sorrow because of the fall due to sin. From there, mortal sorrow continues to be true for every family on earth, until Christ is born and dies for the sin of the whole human race, which began with Adam.

The one father concept is key to biblical genealogy. Even Paul compared Adam and Christ as father figures of humanity. Adam is the father of

---

[15] Matthew Henry, John Gill, Keil & Delitzsch, and Jamieson, Fausset and Brown, to name a few.

[16] Adam and Eve were created in paradise before sin entered the world, while their offspring were born in sin and on a cursed and dying earth.

all born in "the natural." Conversely, Christ is the father of those born in the Spirit. Thus, He is called the "Last Adam."[17]

The Genesis account upholds Paul's "first and last Adam" interpretation because its approach is designed to create a typological platform to draw upon.[18] The higher purpose of Scripture is always evangelical and not historical. Without this intentionality, our understanding of spiritual constructs like the one father concept would be lost.

One might wonder why Adam's third son, Seth, is not a part of the first family's typological equation. He and his line are excluded from the first family because he represents a new type. With Seth, the family's total number of members moves from four to five. On the number chart, five is the number of grace, which means unmerited favor.

Seth's name means "appointed." His position on the Christ-line, as well as the meaning of his name, gives us the clues. When we combine these clues with his mother's referring to him as the appointed seed over another (Gen. 4:25), the picture is complete. Therefore, Seth represents Christ, who is by grace, the appointed replacement line for the two lost lines before him.

The Parable of Two Lost Sons

The "lost and found" concept within Scripture is a central theme. Probably one of the best illustrations of the "father and two sons" idea in the New Testament is from one of Jesus' lost sheep parables known as "The Parable of the Prodigal Son," and is recorded in Luke 15:11-32.

As we read the parable, it appears we have found the necessary New Testament companion narrative to the Cain and Abel story in terms of biblical typology. Notice how it beautifully parallels with Adam's two lost sons by staying consistent with the "father and two sons" theme. Of course, the sons in the parable become "lost" in their own way, as we shall soon see. We learn how each son has a stake in the family inheritance, just like the sons of Adam.

There are two key phrases used in these first few verses that connect the younger son in the Cain and Abel story with the younger son in the parable. The first phrase in the King James Version is, "And he divided unto them

---

[17] **1 Cor. 15:45-46:** And so it is written, The first man Adam was made a living soul; the last Adam was made a quickening spirit. Howbeit that was not first which is spiritual, but that which is natural; and afterward that which is spiritual.

[18] Typology is prophecy in pictorial figures, or types and shadows, and functions in hindsight. The figures, or what the Bible calls "types and shadows," are interpreted by comparing the unified message found in both the Old and New Testaments. Shadows are not considered "the real thing" because shadows have no substance or material themselves. But the language used in Hebrews 10:1 and Colossians 2:17 suggests that Christ is the "reality" and "substance," which is the one casting the "shadows" and causing the "types" in Scripture.

his living" (vs. 11-12b). The second phrase is "and took his journey into a far country" (vs. 13). A.W. Pink gives invaluable insight as to the use of these two phrases in terms of typology and spiritual understanding. Besides natural wealth, as it concerns the first phrase, "And he divided unto them his living," Pink explains:

> "God has given to every one of his creatures a soul. This soul may be regarded as capital in hand with which to do our trading both for time and eternity. It is a most valuable portion, for it is worth more than "the whole world." It was while in his father's house that he received his "portion of goods," and that "he [the father] divided unto them [his] living," so that the portion received was a living portion. This can only refer to the creature, prior to his birth into this world, receiving from "the Father of spirits" (Heb. 12:9) a 'living soul.'" (Pink, *The Prodigal Son*, Lk. 15:11-13).

Here, Pink is suggesting the share of the inheritance is the life given by the father. A fitting perspective, especially if the father in the parable is Jehovah. This first phrase, "divided unto them his living," suggests that the inheritance is not just limited to this world and leaves room for eternal implications that link back to the Cain and Abel story.

Concerning the second phrase, again, we see another common trait of the proverbial "younger brother." This time the connection is to "a far country" (v. 13). This second phrase naturally conjures up mental images of distance. Pink equates this phrase as being "alienated from the life of God" (Eph. 4:18), which is like a "gulf between sinful man and a Holy God."

With the use of these two phrases explained by Pink's insights, the first common trait of the proverbial younger son of the father is the "cashing out" of life early. Note how the parable uses distance to illustrate alienation just as Genesis uses Abel's blood crying out in the grave (Gen. 4:10). We see the second common trait is distance from God, which is the result of the first trait—cashing out one's life. However, there is more.

As the parable continues, we learn how the younger brother suddenly comes to his senses (vs. 17). After being in the faraway land for quite some time, all "cashed out" and in ruin, his spiritual awaking inspires him to journey back home (vs. 20). Even after all this time, the father never stopped watching and waiting for his lost son, who is then joyously received and restored as a legitimate heir of the family (vs. 22-24).

The parable helps us to see how the younger brother became lost almost immediately, followed by alienation. However, unlike the Cain and Abel story, the parable gives us hope because the younger son was "found" (vs. 24, 32). The parable also reassures the elder son when his father said, "Thou art ever with me, and all that I have is thine" (v. 31).

On the other hand, it is not so easy to see the older brother's issue, which also jeopardized his standing for the inheritance. The parable supplies the clues. First, the older brother's jealousy of his lost sibling was because of his brother's acceptance by the father (vs. 25-28). Second, the older brother was outraged by that acceptance (vs. 28). Third, the older brother's refusal to come into the father's house only to continue to work (vs. 29) in the outer field (vs. 25) indicates he was not in the father's house, either. The sons in the parable exhibit the same character traits as Adam's two lost sons and supplement our understanding of the fate of Cain and Abel.

The Biblical Lost and Found Theme

Note how the parable highlights the lost and found theme, while the Cain and Abel story accentuates the need for the blood sacrifice. Together, both stories highlight the critical character traits of two lost sons, in type. The key characteristics, therefore, provide a known pattern to identify both sons throughout biblical history.

The typological profile of the elder brother contains these primary traits throughout Scripture. He is a worker in an outer field. He stays close to the father's house but chooses to work, which keeps him in the outer field. His choice to accept the blood offering is always available. He is jealous of his father and his younger brother's relationship. Lastly, he hates his brother to the point of death and is angry at his father.

In turn, the pattern of the younger brother will always possess these general traits: He is lost early due to a "life cashing-out" experience. This experience results in a period of alienation. He has a spiritual awaking to come back to his father's house. Lastly, he is found and restored without question by the father under his watchful and loving care.

From our comparison of Adam's sons with the two sons of the parable, we can see how each son relates to the father very differently. With the first key to biblical genealogy being the one father concept and the second key being the character patterns of the two lost sons of the father, we are now ready to address the summary statements formed by the Cain and Christ-line in the proper context. At this point, we need to take a fresh look at the story of Cain and Abel found in Genesis Chapter 4.

From the Genesis record, we learn there is a conflict within the family of "man," which is the meaning of Adam's name. From the narrative, we learn how the two sons of the "family of man" show their true colors concerning the offering required by Jehovah (vs. 1-5). Abel brought a blood sacrifice, and his older brother, Cain, offered "fruit of the ground." Jehovah preferred Abel's offering over Cain's offering (vs. 5). Jehovah's preference did not sit well with Cain, even though Jehovah gave him a choice (vs. 7). In the heat of his anger, Cain killed his brother (vs. 8). Because Abel's blood cried out from the grave (vs. 10), Jehovah cursed Cain to live a "marked" lifestyle. Then he was cast out to become a "wandering worker in the outer field" (vs. 11-12).

The blood sacrifice and Abel's application of it is an important feature that the parable about the prodigal son failed to include. Because Genesis establishes a typological precedent, the blood sacrifice represents Christ's work on the cross, which is the only sacrifice that can be accepted by Jehovah. This sacrificial controversy is more of the elder brother's issue, which develops fully in Chapter 3. For now, the focus is on how the two brothers' personal views and responses about the sin-offering divide them.

The negative attitude about Christ as the Lamb of God freely offered to save the world is where Christianity would generally perceive that the division is between believers and nonbelievers. However, in the context of the two lost sons of the father who are in covenant relationship with Jehovah, we must discern how this division is from within the "family of God." In other words, the two basic human approaches to Jehovah are present within the family. These two approaches are first by "the way of works" and second by "the way of blood sacrifice (the gift given by grace) through faith."

Family Ties That Bind

The biblical record confirms that Cain is part of God's eternal family. Most English translations in Genesis exclude this detail. Notice in the story of Cain and Abel, the Hebrew name for God dealing with Adam and his two sons is *Jehovah* (Gen. 4). Compare this with Genesis Chapter 1, which uses *Elohim* as the name for God dealing with creation.

The use of the two different names of God in Genesis is another indispensable tool in the hands of the Bible student. First, Jehovah is always associated with a covenant or family relationship as a Father dealing with His family. Conversely, Elohim is always associated with creation, or a general relationship, such as the Creator dealing with His creation.[19]

The Almighty's involvement as Creator to His creation can only be a general address to the population. He is their maker, and His creation may or may not acknowledge that. However, the name Jehovah indicates a covenant relationship, just like a wedding vow, which begins a family bond of generations without end in a legal context.

This same covenant relationship is at the heart of Jeremiah's prophecy, which we reviewed in part at the beginning of this chapter. The complete verse reads: "Turn, O backsliding children, saith the LORD; *for I am married unto you*: and I will take you one of a city, and two of a family, and I will bring you to Zion [emphasis added]." (Jer. 3:14). Because Jehovah has a "legal" connection to the first family, this same relationship extends to future generations of the Adamic line. Note the wording of Jeremiah's prophecy, which conveys this point.

As far as typology is concerned, we can picture Jehovah dealing with His family in every generation throughout all ages to eternity. The use of these two names of God (Jehovah and Elohim) is consistent throughout Scripture. Because of this consistency, the reader can determine when God is dealing with the general population or His covenant people. This distinction is crucial, just as within our own family connections. As the saying goes, "Blood is thicker than water." So too, family relations become a matter of law when it comes to the family inheritance.

From the Cain-line statement, and from the Bible's use of the name Jehovah to indicate family, we can see how Cain is considered the firstborn son of Father Jehovah. Thinking Cain to be Divine, Eve prophetically hinted this thought at his birth, as if he was the promised seed that would break the serpent's head, when she said, "I have gotten a man, the Lord." (Gen. 4:1). John Gill Commentary provides insight as to this curious statement:

> **"Some render it, "I have gotten a man, the Lord" (x);**
> that promised seed that should break the serpent's head
> to be a Divine person—the true God, even Jehovah, that

---

[19] Bullinger, *Divine Names*, II; IV.

He should become a man. She must have been ignorant of the mystery of our Lord's incarnation or of His being born of a virgin." (Gill, *Exposition of the Bible*, Gen. 4:1).

Gill explains how Eve viewed her firstborn son in a Divine context. He was not Divine as we all know from the Genesis narrative, but Cain's position has always been set apart for Divine purposes. We will discuss this in detail in the next chapter. For now, we are to understand because of the fall, Cain could never reach the level of perfection of which his birthright obligations required on an eternal scale.

Despite his birthright responsibilities, Cain declined in status and became "marked of God" due to his murderous heart. The mark was also a bittersweet blessing for Cain. It stood as a sign of separation and postponed judgment as well as a warning to others. Cain's decline is not only central to the Cain and Abel story, but it is also a central theme in the Bible just as the Cain-line summary statement suggests.

Family Ties That Break

Cain's marked life separated him from the family and his father. He became a fugitive and vagabond due to his crime. The consequences of his actions separated him from his homeland. We also see this reflected in the older brother of the prodigal son parable, who worked in the outer field, indicating his separation from his father's house.

By continuing to study the story of Cain and Abel, the two different approaches to Jehovah—one of works and one of faith—a light bulb comes on. If we are to assume both sons of Adam were lost, then we must ask several questions. Why was Cain's life spared even though he was on a declining path, and why was there a Divine mark on him? Even the Mosaic Law teaches, "A life for a life, an eye for an eye, and a tooth for a tooth?" (Duet. 19:21). Likewise, why did Abel die while his older brother went free?

Furthermore, if Abel is dead, how could the "voice" of Abel's blood cry out from the ground?[20] Maybe this statement implies the universal law of the Creator holds justice in abeyance and is to be carried out later? Could this also be an early hint the grave had no power to silence the blood of the innocent, especially to those who were atoned by the correct appropriation of the blood sacrifice?

---

[20] **Gen. 4:10:** And he said, 'What hast thou done? the voice of thy brother's blood crieth unto me from the ground.'

Questions such as these help us see how the clues supplied by the Genesis account and the prodigal son parable are intentional, which provides a broader spectrum of this untold story about the two lost sons of the Father. If the parable about the two lost sons whom Jesus came to seek and to save has any merit within the context of the Cain and Abel story, then we must ask, what is really going on between these two lost lines of Adam?

Family Ties to be Reformed

Ironically, the lost and found theme of the New Testament is at a loss to us. Its significance is impossible to lose because Jesus has kept it at the forefront with such radical sayings like:

> "The son of man came to seek that which is lost." (Mt. 18:11).
> "Go not into the way of the Gentiles...But go rather to the lost sheep of the house of Israel." (Mt. 10:5b-6).
> "But he answered and said, I am not sent but unto the lost sheep of the house of Israel." (Mt. 15:24).

With statements like these, we see that Jesus understood there was an issue concerning a loss of eternal proportions. The question then becomes, who are the lost sheep of Israel? Modern scholarship maintains humankind was lost at the fall. Although this conclusion is generally correct, it does not represent the complete picture, because the family of God is always couched within the context of covenant relationship.

The creation story in Genesis is rich with visual metaphors and meaning for our understanding in this regard. The family unit is represented as a binding force. The union scene begins with the first man, who is erected from the dust of the ground by the living breath of the Almighty. The fleshly amendments to this earthly medium, which we call "Adam," was then transferred into the Divine "Garden" where Eve was cultivated in "union" with him and the two were as one flesh. (Gen. 2:7-25).

The garden setting draws implications that the desired objective of the "Garden Union" is meant to be understood in terms of "seedtime and harvest." The legal component of the union protects the rights of the family and their inheritance, otherwise the family is left unprotected.

While Adam and Eve are considered direct creations of God like the angels in heaven,[21] their lower estate had eternal purposes for His family.

After they were cast out of the Garden due to sin (Gen. 3:24), their only recourse was to be "fruitful and multiply" in mortal sorrow on a cursed ground. (Gen. 3:16-17). Herein lies the "lost and find theme" of Jesus. But all was not lost because God promised them a new seed would come. (Gen. 3:15). God's "Garden Program" will prevail in time and in due season. (Gal. 4:4).

Hebrews 2:16 picks up the case of the coming seed and speaking of Jesus states, "He took not on him the nature of angels; but he took on him the seed of Abraham." The biological and physical appearance of Christ was made possible after the fall because of the Garden Program's efforts. Christ, as God, being born in the flesh, is a great cosmic wonder. So much so that Peter takes notice of how even the angels were curious (1 Pet. 1:12). Undoubtedly, this act of God being born in fallen flesh so He can "father" a family is beyond the ability for anyone to fathom.

Even though the created class of angel is termed "sons of God" in the Old Testament,[22] the New Testament introduces a new breed of the sons of God.[23] The new spiritual sons of God are "a new creation in Christ Jesus,"[24] because they are "born from above" into the family of God.[25] Because both Christ and Adam were "made a little lower than the angels," Christ's blood sacrifice can be freely offered to all. When we consider the desired end-product of the Godhead is to "birth" children in their image by such a means, the amazement and wonder of the angels make perfect sense.

This "new creation in Christ" is exactly that—new! This "new life" was not offered to the angels, whether fallen or not. Thus, the reason why man was made lower was so he could be re-made at the highest level. The new birthing process was God-ordained and legally binding. Man is not only a new creation in Christ, but he is also "born" as a legitimate child of God.

---

[21] **Heb. 2:6-7:** What is man, that thou art mindful of him? Or the son of man, that thou visitest him? Thou madest him a little lower than the angels; thou crownest him with glory and honour, and didst set him over the works of thy hands.

[22] Gen. 6:2; Ps. 82:6-7; Job 1:6, 2:1, 38:7.

[23] **Lk. 20:34-36:** And Jesus said to them, The sons of this world are married and have wives; But those to whom is given the reward of the world to come, and to come back from the dead, have no wives, and are not married; And death has no more power over them, for they are equal to the angels, and are sons of God, being of those who will come back from the dead. (BBE).

[24] **2 Cor. 5:17:** Therefore if any man be in Christ, he is a new creature: old things are passed away; behold, all things are become new.

[25] **Jn. 3:7:** Do not wonder because I said to you, You must be generated from above. (LITV). King James stated it this way, "Marvel not that I said unto thee, Ye must be born again." The literal translation is "born from above."

Angels are created in glory, but they are not born into the family of God and clothed in His greater glory.

Family Ties to be Reborn

The born-again or regeneration process is precisely why genealogy plays such a vital role in *HIS-Story* and why genetics and biology are the crucial aspects of "fathering." The first family typology helps to illustrate this point. Biological birth is for mortals. This organic material only serves as a starting point through which Divine transfiguration can take place.

The Seed of Truth must bypass corruptible flesh to be sown in the invisible portion of a person called the heart by the hearing of the Word. Biological fathering and family concepts are human-based experiences designed to help us grasp eternal perspectives in preparation for our transition into the eternal family of God.

The concept of fathering suits the lost and found theme because Christ's birth within the family of fallen man qualifies him as a new father figure. Whosoever believes in Him will be "born" from above. (1 Jn. 4:7). By this method, the "lost" in every generation, whether Jew or Gentile, are found, thereby fulfilling Jeremiah's 3:14 prophecy. If we assume the "two of a family" taken to Zion are both Jew and Gentile, how does this relate to the first family and Adam's two lost sons? The surprising answer and more will be revealed in the next two chapters.

CHAPTER 3
Elder "Lost" Son

We learned from the previous chapter that its title, "The Father and His Lost Family," magnifies the first family as the central theme. They are Adam, Eve, Cain, and Abel. Together, the four members represent all families of the earth in eternal "mortal sorrow" because of the fall. The first family typology is a powerful lens to view the family of man in their fallen condition on an eternal scale. It is a foundational concept in the epic saga of *HIS-Story*.

In this chapter, we will turn our focus to Adam's elder son, who represents the first of the two "lost" sons. Since Cain is his firstborn, it is logical to start with him. He is the easiest to trace because of his genealogical record. We cannot say this about his younger brother. Unfortunately, Abel's death automatically excludes him from being listed as a contributing member of the family tree.

We have established that both Cain and Seth begin their genealogies with Father Adam. In so doing, the meaning of Adam's name, "man," becomes the theme. Likewise, since Adam is common to both the Cain and Christ-line, their summary statements have a "man theme" in some way.

When we view the man theme as it applies to Cain and his line, the man refers to the "firstborn of fallen man," in type, because Cain is the firstborn of fallen Adam. When we apply the man theme to the Christ-line, the man refers to Christ as the "Blessed God" born in the likeness of "firstborn fallen man." As we can see, the application of the man theme changes to suit the context of the family lines. So, if Cain and his line represent the "firstborn of fallen man," what does that mean?

The Role of the Family's Firstborn

Once we become familiar with the firstborn concept and its eternal position, we will recognize the intended role Cain and his firstborn line were and still are meant to have. Deuteronomy 21:15-17 illustrates how a father is legally obligated to acknowledge his firstborn son as his principal heir. It also implies the father's obligation to grant his firstborn heir a double portion of his estate. This inheritance right is known as *mishpat ha-bekhorah*—the rule of the birthright.[26] This "rule" rests upon the strong arm of the Law. The verb *yakkir*, which means "he shall acknowledge,"[27] expresses the legal component of the birthright.

The firstborn male is considered the "beginning of the father's strength." Even if the firstborn son was not popular or loved as much as his other siblings, he could not be passed over by his father. We will also add, the only exceptions to this rule were choices made by Jehovah in fulfillment of His eternal purposes. However, even on those rare occasions, the firstborn right was protected by delay. This concept will be discussed briefly in this chapter and more extensively in the final chapters.

There are three critical functions assigned to the firstborn office. First, to become the principal heir and successor of the family's estate. The second function is to maintain the value of that inheritance and ensure legal distribution to the heirs. The last function assumes the spiritual representative of the family and the channel to spiritual blessings because of his mother. In other words, the firstborn is to act as king and priest for the family.

The first family understood this concept very well, which explains why Eve pronounced "I have gotten a man from the Lord." (Gill, *Exposition of the Bible*, Gen. 4:1). We discussed this briefly in the last chapter. However, in the context of the role of the firstborn, we need to make another point. Judging by Eve's proclamation, his parents mistakenly looked to Cain as being the promised "seed" of the woman.[28] They misapplied him as the one who would "bruise the head of the serpent,"[29] and restore the family to their eternal estate. Since the redemptive plan was yet to be fully disclosed by Jehovah, it would seem the first family was looking for their salvation through the wrong son.

Despite their error, the fact they understood the eternal value of the firstborn office is worthy to note. The firstborn right within the family, whether fallen or not, cannot be legally revoked. However, as we remarked earlier, all claims to the eternal birthright can be postponed. Such a delay would give much needed time for Jehovah to deal with other pressing legal matters of concern, such as Adam's sin, which caused the fall, and Cain's murderous crime. (Gen. 4:8).

---

[26] **Deut. 21:17:** But he shall acknowledge the son of the hated for the firstborn, by giving him a double portion of all that he hath: for he is the beginning of his strength; the right of the firstborn is his.

[27] Undoubtedly, the acknowledgment involved certain formal, legal acts which are not indicated in biblical literature but thrives in the Mid-Eastern culture even to this day.

[28] **Gal. 3:16:** Now to Abraham and his seed were the promises made. He saith not, And to seeds, as of many; but as of one, And to thy seed, which is Christ.

[29] **Gen. 3:15:** And I will put enmity between thee and the woman, and between thy seed and her seed; it shall bruise thy head, and thou shalt bruise his heel.

At this point in *HIS-Story*, we must keep in mind how the firstborn office represents the "father's strength" to maintain the value of the family's estate as well as the "mother's vigor" to give life to the heirs of the estate.[30] Unfortunately, due to the fall, man's eternal estate was reduced to mortality. Because of Adam's failure, man's firstborn was also doomed to fail and could only render death to himself as well as to his brethren. Therefore, all claims to the eternal birthright of fallen man were suspended until due process ran its course.

The Role of a Firstborn Nation

Until the Mosaic Law, Cain's firstborn office teaches us how the eldest son in each Hebrew family was appointed as head and priest of the family and became the possession or property of Jehovah.[31] When Israel was pronounced a nation and the firstborn son by Jehovah,[32] a transition was in the making. Once the blood of the Lamb covered the doorposts of each household, the passing of the death angel in Egypt (Ex. 12) changed everything. This one pivotal event not only offered redemption to all firstborns, but it also paved the way for some exciting changes to come in terms of firstborn reform.

The first change was to alter the Hebrew calendar by adding the "set times of the Lord," known as the religious calendar. This topic will be covered mainly in the final chapters of the book, but more specifically as it relates to Chart 11. The second change was when Jehovah split the priestly and kingly responsibilities of the firstborn office between two tribes of the nation. The tribe of Levi, according to Chapter 3 of the book of Numbers, was given the priestly duties. This transfer was partly as a tribute to Moses and Aaron, and partly because the Levites distinguished themselves by their zeal during the golden calf incident in the wilderness (Ex. 32:28-29).

Jehovah's appointment of an entire tribe for Divine service ensured the regular performance of the rites of religion as a nation. Since the Law mandated every firstborn of man and every unclean animal should be redeemed,[33] the Levites, as the newly appointed priestly line, would now be

---

[30] Ex. 13:12; 22:29. Also see, the article on Firstborn, The Jewish Virtual Library (2008).

[31] See, *JFB Commentary*, Num. 3:11-13.

[32] **Ex. 4:22:** And thou shalt say unto Pharaoh, Thus saith the LORD, Israel is my son, even my firstborn.

[33] See, Num.18:15. The laws concerning this redemption of the firstborn of man are recorded in Ex. 13:12-15, 22:29, 34:20; Num. 3:45, 8:17-18, 18:16. The firstborn male of every clean animal was to be given up to the priest for sacrifice (Deut. 12:5-19; Ex. 34:19-26; Num. 18), but the firstborn of unclean animals was either to be redeemed or sold and the price given to the priest (Lev. 27:11-13, 27). Even the firstborn of an ass, if not redeemed, was to be put to death (Ex. 13:13, 34:20).

the facilitators of this practice for the whole nation of firstborns as a religious requirement.

The kingly duties were assigned to the tribe of Judah by their father Jacob (Israel) before his death as he blessed his twelve sons. Judah's blessing by his father is, "The scepter shall not depart from Judah, nor a lawgiver from between his feet, until Shiloh come; and unto him shall the gathering of the people be." (Gen. 49:10). From that directive, the tribe of Judah became the custodians of the Law and assumed the right of rule.

From these significant changes, the birthright position with its kingly and priestly responsibilities was preserved by the two designated tribes of Israel as the "firstborn son" of Jehovah among all nations of the earth. Together, both tribes became joint-firstborn representatives for the whole. Their roles fulfilled the Firstborn Primitive Office established in Cain's day and covered the full spectrum of this responsibility on a global and eternal capacity.

The Firstborn Fix

As we can see so far, the role of the Firstborn Primitive Office stood as the family's representative in charge of the welfare and well-being of the family line as well as its eternal inheritance. This ancient, sacred office is a foreign concept to the Western world and became a point of contention in the story of Cain and Abel. Unfortunately, because of the fall, the firstborn office fell into a firstborn fix from the very beginning. In that context, no matter who became the firstborn of fallen Adam, that man would be the perfect portrayal of the sad "beginnings of the father's strength," and the "sour" renderings of the "first fruit of the womb" as a result.

All eternal rights of "the family of man" are void of any value due to the weakness of the father, which caused all to "fall" into mortal sorrow. Here, we have the introduction of fallen man's first underlying legal issue: bankruptcy. Because of the fall, Adam's estate was bankrupt of eternal life and dominion of the earth. Yes, Adam was able to pass down earthly possessions to his heirs, including ownership of land. Yet, on an eternal scale, his "mortal" or "temporary" estate pales in comparison to his eternal inheritance, which was lost.

Where do we find this Firstborn Primitive Office concept in the story of Cain and Abel? How do we know if we are even on the right track? Unfortunately, this concept vanishes in obscurity due to the various English

translations of the biblical record. With a little digging, the Firstborn Primitive Office surprisingly comes to the forefront in Jehovah's response to
Cain's jealous attitude against his brother Abel:

> **Gen. 4:7:** "If thou doest well, shalt thou not be accepted?
> and if thou doest not well, sin lieth at the door. And unto
> thee shall be his desire, and thou shalt rule over him."

At first glance, the King James Version of this verse appears challenging to decipher. Therefore, if Cain and the Christ-line summary
statements have any basis in truth at all, then somewhere within the
context of this verse, there should be an acknowledgment of Cain's firstborn office. Since there appears to be none in the King James Version,
we must dig deeper.

To help us with the first part of the verse, we look to John Gill and
Matthew Henry's commentaries as it concerns the meaning of "sin lieth at
the door." Both commentators note that other scholars render the word sin
as "sin-offering." One such scholarly work is the Jamieson, Fausset, and
Brown Commentary:

> ***"sin lieth at the door*** — sin, that is, a sin offering - a
> common meaning of the word in Scripture (as in Hos.
> 4:8; 2 Co. 5:21; Heb. 9:28). The purport of the Divine
> rebuke to Cain was this, "Why art thou angry, as if un-
> justly treated? If thou doest well (that is, wert innocent
> and sinless) a thank offering would have been accepted
> as a token of thy dependence as a creature. But as thou
> doest not well (that is, art a sinner), a sin offering is nec-
> essary, by bringing which thou wouldest have met with
> acceptance and retained the honors of thy birthright."
> This language implies that previous instructions had
> been given as to the mode of worship; Abel offered
> through faith (Heb. 11:4)." (*JFB Commentary*, Gen.
> 4:7).

According to the JFB scholars, the use of the term sin-offering has a
common meaning. If the translators of the King James Version of the Bible

would have been consistent with that rendering in Genesis 4:7, then the intent of Jehovah's comments to Cain becomes, in the words of Matthew Henry:

> "That though Cain had sinned, and had done amiss in the offering he had offered, nevertheless, there was a propitiatory sacrifice [a sin-offering] for sin provided, which was at hand, and would soon be offered; so that he [Cain] had no need to be dejected, or his countenance to fall; for if he looked to that sacrifice by faith, he would find pardon and acceptance." (Henry, *Commentary of the Whole Bible*, Gen. 4:7).

From Jehovah's response, as explained by Henry, all Cain had to do was to look to his younger brother's blood sacrifice to receive forgiveness for his sin. Cain's sin at this point was his failure (as well as his inability) to bring the right sacrifice. When Jehovah said to Cain, "If thou doest well shalt thou be accepted?" this was not about Cain's willpower. It was about a choice that was given to him by Jehovah. He must decide to accept or reject the sin-offering "lying at the door." This choice was his, which he could make throughout his lifetime.

Typologically speaking, the sin-offering pictures Christ as the younger brother who ultimately becomes the blood sacrifice for all, which satisfies the family's eternal debt. However, at this point and time, Scripture's focus is on the firstborn's anger at Jehovah's acceptance of the younger brother over him. His rage gave cause for Cain's jealousy and his fear of losing his birthright position and kingly and priestly privileges. His self-centered attitude blinded him to the point that he could not see it was out of Father Jehovah's love for the firstborn that the sin-offering was available in the first place. In continuing to trace *HIS-Story*, this becomes a primary pattern of how Jehovah deals with the firstborn of His fallen family.

Concerning Jehovah's second comment to Cain, both Gill and Henry, once again, agree. A better rendering is, "Unto thee [Cain] shall be his [Abel's] desire, he [Abel] shall continue his respect to thee [Cain] as an elder brother, and thou [Cain], as the firstborn, shalt rule over him [Abel] as much as ever." Matthew Henry commented further:

"God's acceptance of Abel's offering did not transfer the birth-right to him [Abel, which Cain was jealous of], nor put upon him that excellency of dignity and of power which is said to belong to it [The Firstborn Office] Gen. 49:3. God did not so intend it." (Henry, *Commentary of the Whole Bible*, Gen. 4:7).

No doubt, these are curious exchanges, but our digging has proved fruitful. Because of some English translations, the Firstborn Primitive Office has been hidden from plain sight all along. Here, Henry explains how Jehovah's second comment to Cain gave him full assurance that his firstborn office still belonged to him and would not be taken from him. It was his right to become king and priest of the family, and it did not and would not transfer to his sibling. Cain had a right to be protective of his position, but his anger and jealousy blinded his ability to see his fallen spiritual condition. As a result, he refused to see he was in a firstborn fix that called for a sin-offering.

The Firstborn Replacement

The first family's misplaced hope in their firstborn as their "king and priest" is a familiar pattern in the Bible. In the Old Testament, many times, we see the firstborn or the elder son often fall into sin while a younger son follows the path of righteousness. This pattern is true not only in the case of Cain and Abel but also for the successive generations of the patriarchs.[34] Due to the firstborn failure of fallen man, firstborn reform and redemption were always part of the "Garden Program." In the meantime, Jehovah had to suspend the birthright claim of fallen man until further notice.

Even though Cain and Israel share the "birthright" within the family, both failed due to their fallen father's bankrupt estate and because of their own sin and inability to fix it. The firstborn fix demanded a qualified firstborn replacement. Otherwise, the family of fallen man and their eternal inheritance would be eternally lost. Tangible evidence of this change is, once again, seen in Moses' day when he was appointed to lead the Hebrew nation as Jehovah's "firstborn son" out of Egypt:

---

[34] Isaac instead of his older brother Ishmael. Jacob, instead of his older brother Esau. Judah, Levi, and Joseph instead of their older brother Reuben, and David instead of any of his seven older brothers. Each time, the offspring of the elder son or sons expressed hostility towards the offspring of the younger son.

> **Ex. 4:22-23:** "And thou shalt say unto Pharaoh, Thus saith the LORD, Israel *is* my son, *even* my firstborn: And I say unto thee, Let my son go, that he may serve me: and if thou refuse to let him go, behold, I will slay thy son, *even* thy firstborn."

In this account, Jehovah told Moses to call His people His "firstborn" to help Pharaoh understand how the God of the Hebrews personally related to His own. This firstborn association later parallels Pharaoh's refusal to let them go, which resulted in the death of all firstborns of the land that were not "passed-over," including Pharaoh's son.[35]

The New Testament supplies an even fuller meaning of this event as it relates to Israel's Messiah becoming their qualified firstborn replacement. The firstborn replacement theme becomes evident in Matthew's account of the birth of Christ.[36] He purposely links Pharaoh's killing of the firstborn in Egypt to Herod's pursuit to kill the babe born in Bethlehem. Matthew tells us it was because of the prophecy about "their coming King" that fueled Herod's fears. With such a perceived threat, Herod took drastic measures to secure his position of authority within the land. So, he issued a decree to kill all the firstborn males two years old or under[37] as an attempt to destroy any chance the prophecy may be true.

Consequently, Herod's evil decree caused Joseph and Mary to flee to Egypt to save their firstborn son, Jesus. Matthew's record tells us their return became the fulfillment of Hosea's prophecy, "Out of Egypt, I called my son." (Mt. 2:14-15). However, after reading the complete verse of Hosea 11:1, of which Matthew quotes, Hosea spoke of Israel, not Jesus. Hosea's account reads, "When Israel was a child I loved him, and out of Egypt I called my son."

So then, how should we interpret this passage in Matthew? Was Hosea referring to the nation of Israel as Jehovah's son, or was he metaphorically speaking of Jesus, as Matthew is suggesting in his New Testament account? It all goes back to the firstborn office. Since both Israel and Jesus share the

---

[35] **Ex. 12:29:** And it came to pass, that at midnight the LORD smote all the firstborn in the land of Egypt, from the firstborn of Pharaoh that sat on his throne unto the the firstborn of the captive that was in the dungeon, and all the firstborn of cattle.

[36] **Mt. 2:14-15:** When he arose, he took the young child and his mother by night, and departed into Egypt: And was there until the death of Herod: that it might be fulfilled which was spoken of the Lord by the prophet, saying, Out of Egypt have I called my son.

[37] **Mt. 2:16:** Then Herod, when he saw that he was mocked of the wise men, was exceeding wroth, and sent forth, and slew all the children that were in Bethlehem, and in all the coasts thereof, from two years old and under, according to the time which he had diligently inquired of the wise men.

same firstborn status according to Jehovah,[38] then the original Passover event in Egypt was meant to be compared from two sides of the same first-born coin.

From the Old Testament perspective, Israel, as Jehovah's firstborn son, is called out of Egypt and "lives" because of the blood applied at Passover. From the New Testament perspective, Jesus, as the "Firstborn Begotten Son of God" is called out of Egypt to die as the Lamb of God. It was because of the blood of Christ as the replacement firstborn body that caused Israel to live as a national firstborn body.

In the context of viewing Jesus as the "Lamb of God who taketh away the sin of the world" (Jn. 1:29), the offer extends to all nations, not just Is-rael. The invitation is "whosoever will," must apply the blood of the Lamb spiritually on the doorframes of their heart to be "Passed-over." The two sides of the "firstborn" coin prove to be the Garden Program's greatest weapon, not only in terms of Cain and Israel's firstborn fix but as it also concerns the whole world.

The Firstborn Connection

If Cain represents the firstborn of fallen humanity, and Israel repre-sents the firstborn of all the fallen nations in the world—both of which need reform and redemption—then we have found our first common link between Cain and Israel. This firstborn connection between the two shows us why both desperately needed the sin-offering,[39] as the Cain and Abel story highlights.

Unfortunately, the first family did not have the benefit of knowing both sides of the firstborn coin to aid in their understanding. If they did, they would have understood the only reason the birthright had any value was due to the sin-offering, which Jehovah would provide Himself at the ap-pointed time. Instead, the first family depended on their firstborn, which was backed by the legal arm of the birthright. But due to the fall, the eternal value of the family's inheritance remained bankrupt. Their only recourse was to consult with the highest counsel to find another legal remedy for

---

[38] **Mt. 17:5:** While he yet spake, behold, a bright cloud overshadowed them: and behold a voice out of the cloud, which said, This is my beloved Son, in whom I am well pleased; hear ye him.

[39] Christ as the sin-offering appears once "to put away sin by the sacrifice of himself" (Heb. 9:26). Having once died, there re-mains no more sacrifice for sins, "For by one offering he hath perfected forever them that are sanctified" (Heb. 10:14). With-out faith in the sacrificial death of Christ there is no salvation: (a) Christ "was delivered for our offences, and raised again for our justification" (Rom. 4:24-25), and (b) Christ died for the sins of His people, in order to take them away (1 Cor. 15:1-4). All the sacrifices of the Old Testament find their fulfillment in Christ, as the Lamb Slain: (a) Every morning and evening a lamb was sacrificed in the temple, and (b) To show that Jesus Christ was typified by those Old Testament sacrifices, He was declared by John the Baptist to be "...THE LAMB OF GOD, which taketh away the sin of the world" (Jn. 1:29).

their situation. Little did they know, Jehovah, as their counsel, was already on the case with the plan of salvation by way of substitution.

Now that we see biblical confirmation of the firstborn connection between Cain and Israel, we can confidently conclude Cain and the Christ-line ultimately represent two firstborn lines as suggested by the man theme as noted earlier in our introductory paragraphs. The Cain-line looks to firstborn Israel, while the Christ-line looks to Christ as the firstborn replacement line. Christ is the firstborn substitute—both nationally as well as personally. By this design, Christ as the substitute line becomes the legal remedy to the family's bankruptcy issue by paying the family's debt by His blood and restoring their eternal inheritance.

However, because Israel is a "body" on a national level, Christ is unable to pay the family's debt until they are "one national body" of believers. As such, all Israel must recognize Christ as their Messiah. This future event is their destiny as the Cain-line summary statement suggests and the last two chapters of this book will describe.

The Mark of the Firstborn

Now that we realize Cain and Israel share the same firstborn office within the family of fallen man, the Cain and Abel story continues to highlight even more commonalities between the two. For starters, Jehovah accepts Abel's sin-offering of the "firstlings of his flock"[40] over Cain's sin-offering of the "fruit of the ground."[41] Why was one offering selected over the other?

In the previous chapter of Genesis, we learned how Jehovah cursed the ground due to the sin of Adam.[42] This curse was a literal one. Therefore, the state of the earth and anything produced from it was genuinely cursed. Jehovah, bound by His word, was unable to accept any "fruit of the ground" as an offering. That fact alone provides good cause. However, there are still more reasons why Cain's offering was not accepted, which turns the whole Cain and Abel drama into an opportunity to outline the "mark" of the firstborn.

Cain, as the firstborn of fallen man, has five primary characteristics:

---

[40] **Gen. 4:4:** And Abel, he also brought of the firstlings of his flock and of the fat thereof. And the Lord had respect unto Abel and to his offering.

[41] **Gen. 4:3:** And in process of time it came to pass, that Cain brought of the fruit of the ground an offering unto the Lord.

[42] **Gen. 3:17:** And unto Adam he said, Because thou hast hearkened unto the voice of thy wife, and hast eaten of the tree, of which I commanded thee, saying, Thou shalt not eat of it: cursed is the ground for thy sake; in sorrow shalt thou eat of it all the days of thy life.

1. He rejects the true sin-offering. (Gen. 4:3-4).
2. He divides the family line. (Gen. 4:12-14).
3. He has a delayed-salvation pattern. (Gen. 4:15).
4. He has a murderous heart. (Gen. 4:8-11).
5. He has the choice to choose wisely. (Gen. 4:7).

Together, these five traits become the "mark" of the firstborn in terms of his spiritually fallen condition. Therefore, Cain's "mark," as it relates to the "firstborn of fallen man" typology, is not limited to physical appearance. Remember, the fuller meaning of *HIS-Story* stretches far beyond our time, into eternity. So, from Jehovah's perspective on an eternal scale, the "mark" of the firstborn of fallen man is a heart issue.

By identifying Cain's primary traits, we have managed to create a reliable profile to track the firstborn of fallen man throughout biblical history. In the pre-flood period, the firstborn position began by an individual. In the post-flood period, the firstborn role develops into a national body known as Israel. Curiously, Cain's five character-traits are common to National Israel, and that portion stuck "working" under the Law.[43]

The Faces of the Firstborn

Once we see how the five character-traits of Cain, in type, serve as the "mark" of the firstborn of fallen man, it is not hard to recognize how Cain is a type of Jewish Israel. He represents that portion of Israel stuck "working" under the Law. As firstborns, both Cain and Israel bear the firstborn "mark" of Jehovah before the world. As noted previously, Cain's mark was more than just a physical mark—it was a spiritual condition. This same marked condition holds true for National Israel because they rejected Jesus as their sin-offering just as Cain did in his day.

Therefore, the "mark of the firstborn" assumes a spiritual condition only Jehovah can fix. This conclusion becomes evident by comparing the different administrations held within the office. The firstborn office, as administered by both Cain and National Israel, unquestionably portrays a weakness, which leads to "mortal sorrow" and death for the

---

[43] **Jas. 2:10:** For whosoever shall keep the whole law, and yet offend in one *point*, he is guilty of all. According to *JFB*, "The best manuscripts read, "Whosoever *shall have kept* the whole law, and yet *shall have offended* (literally, 'stumbled'; not so strong as 'fall,' Rom. 11:11) in one (point; here, the *respecting of persons*), is (hereby) become guilty of all." The law is one seamless garment which is rent if you but rend a part; or a musical harmony which is spoiled if there be one discordant note [Tirinus]; or a golden chain whose completeness is broken if you break one link [Gataker]. You thus break *the whole law*, though not the whole of the law, because you offend against *love*, which is the fulfilling of the law. If any part of a man be leprous, the whole man is judged to be a leper. God requires perfect, not partial, obedience. We are not to choose out parts of the law to keep, which suit our whim, while we neglect others." (*JFB Commentary*, Jas. 2:10).

family. By the same token, that very same office as administered by Christ portrays a strength, which leads to prosperity and eternal life for the family.

Our last consideration is how the Cain and Abel narrative purposely prefigures death is allotted to the younger brother while life to the older. Figuratively speaking, Christ also is considered Israel's younger brother, who died for all, not just for the firstborn class, but as humanity's next of kin. Christ's birth into the family of fallen Adam offers salvation to all because He lived and died without sin — unlike the rest of us.

If Firstborn Cain is a type of the Jew, or that portion of Israel stuck "working" under the Law, then what about Abel? What is Abel's place within the family? Whom does Abel represent in type? Since Abel appears to have no genealogical record, how can he and his line be established through death? The next chapter will answer these questions and provide more clues as we continue to trace *HIS-Story*.

CHAPTER 4
The Younger "Lost" Son

With the first two chapters as a backdrop, the two main points we must keep in mind as we continue in this chapter is how the first family of fallen man lost their two sons due to their omission on the Christ-line or Christ's genealogy through Seth, the replacement line of Adam. The loss of Adam's two sons in the genealogical record is the Bible's way of saying any name not written in the "Book of Life," which is Christ, has no life.

The other point to keep in mind is both Cain and Israel, in type, are both firstborns of the fallen family on a personal and national level. Both share the family's birthright position. However, because the family inheritance went bankrupt due to the fall, all legal claims are suspended until the family's debt is satisfied, thereby resolving the bankruptcy issue.

In the last chapter on *The Elder "Lost" Son*, we became familiar with the "mark of the firstborn" by identifying the five primary character traits of Cain. He serves as a type of the "firstborn of fallen man." From there, we learned how the sum of Cain's traits mirrors the "mark" of the Jew, or that portion of Israel stuck "working" under the Law. In this chapter, we now turn to the other "lost" son of the "family of fallen man."

If we think of the Cain-line in terms of that visible, "marked," and earthly line of God, then, by contrast, the Abel-line is that heavenly, "unmarked," and spiritual line of God. The Genesis account asserts that even after his death, Abel's blood could still cry out. (Gen. 4:10). Even the prodigal son parable illustrates how the life-estate lost by the younger son was restored instantly upon reconciliation with his father.

What is curious about the younger son in the Cain and Abel story and the prodigal son parable is how both sons lose their life early and in their own way. Both younger sons in each tale are seen and heard by the father. This mental picture naturally conjures additional insights as to how the two younger sons "live," even amidst death and distance, in each story.

In typological terms, Abel stands as that mysterious line, who died—yet lives, because the sin-offering was applied by faith. Because of "His blood," life is freely offered to all who come into the body of Christ by faith. Their genealogical record instantly becomes part of Christ's own record. In this chapter, we will seek to provide support for this conclusion.

The Firstborn of Re-Creation

Even when Scripture is silent, there is a message for our understanding. Silence applies especially in the case of Abel. However, his fate is not clearly understood until we examine the rest of the Cain and Abel story. Up until this point, Adam and his two lost sons, Cain and Abel, have been our primary focus, and with good reason—they were the sons of promise.

It would appear the first family was off to a good start when Eve pronounced at the arrival of the first son she *acquired* (the meaning of Cain's name) from Jehovah. However, as the story unfolded, soon that joy dwindled to a mere *vapor* or *breath* (or in other words, spirit-form), which is the essence of Abel's name. Now with Abel's death and the firstborn cast out of the family, how would the Garden Prophecy (Gen. 3:15) ever be fulfilled? The vision of hope in the abilities of the Adamic offspring is bleak at best.

Due to the failure of Adam's first two sons, Adam had to begin again because the Garden Prophecy intended human genetics to be its vehicle. This expectation makes Adam's third son a significant figure on the Christ-line. As the replacement son, Seth, in type, points to Christ as the sin-offering, which is freely offered to redeem all born in the family of fallen man so they can live in Him as a new creation, as typified by Abel.

As number typology dictates, Seth's two older brothers before him prophetically became a witness to the world by their very own stories of inadequacy. In other words, by Cain and Abel's very absence in the Christ-line record, they both bear witness to this fundamental fact: fallen man and its corrupt seed have no power and no hope to continue the family line into eternity. Their "mortal sorrow" is a consequence of sin. Sin caused the curse given in the Garden and provides the reason why the Firstborn Primitive Office went bankrupt and lost the inheritance of eternal life and dominion of the earth.

The Apostle Paul beautifully summarizes the effects of the "Garden Curse" by stating the "wages of sin is death." (Rom. 6:23). So too, it can be said that fallen man, laboring under the curse of sin, can only produce death within his family line. In graphic terms, the genetic code of humanity is literally "cursed to death," and its ability to continue its line stopped for all eternity.

Thankfully, things take a turn after the birth of Adam and Eve's third son:

> **Gen. 4:25:** "And Adam knew his wife again; and she bare a son, and called his name Seth: For God, *said she*, hath appointed me another seed instead of Abel, whom Cain slew.

Under the Divine inspiration of the Holy Spirit, Scripture memorialized the birth of this new son as the "appointed replacement seed" for the fallen family line. Eve, whether intentionally or unintentionally, finally captures the true meaning of the Garden Prophecy of Genesis 3:15 as more of a Garden *Promise* instead of a Garden *Curse*. Typologically speaking, this incident highlights the inadequacies of Adam's firstborn son and the need for a *qualified* replacement line.

Abel is supernaturally associated with death in the Genesis record. This concept highlights his ability to speak and be heard by Jehovah, even in death. (Gen. 4:10). Therefore, Abel typifies Christ at His first coming as one who is born to die in the likeness of "mortal flesh," yet, innocent of deserving death. In this way, typology is highlighting an important and very significant attribute of Christ; namely, Christ knew no sin.[44] Due to His total obedience at Calvary,[45] Jehovah, being faithful to His word, raised His only begotten Son because mortal flesh, as typified by the cry of Abel's blood from the grave, has no power of its own to do so.

With Abel's death becoming the type of Christ as a natural-born innocent man who came to die in place of a guilty man, we can understand how the death penalty was satisfied.[46] With that part of the equation removed, the Garden Program could move toward the restoration and harvest efforts on new ground. Typologically speaking, the new son, Seth, was given to the first family to reflect a fresh start and a new beginning apart from the old family model and its contaminated fleshly material.

Seth, in type, represents the only son of fallen Adam, who is free from sin and the grave because his line ends with Christ. This is the only redeeming quality of the man Seth because he, too, is a sinner like the rest of us.

---

[44] **2 Cor. 5:21:** Him who knew no sin he made to be sin on our behalf; that we might become the righteousness of God in him.

[45] Before the creation of the world, Christ had committed Himself willingly to the Cross (Isa. 50:4-7; Heb. 10:5-10; 1 Pet. 1:19-20). He laid down His life (Jn. 10:11, 18). He poured out His life to death (Isa. 53:12), and He gave Himself up as an offering and a sacrifice to God (Eph. 5:2).

[46] **Rom. 6:23:** For the wages of sin is death; but the free gift of God is eternal life in Christ Jesus our Lord.

Typology also purposely uses a ten-member scale on the Christ-line in the pre-flood period as a prophetic timeline for the ages.[47] With this in mind, the leap between Adam to Seth on the Christ-line's timeline represents a monumental break-through from the old creation to the new creation, in type.

New Life, New Blood

The idea of Abel's life representing the sinless side of Christ as a literal "son of mortal man" is portrayed by Abel's unjust death at the hands of his own brother, Cain. (Gen. 4:8). Since Jehovah confronts Cain in the very next passage, and the New Testament confirms Abel's righteousness (Heb. 11:4), we can conclude that Abel did not deserve death. From that conclusion alone, we can view Abel as innocent of the crime, which caused his death. Here, the typological focus carefully stresses the idea of "innocence" of a crime that deserves death.

Abel, although not sinless, was innocent because he did not deserve death for a crime that he was falsely considered guilty of. This fact alone directly parallels Christ's circumstance that concerns His own undeserving death on the cross. However, Paul stated Christ's innocence in this way, "For he [God] hath made him [Christ] to be sin for us, who knew no sin; that we might be made the righteousness of God in him." (2 Cor. 5:21).

Because of Abel's associations in the Genesis narrative, typology can move forward to point out how death and the grave had no right to keep those who do not deserve death. The strange crying out of Abel's blood from the tomb helps to support this understanding. However, while the Cain and Abel story can only represent Christ's innocence through types and shadows, Paul's letters clearly explain there is "life in the blood" because of Christ's sacrificial death on the cross as the sin-offering. Christ alone paid the penalty of the death curse upon mankind pronounced in the Garden.[48]

The meaning of the sacrificial death in Cain and Abel's day was legally defined later by Moses as, "life resides in the blood."[49] By this definition, life depends on that liquid or fluid state of the blood. This fluid quality of the Godhead points to the Holy Spirit because He is frequently described in terms of wine and water in Scripture. With such a description, the transitional counterparts, such as air or breath, also apply to the Holy Spirit.

---

[47] This will be fully demonstrated in the final chapters of *HIS-Story*.

[48] 1 Cor. 1:20-23, 10:16; Eph. 2:13-14; Rom. 6:4, 8:10; Gal. 2:20; Phil. 1:20; Col. 3:3-4; 2 Tim. 1:1.

[49] **Lev. 17:11:** For the life of the flesh is in the blood: and I have given it to you upon the altar to make an atonement for your souls: for it is the blood that maketh an atonement for the soul.

Remember, the meaning of Abel's name is "vapors," and is a transitional form of liquid and foreshadows the ghostly or a spiritual presence of a being. In this light, typology focuses on the spiritual life of Abel as a believer in Christ because He did not deserve death, yet died, nonetheless. Hebrews 11:4 confirms Abel's faith and righteousness by stating, "By faith, Abel offered unto God a more excellent sacrifice than Cain, by which he obtained witness that he was righteous, God testifying of his gifts: and by it, he being dead yet speaketh." Abel not only represents spiritual life by faith despite his physical death, but he also can be thought of as a "life hid in Christ," deemed righteous.

New Life, New Body

There are many verses by Paul, but the select few listed below will serve to establish the "life in Christ" concept, which is always a life that identifies with His death and is deemed righteous, like Abel.

> **Gal. 2:20-21:** "I am crucified with Christ: nevertheless I live; yet not I, but Christ liveth in me: and the life which I now live in the flesh I live by the faith of the Son of God, who loved me, and gave himself for me. I do not frustrate the grace of God: for if righteousness *come* by the law, then Christ is dead in vain."

> **Rom. 8:10-11:** "And if Christ be in you, the body is dead because of sin; but the Spirit is life because of righteousness. But if the Spirit of him that raised up Jesus from the dead dwell in you, he that raised up Christ from the dead shall also quicken your mortal bodies by his Spirit that dwelleth in you."

> **Col. 3:1-4:** "If ye then be risen with Christ, seek those things which are above, where Christ sitteth on the right hand of God. Set your affection on things above, not on things on the earth. *For ye are dead, and your life is hid with Christ in God.* When Christ, who is our life, shall appear, then shall ye also appear with him in glory [emphasis added]."

2 Cor. 5:17: "Therefore if any man *be* in Christ, *he is* a new creature: old things are passed away; behold, all things are become new."

Gal. 6:15: "For in Christ Jesus neither circumcision availeth anything, nor uncircumcision, but a new creature."

Gal. 3:28: "There is neither Jew nor Greek, there is neither bond nor free, there is neither male nor female: for ye are all one in Christ Jesus."

From these passages, Paul's concept of a "life in Christ" carries a unifying element, eliminating all divisions of people to form one glorious spiritual body that spans across the ages outside of time and space. It is a body that is unidentifiable in the natural. It is a body that is unseen and "dead" to the world and a body that is only identifiable in Christ, which takes on His image and His righteousness. It is a body of individuals who live a life filled and guided by the Holy Spirit, who was sent as the Comforter to abide with believers—both Jew and Gentile—in Christ forever (Jn. 14:16) and who will teach all things (Jn. 14:26).

We have noted how Scripture uses liquid (and its transitional forms), in type, to highlight the influences of the Holy Spirit and the spiritual life of a body. Scripture also views the Levitical Law's "life in the blood" in terms of the physical, while "life in the Spirit" applies to the spiritual. This makes the spiritual body of Christ, a body of flesh, which has emerged from death to life as a "new creation" on new, resurrection ground.

Likewise, the unique creation of Eve rests on resurrected ground. She was formed from Adam's pierced side while he slept, and both become "one" body as a result. (Gen. 2:21-24). Similarly, Christ is one with His Church, known as the "body of Christ." Because Christ experienced the "sleep of death" literally as Adam did figuratively, and because both were pierced in the side, the bride, as represented by both Eve and the Church, lives.

This idea fits nicely with the Jewish concept of sleep and death, which relates to three Hebrew words: *shakab, yashen,* and *shenah.*[50] Collectively, the three words express death as a form of sleeping or rest. For example,

---

[50] Strong's #7109, #3462, and #8142 respectively.

38

Job speaks of death as to "lie down in the dust."[51] When dead, an Israelite's body is said to be "resting with their ancestors."[52] In Psalms, death is simply the "sleep of death."[53] In the New Testament, both Jesus and Paul continued this same style in their day.

Furthermore, by comparing Eve's strange "generation," and Abel's stranger "regeneration," it becomes clear that both share a kind of *spiritual existence* because both "live through death." Once we place Eve and Abel in the spiritually "born-again" category of existence, the primary difference between Eve and Abel is their gender and their relationship with the Father.

When Scripture refers to Jehovah's people in the feminine, it relates to the idea of fertility, which carries the expectation of seedtime and harvest. A perfect example is Revelation 12, where Israel is referred to as the "woman," who delivered a "man child" (Christ).

Jehovah's children, on the other hand, are typically characterized in the masculine to underscore the product of the "Garden Union." This practice gives Scripture the ability to address the sons collectively or by their divisions. Such insight explains why the Old Testament prophets refer to God's people in the feminine on some occasions and later in the masculine.

Such spiritual life is not active in Cain, who represents Jewish National Israel, or that portion of Israel stuck "working" under the Law, as the firstborn of the "family of fallen man." Both Cain and Israel exist in the natural with a carnal mindset and live in the *material realm* in an *earthly existence* outside of death in Christ. Thus, Jewish National Israel and Cain need the sin-offering, which continually lies at the door to be "born" of the Spirit.

New Life Restores the Family

We continue to see the different approaches to Jehovah by the two lost lines of Adam are exact opposites. For example, the firstborn works, while the younger rests. The older teaches Law, while the younger teaches grace. The blood sign of the elder is physical circumcision as it relates to Passover. At the same time, the younger's is spiritual circumcision[54] as it relates to

---

[51] Job 7:21, 20:11, 21:26.

[52] Gen. 47:30; Duet. 31:16; 2 Sam. 7:12; 1 Ki. 2:10.

[53] Ps. 13:3, 90:5.

[54] Jesus speaking of Lazarus (Jn. 11:11-14), and Paul speaking of "sleeping in Jesus (I Thes. 4:13-14).

communion[55] by drinking from the cup[56] and feeding on the "Bread" of Life."[57] The older has a physical, literal temple, while the younger's temple is spiritual.[58]

With differences so extreme, it is hard to believe they are even related at all. The truth is they are brothers because they are the lost sons of the Father. So too, Firstborn Israel is the older brother to the Christian Church. Both are sons of the Father, yet both lost in their own way. As such, He sent His only begotten Son, Christ, as the replacement line to reconnect all lost family lines of the ages.

At this point, the identification of the cast of characters for *HIS-Story* is now complete and the stage is set. With Cain serving as an early portrait of Firstborn National Israel and Abel's spiritual life reflecting the Christian Church, we can now turn to the Garden Program's rescue plan. As we begin tracing *HIS-Story,* His bloodline will serve as our tour guides. Since Adam is the first member in on the Christ-line, the next chapter will start there.

---

[55] **Rom. 2:29:** But he *is* a Jew, which is one inwardly; and circumcision *is that* of the heart, in the spirit, *and* not in the letter; whose praise *is* not of men, but of God.

[56] **1 Cor. 11:24-32.** Communion was to be observed at the table by drinking the cup with wine representing Christ's blood, and eating broken bread representing Christ's broken body. Christ's blood represents His Life. (1 Cor. 11:24-32 and Lev. 17:11).

[57] **Jn. 6:35:** And Jesus said unto them, I am the bread of life: he that cometh to me shall never hunger; and he that believeth on me shall never thirst.

[58] **1 Cor. 3:16:** Know ye not that ye are the temple of God, and *that* the Spirit of God dwelleth in you?

CHAPTER 5 – ADAM
"Christ Comes in the Office of Man"

The Christ-Line Summary Statement

Now that we understand how fallen Adam's two sons, Cain and Abel, represent, in type, two lost lines of the family of man in "mortal sorrow" on an eternal scale, we can move forward with *HIS-Story* as told by *HIS-Blood-line*. To do this, we will begin tracking the contributions made by each member listed within the Christ-line in the pre-flood period. The Cain-line will be included in our considerations once we get to the final chapters for reasons that will become clear during the process.

Since the Cain-line stops in the eighth generation of Adam in the pre-flood period, by default, the Christ-line becomes the plumb-line. In terms of typology, the Christ-line provides the standard because it is the only line that survived judgment by the flood in Noah's day. This scenario echoes Christ's own salvation model as He is *the Way, the Truth, and the Life.*[59] As far as the Bible is concerned, Christ is the only way to be saved.[60] For us to deviate from that perspective is to know with certainty that our path to "Truth" will never begin.

Before we can continue our excavational quest, we need to review the Christ-line summary statement once again:

Christ-Line Summary Statement:
Man, appointed mortal sorrow, [but] the Blessed God shall come down teaching, His death shall bring the despairing rest."

Again, we cannot help but note the statement's overall evangelical tone. However, we must not forget that the theme of the message will take on the meaning of the first name listed in the line. Since Adam means "man" in Hebrew, then the summary statement of both lines will take on that theme in some unique way. As noted earlier, this applies to both the Cain and the Christ-line because both lines begin with Father Adam. In the case of the

---

[59] **Jn. 14:6:** Jesus saith unto him, I am the way, the truth, and the life: no man cometh unto the Father, but by me.

[60] **Jn. 10:9:** I am the door: by me if any man enter in, he shall be saved, and shall go in and out, and find pasture.

Christ-line, the man theme relates to Christ's perfect firstborn position within the family of fallen man. While the Cain-line keeps to the theme of the imperfect firstborn of fallen man.

Adam: First in Order and First in Meaning

To gain an understanding of Christ fulfilling His appointed role as man, we must, once again, pause to review Adam in type. Except now, we will conduct this review in terms of the man theme as it relates to the meaning of the Christ-line's statement. Not only is Adam listed first in the Christ-line, but he is also first for all lines. Every human being traces back to Adam genetically. Thus, the reasons why Adam's actions in the Garden affected all of humanity.

Because of Adam's position, again we are reminded of Paul's letter to the Corinthians[61] as he draws comparisons of the first Adam in his "perfect state" to Christ as the second Adam in His "perfect state." As noted earlier, Paul refers to Christ as the Last Adam. In terms of this typological focus, we can view the man theme as it compares with Adam in his unfallen, incorruptible state to Christ as the last Adam in His perfect and incorruptible state.

Consequently, the firstborn position as it relates to the creation of man applies *before* and *after* the fall. Unlike Cain, who was the firstborn of fallen man, Christ, in the context of Adam (in his perfect state), is the firstborn of creation. Christ has a superior firstborn position to both Cain, and Adam simply because He "is the firstborn of all creation." (Col. 1:15).

Firstborn Model

Paul said, "[Christ] is the image of the invisible God, the *firstborn* of every creature: for by him all things were created." (Col. 1:15-16a). Besides learning about the preeminence of Christ, what makes this verse more notable is the Greek word used by Paul that was translated as "firstborn" in this verse is "prōtotokos." The word *prototype* derives from this same Greek word. A prototype, remember, is a model used to make copies on the manufacturing line. Let that sink in.

So, just as Adam became the substance to create the world's population, so too, Christ before him was the substance used to create Father Adam. Centuries later, Christ was then "born" of the substance of the

---

[61] 1 Cor. 15:45-49.

woman to "father" an eternal race. By this, Christ, as the Last Adam, becomes the re-creation model (or prototype) "from which all things are made."[62] From that perspective, we can somewhat understand how Christ really can be *before* and *after* Adam.

Adam: First in Title and First in Reformed Office

Since Adam is first in order, it follows the meaning of his name must also be first in theme. From a Christian perspective, it is not difficult to understand how the meaning of Adam's name "man" points to the two natures of Christ. He is both God and man. To help illustrate this, we look to Bullinger to explain how the phrase "Son of Man" has two meanings:

> "**As applied, without the article**, to men, it means merely a descendant of Adam, a human being. But as used of Christ with the article—"The Son of Man" it is different, for He was not a descendant of the first Adam, at any rate on the father's side. He was man 'of the substance of His mother,' but His generation was by the Holy Ghost. Herein lies the difference between Christ and mere man. He was "the Second Man—The Lord from heaven." Applied it relates to his dominion rights to the possession of the earth. …We can never dissociate this thought from "The Son of Man." He is "the Last Adam"- not another man like all the other sons of Adam, but a different man. "In the likeness of sinful flesh," of course, with the 'infirmities' of the flesh, but not with its sins. We must not confound 'infirmities' with sins." (Bullinger, *The Divine Names*, XIII).

Bullinger's insights beautifully complement the man theme in the Christ-line summary statement. Christ must satisfy the first function of the Man Office (or the "Adam" Office) before He can assume the second function of His office of which His title speaks. The Christ-line summary statement supports this idea, which is the reason why the "Blessed God's death" is mentioned before the Despairing can find rest.

The distinction Bullinger makes is necessary because it clarifies how the first stage of Christ as a man born in "mortal sorrow" has "no life in Himself."

---

[62] Gen. 1:27; Col. 1:15.

His resurrection was solely dependent upon the resurrection power supplied by the Father.[63] Scripture maintains that Christ is unique because He is not only born within the family of fallen man on His mother's side, but He is also the only begotten Son of His Father, Jehovah.

It is paramount that we understand the term "begotten" because it denotes explicitly *resurrection* power supplied by Jehovah. This concept is represented in the book of Hebrews:

> **Heb. 1:5:** "For unto which of the angels said he at any time,
> Thou art my Son, this day have I begotten thee? And again,
> I will be to him a Father, and he shall be to me a Son?"

Now add Peter's address to the Jewish congregation in the book of Acts, which provides a fuller meaning of this word begotten that we are considering:

> **Acts 13:33-34:** "God hath fulfilled the same unto us their children, in that he hath raised up Jesus again; as it is also written in the second psalm, *Thou art my Son, this day have I begotten thee. And as concerning that he raised him up from the dead, now no more to return to corruption* [emphasis added]."

Both the Hebrew writer and Peter are quoting Psalm 2:6-7, "Yet have I set my king upon my holy hill of Zion. I will declare the decree: the LORD hath said unto me, Thou art my Son; this day have I begotten thee." When was Christ pronounced "begotten"? The verse before in the same Psalm gives us the answer—in the time of His wrath, He will speak sour displeasure to the nations.[64]

Because Psalm 2 links Christ's "begotten" status with His second coming, we are instantly transported to the tribulation period as described by the book of Revelation. On that day, Christ comes as "The Son of Man" in His resurrected state to judge the nations,[65] initiate the first resurrection,[66]

---

[63] Acts 13:33; Rom. 6:4.

[64] **Ps. 2:5:** Then shall he speak unto them in his wrath, and vex them in his sore displeasure.

[65] **Rev. 15:4:** Who shall not fear thee, O Lord, and glorify thy name? for *thou* only *art* holy: for all nations shall come and worship before thee; for thy judgments are made manifest.

[66] **Rev. 20:5-6:** But the rest of the dead lived not again until the thousand years were finished. This is the first resurrection. Blessed and holy is he that hath part in the first resurrection: on such the second death hath no power, but they shall be priests of God and of Christ, and shall reign with him a thousand years.

and take His royal seat at Mount Zion[67] in the Millennial Kingdom as King of Kings and Lord of Lords. His begotten state qualifies Him as the "Firstborn of the Dead."[68] Remember, the Garden Prophecy is about the coming "seed of the woman." Therefore, Christ must be generated and sown within the substance of the woman. This detail is evident in Luke's description of the Christ child by stating:

> **Lk. 1:35**: "And the angel answered and said unto her [Mary], The Holy Ghost shall come upon thee, and the power of the Highest shall overshadow thee: therefore also *that holy thing* which shall be born of thee shall be called the Son of God [emphasis added]."

Firstborn of All Firstborns

Now that we have some background about Christ's role in the context of Adam, or rather, the office of man, we turn to the portion of the Christ-line summary statement, where it reads, "the Blessed God who shall come down." In terms of Christ, this phrase highlights His first coming when He came to correct what went wrong with humanity. Namely, to pay Adam's debt, which became the death sentence for all mankind.

From the Cain and Abel story, the firstborn concept powerfully demonstrates typological principles within a family drama. We learn how Cain is the first to be born. As firstborn of a fallen race, Cain's firstborn office was to maintain the strength of his father's house and distribute the family's inheritance to subsequent heirs within the line. From our present chapter, two additional considerations add to this perspective. First, Adam, much less Cain, failed to have the strength to conquer death. Moreover, Adam's "house" stood bankrupt due to the fall.

Merely reforming and replacing Cain and his firstborn office is not enough. Fallen humanity required Christ to go back further than Cain. To cure the defective line, we must go back to the source—fallen Adam. To do this, Christ had to become the "Firstborn of Creation."[69] This status is far superior to all God's creations, including Adam and the angels. In His begotten state, He is also the "Firstborn of the Dead,"[70] who conquered death,

---

[67] **Rev. 2:27:** And he shall rule them with a rod of iron; as the vessels of a potter shall they be broken to shivers: even as I received of my Father.

[68] 1 Cor. 15:21, 42; Col. 1:18; Rev. 1:5, 13, 14:14.

[69] **Col. 1:15:** Who is the image of the invisible God, the firstborn of every creature.

hell, and the grave. He alone has the keys to free the captives, just as Abel's blood crying out from the grave signifies.[71]

With Christ being the Firstborn of Creation, the Firstborn of the Dead, and the Firstborn of the Father,[72] He covers the full spectrum of the firstborn office as it relates to both the spiritual and material realms. Not only is the value of the Father's house restored to Christ as the Last Adam, but He maintains the strength and the inheritance of the Father's house, without interruption, on an eternal scale. Nothing can jeopardize the Father's house if Christ as the firstborn is alive and fulfills his role as King and Priest for the family.

Legal Remedies in the Absence of the Firstborn

However, in the realm of fallen men, legal remedies had to be established if, and when, a firstborn was not available. An additional office known as the "Kinsman-Redeemer" was in place to save an Israelite's family from being cut off from the homeland. Unlike Cain's firstborn office, this office speaks of Christ, in type, as "next of kin" to any individual born within the family who is willing and able to be their "redeemer."

According to Israelite inheritance laws, a male blood relative qualifies as a *kinsman* or next of kin. There are three primary objections to this office: (1) redemption of property, (2) redemption of person, and (3) and redemption of blood (vengeance) as outlined in this next chart:

The Role of the Kinsman Redeemer		
Redemption of Property (Lev. 25:25-28)	Redemption of Person (Lev. 25:47-55)	Redemption of Blood (Num. 35:16-21, 31)
The kinsman acts on behalf of an impoverished relative to purchase and return the land that a poor relative was forced to sell. He, the kinsman, redeems or buys back the land.	The kinsman redeems a relative who was forced to sell himself into slavery and "buy" him out of slavery to set him free.	The kinsman is an avenger. When a relative of his is murdered, he is to avenge the death. It is his duty as "goel" to protect the honor of the family and exact vengeance.

Chart 5 – The Role of the Kinsman Redeemer

---

[70] **Col. 1:18:** And he is the head of the body, the church: who is the beginning, the firstborn from the dead; that in all things he might have the preeminence.

[71] **Rev. 1:17-18:** And when I saw him, I fell at his feet as dead. And he laid his right hand upon me, saying unto me, Fear not; I am the first and the last: I *am* he that liveth, and was dead; and, behold, I am alive for evermore, Amen; and have the keys of hell and of death.

[72] **Rom. 8:29:** For whom he did foreknow, he also did predestinate to be conformed to the image of his Son, that he might be the firstborn among many brethren.

As we can see from the chart, the Kinsman Redeemer protects the family in three primary ways: (1) the family's honor, (2) the family's inheritance to the homeland, and (3) family members from personal debts that would jeopardize their freedom. If the firstborn of the family died, the subsequent heirs looked to a kinsman to redeem their legal rights as an Israelite.

Consequently, widows also had a statutory provision known as the Levirate Marriage Law. This legal remedy required a dead man's brother[73] to marry the childless widow and to father a son. The son would assume the dead man's name on behalf of the widow and the rest of the dead brother's family to claim their inheritance in the homeland.[74] The book of Ruth gives us a textbook example of how the Israelite inheritance laws work. It is also a story that highlights how the Kinsman Redeemer[75] plays a vital role, should the other legal provisions fail the family.

Ruth was a Moabite who embraced the Jewish faith. She married into an Israelite family who settled in the land of Moab.[76] Due to unfortunate circumstances, childless Ruth, along with her mother-in-law, Naomi, became widows. Worse, Naomi lost both her sons, leaving no one left to father a son in place of Ruth's deceased husband, according to the Levirate Law. This situation left both women destitute. Since the ladies lived in Ruth's homeland, amidst a people known for their hatred towards Israel,[77] both were a likely disgrace to their Israelite kin.

Fortunately for the two women, their desperation and their faith gave them the courage to journey back to Israel. From there, providence led them to find a next of kin, Boaz. Out of his own volition, he lovingly looked past their offenses and accepted the role of their Kinsman Redeemer. With that, their family's inheritance was restored.

---

[73] The brother fulfilling the family's duty to a widow is called "levirate," which means "brother-in-law." See, Gen. 38:8.

[74] Deut. 25:5-10.

[75] Ruth 2:20, 3:2, 9-13, 4:1-11.

[76] The story of Ruth takes place during the period of the judges where, "in those days Israel had no king; everyone did as he saw fit." (Judges 17:6). Some commentators note that Naomi's husband, Elimelech, was a man of wealth and good standing in Judah, and sinned by leaving his Israelite homeland in a time of famine to preserve his own family. He took his wife Naomi, and his two sons, Mahlon and Kilion, to Moab, which was intended to be temporary, but turned out to be a period of about ten years.

[77] The implications of Ruth being a Moabite is significant because racial differences and hostilities are passed down through many generations. Ruth belonged to a people who had tried to put a curse on the Israelites. The Lord promised Abraham that He would make him into a great nation and that through him all nations would be blessed. Balak, King of Moab, was terrified by the Israelites so he summoned Balaam to come and curse them but was unable to because of Jehovah. Instead, Balaam taught the Moabite women to seduce the Israelites by enticing them to commit sexual immorality and to participate in their pagan festivals where they offered sacrifices to their gods. As a result, the Moabites were excluded from entering the assembly of the Lord.

Ruth and Naomi's story is a beautiful lesson as to how the inheritance for all Israelite families depended upon the firstborn son. From this lesson, we learn why the firstborn position is an essential role within the family's structure. Without him, the dependents (whether Jew or Gentile) fall into great peril. Unless a willing and able next of kin steps in, restoration back into the family's inheritance of the Promised Land is lost *forever*. Naomi and Ruth's story exemplifies Christ, who qualifies for both positions within the family.

Because Christ was born into the family of fallen Adam, He alone qualifies for both roles—as the firstborn of all firstborns and as Kinsman Redeemer. Together, both offices become the remedy for the human condition. Christ truly is the lifeline and keeper of all family lines. Consequently, since Christ first came as "son of man" and returns in His glorified title as "The Son of Man," the man theme of the Christ-line is confirmed to be more of a "man office," which is fulfilled by Christ.

Now that we understand the need for Christ to be born within the family of fallen Adam (or fallen "man" as his name means) to become the replacement line that redeems all family lines, the man theme makes perfect sense. With the biblical concept of substitution as a background, the next chapter on Seth will concentrate more on his remaining contributions to the fuller story to *HIS-Story*.

CHAPTER 6 – SETH
"Christ, the Rejected Substitute Firstborn Son"

Then Began Men to Call

Because Seth represents Christ's foundational role as the substitute line for all family lines of the earth born in "mortal sorrow," this concept was addressed early within the framing chapters. It was necessary because Seth plays an integral part within the cast of characters as it relates to their typological roles. Accordingly, this chapter, which bears his name, will proceed to concentrate on his remaining contributions to *HIS-Story*.

In addition to describing Seth as the son born in the "likeness and image"[78] of his father, the Genesis record stands firmly reserved. The only other information given to us concerns a strange event, which happened around the birth of Seth's own son, Enosh:

> **Gen. 4:25-26:** "And Adam knew his wife again; and she bare a son, and called his name Seth: For God, said she, hath appointed me *another seed* instead of Abel, whom Cain slew. *And to Seth, to him also there was born a son; and he called his name Enos: then began men to call upon the name of the LORD* [emphasis added]."

Surprisingly, this strange reference has produced one of the first major theological arguments between scholars and denominations. Some think that this scene points to the root cause of global apostasy, while many see it as support for the "Sethite" view. Saint Augustine was one of the early leading proponents of this view, which sees Cain as the wicked line of humanity. But Seth and his line, known as "Sethites," were considered the godly line of humanity charged with preserving the true worship of God.

At face value, the two passages in view seem to support Augustine's viewpoint. As Augustinian theology progressed within Catholicism worldwide, the prodigy of Seth was understood to be the only means to produce

---

[78] **Gen. 5:3:** And Adam lived an hundred and thirty years, and begat a son in his own likeness, after his image; and called his name Seth.

"purity of race." By default, his lineage assumed to be those "men calling on the name of the Lord." However, as we shall soon see, nothing could be further from the truth and more detrimental to biblical interpretation.

What is Purity of Race

First, let us talk briefly about the purity of race and the mixing of the bloodlines as a means for the contamination of men. Scripture teaches that due to the fall of Adam, all born of flesh are corrupt.[79] This statement unequivocally means that no matter what "line" mixed with the offspring of Adam, be it, Cain, Seth, or fallen angels, the end product will always be incurably defective and degenerate unless Divine intervention takes place.

When Adam and Eve sinned, instantly, their earthly bodies became a "temporary dwelling place" for their spirit-being. In this regard, the couple left their first estate, like the sons of God in Genesis 6. When the sons of God left their celestial habitation to live on earth with the daughters of men, they were considered "fallen" by "leaving their first estate."

This "fallen state" in terms of man becomes the reason why Jesus taught all men must be "born again."[80] Alternatively, all must be "born of the Spirit," or "born of God," to be able to live in eternity. These are all phrases used to illustrate the concept of regeneration and recreation by the process of resurrection.

The *seed* of God that germinates new life (or a new creation in Christ) is simply the *Word of Truth.*[81] Seth, in type, represents Christ in this way, being the "appointed seed of another." By introducing substitution as a new theme, typology's focus changes to Christ as a new seed, which is apart from fallen flesh and is sown by the simple act of hearing.[82] There is absolutely no sexual transmission involved in spiritual reproduction. Jesus, as the Word,[83] organically includes ideas and thoughts. As such, He becomes the literal eternal seed that is incorruptible and imperishable. His seed can only germinate within that lasting portion of a person. The immortal part

---

[79] The Apostle Paul clearly taught that "no one is righteous, and all have sinned and falls short of the Glory of God." (Rom. 3:10- 11, 23). Paul concludes that "For the wages of sin *is* death; but the gift of God *is* eternal life through Jesus Christ our Lord." (Rom. 6:23). Old Testament confirms, "All we like sheep have gone astray; we have turned every one to his own way; and the LORD hath laid on him the iniquity of us all." (Isa. 53:6).

[80] **Jn. 3:3:** Jesus answered and said unto him, Verily, verily, I say unto thee, Except a man be born again, he cannot see the kingdom of God.

[81] 1 Pet. 1:1, 23; Lk. 8:11; Jn. 1:14; Jam. 1:18.

[82] **Rom. 10:17:** So then faith *cometh* by hearing, and hearing by the word of God.

[83] **Jn. 1:14:** And the Word was made flesh, and dwelt among us, (and we beheld his glory, the glory as of the only begotten of the Father,) full of grace and truth.

of a person is what the Bible calls "the heart."[84] Because the body is now mortal, it requires transfiguration to live in eternity.[85]

Another interesting aspect to note in terms of Jesus as "the seed of Truth" is that He constantly affirmed that He is not a liar like the Devil, who is the father of lies. Satan has "no truth in him."[86] As the invisible seed of Christ is sown upon the hearts of men, make no mistake, "the father of lies" continues to sow his counterfeit seed. However, both types of seed, be it from the Devil or Christ, are sown by hearing[87] and not by physical (sexual) reproduction.

The angels had full knowledge that to disobey Divine Law is to face Divine judgment. When they determined to exchange their celestial existence for a lower one (Jud. 1:6), they were fully aware of the repercussions of that act. The option to turn back to their original estate was lost.

This same principle applies to fallen men at a certain point, whether they understand it or not. Thus, the reason why Lot's wife turned into a pillar of salt when she turned back to "face" judgment upon the city of Sodom and Gomorrah. It is only through re-creation that fallen men live unless they exercise the option to face judgment. Once we understand the "re-creation" or the "born-again" model has no association with the fallen condition, then the purity of race argument, as far as human genetics is concerned, provides no support for the Sethite view.

The Global Apostasy

What about the global apostasy context in connection with the Sethite view? At face value, English translations of the Genesis 4:26 passage imply that some public revival occurred in Seth's day. The Geneva Bible, which precedes the King James Version by 51 years,[88] states, "God began to move the hearts of the godly to restore religion, which had been suppressed by the wicked for a long time." This attitude may be one of the reasons why Saint Augustine's doctrine continues even in our day.

---

[84] Eph. 6:6; Heb. 4:12; 1Pet. 3:4.

[85] **Rom. 8:10-11:** And if Christ *be* in you, the body *is* dead because of sin; but the Spirit *is* life because of righteousness. But if the Spirit of him that raised up Jesus from the dead dwell in you, he that raised up Christ from the dead shall also quicken your mortal bodies by his Spirit that dwelleth in you.

[86] **Jn. 8:44-45**: Ye are of *your* father the devil, and the lusts of your father ye will do. He was a murderer from the beginning, and abode not in the truth, because there is no truth in him. When he speaketh a lie, he speaketh of his own: for he is a liar, and the father of it. And because I tell *you* the truth, ye believe me not.

[87] True hearing involves an active awareness using all the physical and spiritual senses that are available to the body that results in the transmission of understanding to the heart; it is not limited to taking in sound through the ear.

[88] Geneva Bible (1560); King James (1611). The Geneva Bible is an early English translation of the Bible. Its name comes from the fact it was first published in Geneva by Hebrew and Greek scholars who were refugees there. It is a small quarto with marginal notes and was divided into chapters and verses and became popular at once.

However, none of this is evident in the rendering of the King James Version of the Bible. It reads, "Then began men to call upon the name of the LORD," and also includes a curious marginal note, "themselves," which suggests men were calling themselves Jehovah. There was a global happening. The question is, what kind? For that answer we look to Bullinger once again:

> ***"Then began men to call upon the name of Jehovah."***
> If this refers to Divine worship it is not true: for Abel and Cain both began, and their descendants doubtless followed their example. What was really begun was the profanation of the Name of Jehovah. They began to call something by the Name of Jehovah. The Authorized Version suggests "themselves," in the margin. But the majority of the ancient Jewish commentators supply the Ellipsis by the words "their gods;" suggesting that they called the stars and idols their gods, and worshipped them. The Targum of Onkelos explains it: "then in his days the sons of men desisted from praying in the Name of the Lord." The Targum of Jonathan says: "That was the generation in whose days they began to err, and to make themselves idols, and surnamed their idols by the Name of the Word of the Lord." Kimchi, Rashi, and other ancient Jewish commentators agree with this." (*The Companion Bible*, App. 21).

Here, Bullinger points out the obvious. Divine worship existed well before Enosh's birth. What was different, as well as disturbing, was what Jewish scholarship claimed all along. They understood that all human rebellion traces back to this one occurrence as the earliest roots, but those roots continue to thrive today. This explains why the tower of Babel (Gen. 11:8-9), suddenly breaks on the scene almost immediately after the flood.

On that note, the mentioning of the celestial revolt in Genesis 6 is another marker involving end-time apostasy. Notice that when the two fallen races (fallen angels with fallen humanity) unite great wickedness descends.[89] Together, this unholy union produces universal apostasy against their Creator, if left unchecked.

This kind of insurrection gives cause for Divine judgment to cleanse the earth and to start over, as Noah's day represents. All to serve as a collective memory to warn us how history will, once again, repeat itself in the end (2 Pet. 3:4-7), as depicted in the Bible's last book as well as the final chapters in this book.

He Came Unto His Own, and His Own Knew Him Not

It is shocking to think how the world in Seth's day had the replacement line of Adam, whose line would eventually bring forth the true promised "seed of the woman" in Jesus' day. It is even more shocking to think how, at the very onset, the pre-flood world so easily aligned itself with the spreading of the seed of the serpent instead of the seed of the appointed Son, which was left unchecked and grew into worldwide rebellion in Noah's day.

In this chapter, we face the hard and sober truth about sinful flesh. Even the blessed-line produces "sons" that are no better than the Cain-line. Worse still, is how all the fallen sons of God, celestial and terrestrial, will once again unite in the last day to continue their rebellious take-over, as represented by apocalyptic Babylon. Except in that day, the plan of cosmic overthrow will *not* be interrupted by the Almighty like it was at the tower of Babel. Instead, the issue will be finally dealt with as Noah's flood represents and Revelation foretells.

At this point in *HIS-Story*, we see the replacement line begins with Seth, but the ability to save that which is lost is still unobtainable. Just as the world rejected Jesus, so too, Seth is treated in like manner. Thanks to the ancient Jewish sages, we can now understand that the influence of the serpent continues to rally for a worldwide rebellion to stop the success of the Garden Program's rescue mission. Nevertheless, according to the Garden Prophecy (Gen. 3:15), the fate of the serpent will be stopped by the "seed of the woman," which the next chapter on Enosh and Kenan will introduce.

---

[89] Gen. 6:5-8: And GOD saw that the wickedness of man was great in the earth, and that every imagination of the thoughts of his heart was only evil continually. And it repented the LORD that he had made man on the earth, and it grieved him at his heart. And the LORD said, I will destroy man whom I have created from the face of the earth; both man, and beast, and the creeping thing, and the fowls of the air; for it repenteth me that I have made them. But Noah found grace in the eyes of the LORD.

CHAPTER 7
ENOSH AND KENAN
"Christ Comes in Mortal Sorrow"

The Appointed Passion

Upon approaching the Christ-line's third and fourth members, we now come to the contributions of Enosh and Kenan. Enosh's name means "mortal," and Kenan's name means "sorrow." As we learned from the chapters on Adam and Seth, Christ's first order of business as "man" is to come as the substitute seed of the substance of the woman. With the addition of these next two members, Christ's divinity and right to the throne of David, as well as his human qualifications, come into question.

If Abel pictures Christ as an innocent life who dies in place of another, and Seth represents Christ as the appointed replacement seed of a new kind in fulfillment of the Garden Prophecy (Gen. 3:15), then the virgin birth becomes the critical component to the success of the Garden Program. The Gospel letters are beneficial in providing support to Jesus' true genetic identity. From the very first angelic announcement to Mary,[90] Jesus was called "the Son of the Highest" and "the Son of God." Even at the age of twelve, Jesus claimed God as His "Father" in the Temple.[91] In an explanation of His unique status, Jesus testified, "I proceeded forth and came from God."[92]

With the claims of Jesus aside, what about His record? Does His biological pedigree confirm He is the true *Seed* of God from the substance of a woman? Fortunately, two of Jesus' disciples, Matthew and Luke, preserved Christ's ancestry. Matthew's record aims to show Christ is the "seed" of Abraham,[93] in whom *all the families of the earth are blessed,*

---

[90] **Lk. 1:31-35:** And, behold, thou shalt conceive in thy womb, and bring forth a son, and shalt call his name Jesus. He shall be great, and shall be called the Son of the Highest: and the Lord God shall give unto him the throne of his father David: And he shall reign over the house of Jacob forever; and of his kingdom there shall be no end. Then said Mary unto the angel, how shall this be, seeing I know not a man? And the angel answered and said unto her, The Holy Ghost shall come upon thee, and the power of the Highest shall overshadow thee: therefore also that holy thing which shall be born of thee shall be called the Son of God.

[91] **Lk. 2:49:** And he said unto them, How is it that ye sought me? wist ye not that I must be about my Father's business?

[92] **Jn. 8:42:** Jesus said unto them, If God were your Father, ye would love me: for I proceeded forth and came from God; neither came I of myself, but he sent me.

[93] **Gal. 3:16:** Now to Abraham and his seed were the promises made. He saith not, And to seeds, as of many; but as of one, And to thy seed, which is Christ. **Gal. 3:29:** And if ye be Christ's, then are ye Abraham's seed, and heirs according to the promise.

as it revolves around His royal heritage.[94] Thus, he begins with Father Abraham,[95] then traces through King David and ends with Jacob, who was the father of Joseph, Mary's husband.

The New Testament Genealogy of Christ

Matthew's way of exacting the virgin birth is by ending his genealogy with, "And Jacob begat Joseph, the husband of Mary, *of whom was born Jesus*, who is called Christ [emphasis added]."[96] The phrase, "Jacob *begat* Joseph," is biological. In contrast, Joseph is simply the husband of Mary, which leaves Mary, *of whom was born Jesus*. The remarks are subtle but prove invaluable.

Luke, on the other hand, is more direct. He simply traces Jesus' lineage through Mary's family tree and ends with Father Adam to show that Christ is the *Seed* of God born of a virgin. In this way, Luke's approach stresses Jesus' humble capacity as "son of man." Matthew's approach exalts Christ in His glorified position as "The Son of Man."

Another example is how the two men count and organize their genealogies to form their two separate narratives. Chart 6 helps to illustrate this point. Notice how Luke's record has a total of 77 members, yet Matthew's focus is about arranging the members into three sets of fourteen. Each makes use of the number 7 but differently. The number 7 is appropriate because it looks to the weekly Sabbath-Rest in principle.

According to Exodus 31:16-17, the Sabbath is a sign between Jehovah and Israel, as well as a perpetual covenant.[97] With that in mind, Luke's 77 members bear witness (remember two is the number for witness as represented by the double sevens) that there is a perfect and complete rest from the Law to those in Christ. Christ is not only the Lord of the Sabbath (Mk. 2:28), but He is also the *Seed* of Abraham, who was credited as righteous before the Law was given and before circumcision[98] was required.

---

[94] Because Matthew's focus is on Jesus' royal descent, he is the only disciple that mentions the wise men from the East searching for the King of the Jews by following His star. Thus, fulfilling the following prophecies: The scepter will not depart from Judah (Gen. 49:10); The star that shall come forth from Jacob (Num. 24:17); The sign of Immanuel's virgin birth (Isa. 7.14); A great light that shines (Isa. 9.1-2); A ruler in Bethlehem-Ephratah (Micah 5:2; regarding "Ephratah" see Gen. 48:7); The coming of Messiah (Dan. 9:26); and the kings bring gifts to the Son (Ps. 72:1, 10-11; Isa. 60:6). Matthew also shows the fulfillment of the virgin birth prophecy (Mt. 1:22-23) and Christ as the Messiah (Mt. 3:1-3; 16:15-17; 27:46, 54).

[95] **Mt. 1:1:** The book of the generation of Jesus Christ, the son of David, the son of Abraham.

[96] **Mt. 1:16:** And Jacob begat Joseph the husband of Mary, of whom was born Jesus, who is called Christ.

[97] The 7-day Sabbath-Rest is the Old Testament sign based upon God's rest from His work of creation, which fell into eternal death, due to the fall of Adam. Christ's rest is the New Testament sign of "re-creation" based upon His finished work on the cross, which brings eternal life to all who are "born-again."

[98] Gen. 15:6; Neh. 9:8; Ps. 106:31; Rom. 4:3, 9-12.

Matthew's use of the number fourteen is proper because it speaks of deliverance and birthright blessing in a kingdom context, as we will discover in a moment. For now, we need to pause and review both genealogies in their entirety, as represented in this next chart. While comparing, notice how both records are identical from Abraham to David then change from that point on.

New Testament Genealogy Chart of Christ

MATTHEW'S GENEALOGY (Total of 41 members in three sets of 14 from Abraham to Christ.) Matthew 1:1-17	Both Genealogies Have This Section in Common	LUKE'S GENEALOGY (Total of 77 members from Adam to Christ.) Luke 3:23-38
		GOD (1)
		ADAM, the Son of God (2)
		SETH (3)
		ENOS/ENOSH (4)
		CAINAN/KENAN (5)
		MAHALALEEL (6)
		JARED (7)
		ENOCH (8)
		METHUSALEH/MATHUSALA (9)
		LAMECH (10)
		NOAH/NOE (11)
		SHEM/SEM (12)
		ARPHAXAD (13)
		CAINAN/KAINAN (14)
		SALA/SHELAH (15)
		EBER/HEBER (16)
		PHALEC/PELEG (17)
		RAGAU/REU (18)
		SARUCH/SERUG (19)
		NAHOR/NACHOR (20)
		TERAH/THARA (21)
Matthew's 1st Set of 14 *From Abraham to David* (1) ABRAHAM	**(1) ABRAM / ABRAHAM (22)**	ABRAHAM (22)
(2) ISAAC	(2) ISAAC (23)	ISAAC (23)
(3) JACOB / ISREAL	(3) JACOB / ISRAEL (24)	JACOB / ISRAEL (24)
(4) JUDAS/JUDAH	(4) JUDAH *m.→* Tamar (25)	JUDA/JUDAH (25)
(5) PEREZ/PHARES	(5) PEREZ/PHARES (26)	PEREZ/PHARES (26)
(6) EZRON/ESROM	(6) HEZRON/ESROM (27)	EZRON/ESROM (27)
(7) RAM/ARAM	(7) RAM/ARAM (28)	RAM/ARAM (28)
(8) AMMINADAB	(8) AMMINADAB (29)	AMMINADAB (29)
(9) NAHSHON/NAASSON	(9) NAHSHON/NAASSON (30)	NAHSHON/NAASSON (30)
(10) SALMON	(10) SALMON *m.→* Rachab (31)	SALMON (31)
(11) BOAZ/BOOZ	(11) BOAZ/BOOZ *m.→* Ruth (32)	BOAZ/BOOZ (32)
(12) OBED	(12) OBED (33)	OBED (33)
(13) JESSE	(13) JESSE (34)	JESSE (34)
(14) DAVID	**(14) DAVID (35)**[99] *m.→* Bathsheba	DAVID (35)
Matthew's 2nd Set of 14. **(1) SOLOMON** (Matthew 1:6)		**NATHAN (36)** (2 Sam.5.14)
		MATTATHA (37)
(2) REHOBOAM/ROBOAM		MENNA (38)
(3) ABIJAH/ABIA		MELEA (39)
(4) ASA		ELIAKIM (40)
		JONAM/JONAN (41)
(5) JEHOSHAPHAT/JOSAPHAT		JOSEPH (42)
(6) JORAM		JUDAH/JUDA (43)
(7) UZZISH/OZIAS		SIMEON (44)
		LEVI (45)
(8) JOTHAM/JOATHAM		MATTHAT (46)
(9) AHAZ/ACHAZ		JORIM (47)
(10) HEZEKIAH/EZEKIAS		ELIEZER (48)
		JOSHUA/JOSE/JESUS (49)
(11) MANASSEH/MANASSES		ER (50)
		ELMADAM (51)
(12) AMON		COSAM/KOSAM (52)
(13) JOSIAH/JOSIAS		ADDI (53)
(14) JECONIAH/JECHONIAS/CONIAH *and his brethern (Mt. 1:11)*		MELCHI (54)
From the carrying away into Babylon unto Christ (Mt. 1:11).		NERI (55)

[99] In 2 Sam. 7:12-17, God tells David (through the prophet Nathan) that David's kingdom would remain forever and his royal line would go through the son who would build the temple or as it is also called, the house of God. This son of David is Solomon. (1 Chron. 22:7-10).

Matthew's 3rd Set of 14.		Luke's Genealogy
(1) KING DAVID		SALATHIEL (56)
		ZERUBBABEL/ZOROBABEL (57)
(2) SALATHIEL	(2) SALATHIEL/SHEALTIEL (56)[100]	RHESA (58)
(3) ZERUBBABEL/ZOROBABEL		JOANAN (59)
	(3) ZERUBBABEL / ZOROBABEL (57)	JODA/JUDA (60)
(4) ABIUD		JOSECH/JOSEPH (61)
(5) ELIAKIM		SEMEI (62)
		MATTATHIAS (63)
(6) AZOR		MAATH (64)
(7) ZADOK/SADOC		NAGGE (65)
		ESLI (66)
(8) ACHIM		NAHUM (67)
(9) ELIUD		AMOS (68)
		MATTATHIAS (69)
(10) ELEAZER		JOSEPH (70)
(11) MATTHAN		JANNA/JANNAI (71)
		MELCHI/MELKI (72)
(12) JACOB		LEVI (73)
		MATTHAT (74)
(13) JOSEPH	(13) JOSEPH m.→ MARY (76)[101]	HELI/EI (75)
		MARY m.→ JOSEPH (76)[102]
Matthew's Genealogy "The Son of Man" Son of David and Seed of Abraham	(14) JESUS, the Son of God (77)	Luke's Genealogy "Son of Man" Son of God, Seed of the Woman, Last Adam

Chart 6 - New Testament Genealogy Chart of Christ

The Cure for a Curse

As we are beginning to see, all difficulties fade when we view the two genealogical records together as presented in Chart 6. Since we know the number two typologically conveys the legal concept of "adequate witness," the two New Testament writers provide sufficient evidence for Christ's claims about Himself. This "witness principle" is particularly true as it relates to the question of Christ's legal right to the Davidic throne. But due to Matthew listing King Jechonias and "his brethren" in his record,[103] we have another problem to solve because Jeremiah prophesied against this particular section of the royal line:

[100] Pedaiah is the father of Zerubbabel, not Salathiel (1Ch. 3:19). However, Salathiel is legally listed as the father of Zerubbabel by both Matthew and Luke, which appears as a contradiction. Henry states, "Matthew draws the pedigree from Solomon, whose natural line ending in Jechonias, the legal right was transferred to Salathiel, who was of the house of Nathan, another son of David, which line Luke here pursues, and so leaves out all the kings of Judah. It is well for us that our salvation doth not depend upon our being able to solve all these difficulties, nor is the divine authority of the gospels at all weakened by them; for the evangelists [Matthew and Luke] are not supposed to write these genealogies either of their own knowledge or by divine inspiration, but to have copied them out of the authentic records of the genealogies among the Jews, the heralds' books, which therefore they were obliged to follow..." (Henry, *Commentary of the Whole Bible*, Lk. 3:27. Also see, 1Ch. 3:17 for further comments).

[101] For clarity, Chart 6 lists Mary. However, Luke names her husband, Joseph, Jesus' step-father instead. Clarke states, "As the Hebrews never permitted women to enter into their genealogical tables, whenever a family happened to end with a daughter, instead of naming her in the genealogy, they inserted her husband, as the son of him who was, in reality, but his father-in-law." (Clarke, *Commentary on the Bible*, Lk. 3:23).

[102] "Joseph, son of Jacob, and Mary; daughter of Heli, were of the same family: both came from Zerubbabel. Joseph from Abiud, his eldest son, Mat. 1:13, and Mary by Rhesa, the youngest. See Luk, 3:27." (Clarke, *Commentary on the Bible*, Lk. 3:23).

[103] **Mt. 1:11-12:** And Josias begat Jechonias and his brethren, about the time they were carried away to Babylon: And after they were brought to Babylon, Jechonias begat Salathiel; and Salathiel begat Zorobabel.

Jer. 22:28-30: "Is this man Coniah a despised broken idol? is he a vessel wherein is no pleasure? wherefore are they cast out, he and his seed, and are cast into a land which they know not? O earth, earth, earth, hear the word of the LORD. Thus saith the LORD, Write ye this man childless, a man that shall not prosper in his days: for no man of his seed shall prosper, sitting upon the throne of David, and ruling any more in Judah."

Jer. 36:30: "Therefore thus saith the LORD of Jehoiakim king of Judah; He shall have none to sit upon the throne of David: and his dead body shall be cast out in the day to the heat, and in the night to the frost."

According to Jeremiah's prophecy, no man of the seed of Coniah, who is the son of Jehoiakim (Jer. 22:24), is to sit upon the throne of David. The word seed, in this instance, refers to all his future descendants. This prophecy holds true, which includes Jesus, who "is of the throne of his father, David." (Lk. 1:32). Such an assertion appears to contradict Jeremiah's prophecy. What then, is the answer? Once again, Luke's genealogy comes to the rescue.

Remember, Matthew's record is from Joseph (Mary's husband) to Abraham, which shows Jesus is from the royal line of David as well as a descendant of Jechonias. But we must keep in mind, Joseph is not the biological father of Jesus. Thereby, the reason for a second genealogy. Luke traces Jesus' lineage through His mother Mary to show she is a descendant of Prince Nathan,[104] the younger brother of Solomon, born to David and Bathsheba. Thereby, Luke's genealogy avoids the curse of King Jehoiakim.

Fourteen Finds the Kingdom

With such distinctions in the New Testament genealogies, we can see the fulfillment of prophecy. As noted earlier, Matthew divides his genealogy into three groups of fourteen generations in terms of the rise and fall of two diametrically opposed kingdoms, and sums it up this way:

---

[104] **Lk. 3:31:** Which was the son of Melea, which was the son of Menan, which was the son of Mattatha, which was the son of Nathan, which was the son of David.

Mt. 1:17: "So all the generations from Abraham to David are *fourteen generations;* and from David until the carrying away into Babylon are *fourteen generations*; and from the carrying away into Babylon unto Christ are *fourteen generations* [emphasis added]."

Note how he does not explicitly state there are 42 generations. Instead, Matthew carefully arranges his genealogy into three sets of fourteen. This arrangement is significant because there are only 41 members in a straight count. Moreover, notice how King David is listed in the first set of fourteen from Abraham, as well as the second set of fourteen generations. This double reference of David's name causes the total count of Matthew's genealogy to be 41 instead of 42 individual names.[105]

Why such an unusual summation in Matthew's lineage? From a practical standpoint, maybe it was intended to aid in memorization. Or perhaps the emphasis on fourteen is meant to reflect King David since the numerical value of his name in Hebrew curiously equals fourteen. There could be a third reason that relates to kingdoms. Notice how Matthew's tri-configuration stresses how the heirs to the promises become a kingdom under David only to fall captive to Babylon.

The mystery theme of Babylon is spread strategically throughout Scripture. In type, Ancient Babylon represents a world system intrinsically hostile to Divine rule. Chapter 17 of Revelation exposes this "great city" as Satan's harlot queen in his aspired counterfeit kingdom. Is Matthew calling our attention to the two competing kingdoms that seek claim to rule this earth? By ending with Christ, his outline leaves no question who the prevailing party will be in this cosmic war.

What glorious hope Matthew sought to bring to his fellow countrymen far and wide. Every time they reviewed his genealogical record of Christ, he hoped they would receive a message of deliverance and restoration.

Fourteen Finds the Firstborn

Double blessings are part of the firstborn package, but in terms of Israel, that portion of the package has been delayed. Our example comes from Abraham's son, Isaac, who inadvertently gave the birthright blessing to his younger son Jacob. In this story, Scripture places Esau

---

[105] The total count of 42 assumes multiplying 3 sets of 14 generations, but because King David's name is listed twice in Matthew's genealogy, the total count is really 41 individuals.

and Jacob on a national level. We know this because their mother received Divine revelation that she had two "nations" struggling inside her womb, and the elder would serve the younger. (Gen. 25:23). Such brotherly struggles are reminiscent of Cain and Abel, except they are viewed individually rather than nationally.

Upon discovery, his elder son, Esau, cried out to his blind father in complete despair and said, "He took my birthright, and now he's taken my blessing!" (Gen. 27:36). Esau, then, begged for some type of blessing to be given to him, which his father granted. However, it was an inferior blessing compared to Jacob's blessing. (Gen. 27:38-40).

From a typological viewpoint, Isaac, who is Abraham's son of promise, is a type of Christ as God's only son, who goes on to father and bless his own on an eternal scale. At this point, the sons are again competing for the firstborn position, except now as a "governing body." The blessing allotted to the elder may be inferior, but it does have a silver lining.

Esau's blessing included the firstborn right of rule at some undisclosed time in the future. Until then, the older will "serve thy [younger] brother, and it shall come to pass when thou shalt have the dominion that thou shalt break his yoke from off thy neck." (Gen. 27:40). This means, for now, the firstborn birthright must pass temporarily to the younger, until such time the older takes his rightful place.

By now, it should be no surprise why the younger was selected over the older *before* they were even born.[106] That is because the pattern of the firstborn of fallen man, by virtue of his birth order, will forever continue to run its course on cursed ground. Therefore, the Garden Program initiated the pattern of "firstborn reform" to run its course to catch the heel of the firstborn's fallen path.

Appropriately, Jacob's very name means "heel-catcher" and "supplanter." The meaning of Jacob's name perfectly describes the Garden Program's solution to fallen man's firstborn plight. Jacob finally caught the "heel" of the firstborn so he could ultimately "supplant" a far superior firstborn from his line, which is Christ. But since Christ is the Firstborn of all firstborns, He comes again with blessings that far exceed that of the birthright, which is what the number fourteen represents.

---

[106] Mal. 1:2; Rom. 9:13.

Christ's Appointed Sorrow

In terms of the Christ-line's third and fourth members, their collective meaning of "mortal sorrow" draws out the imagery of the type of work Jesus must do to achieve His glorified status. It is a work filled with unimaginable pain and rejection as foretold by the prophet Isaiah:

> **Isa. 53:3, 5, 10:** "He is despised and rejected of men; a man of sorrows, and acquainted with grief; and as it were a hiding of faces from Him, He being despised, and we esteemed Him not... But he was wounded for our transgressions, he was bruised for our iniquities: the chastisement of our peace was upon him; and with his stripes we are healed...Yet it pleased the LORD to bruise him; he hath put him to grief: when thou shalt make his soul an offering for sin, he shall see his seed (offspring), he shall prolong his days, and the pleasure of the LORD shall prosper in his hand."

Isaiah's Messianic writings reflect the Garden Prophecy of Genesis 3:15, where Christ as the "seed of the woman" is to be "bruised" on the heel by the serpent. Since we know He rose on the third day, Jesus' death served as a "temporary bruising." The position of the "heel" implies this understanding. However, the bruising of the serpent's head is yet to come and will be fatal, once rendered by Christ at the appointed time.[107]

Being temporary did not dismiss the fact that death would have been a sweet relief compared to the horrifying events Christ endured. But Isaiah's prophecies come with a promise. Once the full effects of His sin offering are complete, "the pleasure of the Lord will prosper in His hands," and he will see many heirs into His kingdom everlasting.

This chapter reinforces that the Garden Prophecy of Genesis 3:15 was fulfilled by Christ when he was born into the DNA of "mortal sorrow" as the lowly "seed of the woman." Our examination of the two New Testament genealogies testifies to that fact. Moreover, Matthew's tri-configuration of Christ's lineage confirms such a conclusion.

Matthew's unusual genealogical arrangement goes the extra mile to bring hope to the heirs of Christ, via physical or spiritual. His record

---

[107] **Rev. 20:10:** And the devil that deceived them was cast into the lake of fire and brimstone, where are also the beast and the false prophet; and they shall be tormented day and night for ever and ever.

looks forward to the future victory of the Davidic Kingdom through Christ, who brings double blessings when He is crowned King of Kings at His second coming.

The next chapter will concentrate on the teaching of the "Blessed God," as told by the fifth, sixth, and seventh members of the Christ-line. Because the two lost lines of Adam are extreme opposites, the teaching exhibits the same characteristics that is perfectly tailored to suit each of their needs.

As unbelievable as that sounds, the truth is God knows our differences and respects that. He easily accommodates individuality and free will as He accomplishes His plan set before the world was formed. There is no stopping His Garden Program and the progress of Christ fulfilling His mission "to seek and to save" what has been lost. The coming chapters are about to unpack those details as the family members continue their private reveal of *HIS-Story*.

CHAPTER 8 – MAHALALEEL, JARED, AND ENOCH
"Christ, the Blessed God Shall Come Down Teaching"

Enoch Models "The Walk and The Way"

Keeping to the sequential order of the members in the Christ-line, we now have in view the fifth, sixth, and seventh generations. They are, Mahalaleel, Jared, and Enoch, which collectively means: "the Blessed God shall come down teaching." By pointing out there was a problem with the human condition, namely, "Man is appointed mortal sorrow," the need for the coming of the "Blessed God" follows.

Since we already covered why the "Blessed God" came down, this chapter will concentrate on His "teaching." The term teaching is directly connected to Enoch because "teaching" is one of the meanings of his name in Hebrew. We could also include the adjective "dedicated" or even say "instruction or discipline" as the other renderings of his name suggest.

We can learn a great deal from Enoch, although Genesis is incredibly brief. The biggest attention-getter is his curious fate. In Genesis 5:24, we read, "And Enoch walked with God, and then he was not, for God took him." This verse alone suggests that Enoch did not die a natural death. His unusual "translation," as the book of Hebrews tells, was due to his testimony of faith. (Heb. 11:5).

The Pre-Flood and Post-Flood Teaching Difference

Since the prophet Elijah[108] was also *"caught up"* and escaped physical death like Enoch, we need to look to him to supply more clues about the *teaching.* As we begin our comparison, typology kicks into overdrive, as we are about to see. For starters, we must keep in mind that Enoch and Elijah are under two different administrations. Enoch administered within pre-judgment times, while Elijah administered within post-judgment times and is considered Israel's greatest prophet.

---

[108] **2 Ki. 2:11:** And it came to pass, as they still went on, and talked, that, behold, *there appeared* a chariot of fire, and horses of fire, and parted them both asunder; and Elijah went up by a whirlwind into heaven.

Elijah was famous for personalizing the common phrase, "As the Lord God of Israel liveth." Every time Elijah would say this phrase, he would conclude, "in whose presence I stand." This added ending was intentional, as well as testimonial. It signified his perceived standing position before Jehovah. In his mind, Elijah always stood in the presence of God. He saw his Lord in every circumstance and every occasion. He walked not by sight, but his walk was a walk of faith.[109] Faith "sees" the invisible God continually in the natural realm and stands in the right position for "without faith, it is impossible to please God." (Heb. 11:6).

Since Israel looks to the Law as well as the prophets,[110] Moses, on the other hand, is considered Israel's most notable leader. Moses, compared to Elijah, had a vastly different fate. Unlike Elijah, Moses died a natural death, and he was not *translated*, which we would expect, considering his close relationship with Jehovah.

To make matters worse, Moses was forbidden entry into the Promised Land. After being permitted to view the land from afar, he died shortly afterward, still full of strength and vigor. (Deut. 34:1-7). It was not due to his lack of faith as the book of Hebrews informs us. (Heb. 11:24-25). The issue was his disobedience. Jehovah told Moses to speak to the rock in the wilderness to bring forth its water for the people, but instead, he struck it. (Num. 20:8-12).

From our modern-day perspective, his denial of the Promised Land appears a bit harsh. However, since we know Jehovah is just, this incident must serve as an object lesson to those who look closer. Besides being viewed as Israel's most notable leader, Moses was also the great dispenser of the Law. His life represents, in type, service under the Law will always result in being judged by that same Law.

Moses' experience is put on display as a public example only, and by no means indicates he is not among the saints of God. The take-away is, if Moses, as the great dispenser of the Law, was condemned by the Law because he failed to keep it, then how can anyone else keep it?

This quick assessment of Israel's two prominent leaders who lived and operated within an economy different from Enoch's generation provides an important principle. Those who choose to "walk by faith" live under no condemnation (as modeled by Elijah), while those who choose to "live by the

---

[109] **2 Cor. 5:7:** For we walk by faith, not by sight.

[110] **Mt. 22:40:** On these two commandments hang all the law and the prophets.

Law" find no rest from judgment (as modeled by Moses). Moses never reached the Promise Land, which is considered God's Rest.[111]

Enoch lived in a time of "no Law and pre-judgment." The only means of salvation in his day was by faith. From that view, it becomes clear that the Mosaic Law was added later to the salvation menu as an alternate means of righteousness. But as the record stands, keeping the Law proved impossible and that was the point. Cain's offering of his produce on a cursed ground exemplifies such an erroneous notion.

The Ministry of the Spirit (Life) or the Ministry of Law (Death)

So far, we have learned "grace through faith" qualifies us to be "caught up" just like Enoch and Elijah were. Because the two prophets lived in two different periods or administrations, different rules apply to the "teaching" each period received from the "Blessed God." Enoch models those who live within a timeframe of pre-law and pre-judgment, like the Christian Church. As such, both escape judgment as typified in Noah's day and the 7-year-tribulation period of Revelation.[112]

Both Elijah and Moses, on the other hand, lived and operated in the post-judgment and post-law world. The two are considered Israel's most prominent leaders who represent "the Law and the Prophets." Elijah is Israel's model of a life lived by grace through faith, while Moses is Israel's model of a life lived by works of the Law. The two models represent the choice given to Israel. Moses put it this way, "I have set before you life and death, blessing and cursing: therefore choose life, that both thou and thy seed may live." (Duet. 30:19b).

Paul maintains we have "life and liberty" only because of the Spirit's ministry. Conversely, the Law can only offer "judgment and death." In his letter to the Corinthians, he points out the two different administrations: The Spirit and the Law. (2 Cor. 3:7-17). He goes on to explain how the ministry of the Spirit is more glorious than the administration of the Law.

From Paul's comparison of the two administrations, he makes it plain why Moses failed to enter the Promised Land—especially since the Promised Land is a type of rest and not heaven. Paul argues that because a veil was over the fading glory of the Mosaic Law, the children of Israel did not discern how Christ fulfilled the Law, leaving only rest. The veil

---

[111] Ps. 95:11; Heb. 3:11, 4:3.

[112] Israel's destiny will be discussed in greater detail in Chapters 10 and 11.

prohibited them from seeing Christ, the Messiah, as the greater glory compared to the Law.

Since Christ was appointed death once (Heb. 9:28), Moses' striking "the Rock" twice is an apparent deviation from that plan. Moses was blind to the "Rock" of salvation because he lived by the Law. As such, the veil of the Law covered his eyes and made him blind to the truth about Christ.

By using Paul's standard, we can conclude if Moses had been under the law of grace, the covering of the "veil" would give way to true spiritual discernment. He would not have been blind as to the importance of not hitting "the Rock" a second time because he would have immediately understood that Christ was stricken only once to die for all.

Rest Means No More Work

Armed with Paul's teaching to the Corinthians, we gain a contextual filter with which to review the Mosaic Law. As glorious as it was, Paul teaches his converts, it was not the true glory, and it miserably failed because it had no power of its own to give anyone rest. The Law's only purpose was to be an instructor. (Gal. 3:24).

Truth is, Moses, whose name is synonymous with endless work under the Law, never had a chance in reaching the "promised rest." As the great dispenser of the Law, which was written on a cold and hard material, Moses found out firsthand the Law could not offer personal comfort to its transgressor. By the Law's own shortcomings and the shortcomings of the sinner, a more excellent method was necessary. Paul also taught the Romans this truth and stated it this way:

> **Rom. 3:19-24:** "Now we know that what things soever the law saith, it saith to them who are under the law: that every mouth may be stopped, and all the world may become guilty before God. Therefore by the deeds of the law there shall no flesh be justified in his sight: for by the law is the knowledge of sin. *But now the righteousness of God without the law is manifested, being witnessed by the law and the prophets; Even the righteousness of God which is by faith of Jesus Christ unto all and upon all them that believe: for there is no difference: for all have sinned, and fall short of the glory of God; being justified*

freely by his grace through the redemption that is in Christ Jesus [emphasis added]."

Although the Law was unable to save its subjects, the Law was still good. Paul confirms the Law's purpose was for our preparation and preserving the knowledge and worship of the true God.[113] Grace, on the other hand, not only offers redemption individually by faith but also offers complete rest from the Law. Salvation is a level the Law could never reach, and a level crucial to the Garden Program's success.

Christ is the Lord of the Sabbath-Rest

Just as God rested from His finished work on the seventh day of creation, so rest is found in Christ's finished work, which completes the seven-day cycle to begin anew. Christ's title as the "Lord of the Sabbath" reflects this very idea because the meaning of the word Sabbath is rest. Remember, the Sabbath day is also the seventh day that constitutes work is complete. From this imagery, typology points to the time when Christ is Lord of the Sabbath-Rest, because He brought the Law to "rest" by His finished work on the cross.

Curiously, Paul teaches just as the body undergoes one baptism,[114] so too, Firstborn National Israel must undergo baptism as one national body. He uses the crossing of the Red Sea as an example. However, not every member of Israel agreed, which is the reason for the "wilderness experience."[115]

It was in the wilderness that we are introduced to the tablets of stone. Some scholars guess it was a matter of weeks after the parting of the Red Sea. Then, precisely on the day of the very first Feast of Pentecost,[116] the Lord, through Moses at Mount Sinai, laid the Law down in full demonstration of supernatural power and angelic presence. In fear and awe, the "Church in the Wilderness," as Peter addresses them,[117] accepted the terms under the Law. (Ex. 19).

---

[113] **Gal. 3:22-23:** But the scripture hath concluded all under sin, that the promise by faith of Jesus Christ might be given to them that believe. But before faith came, we were kept under the law, shut up unto the faith which should afterwards be revealed.

[114] **Eph. 4:5-6:** One Lord, one faith, one baptism, One God and Father of all, who is above all, and through all, and in you all.

[115] **Deut. 8:16:** Who fed thee in the wilderness with manna, which thy fathers knew not, that he might humble thee, and that he might prove thee, to do thee good at thy latter end.

[116] "The date of that great charter by which Israel was incorporated. 1. The time when it bears date (Ex. 19:1) - in the third month after they came out of Egypt. It is computed that the law was given just fifty days after their coming out of Egypt, in remembrance of which the feast of Pentecost was observed the fiftieth day after the passover, and in compliance with which the Spirit was poured out upon the apostles at the feast of pentecost, fifty days after the death of Christ." (Henry, *Commentary of the Whole Bible*, Ex. 19).

[117] **Acts 7:38:** This is he that was in the church in the wilderness with the angel that spake to him in the Mount Sinai, and with our fathers: who received lively [living] oracles to give unto us.

Unfortunately, the first fruits of the very first Feast of Pentecost ratified under the Mosaic Law caused "undue rest," which resulted in the death of three thousand Israelites. Exodus 32 gives the full account. It appears just as quickly as the congregation confessed their allegiance to the Law at the foot of Mount Sinai, their affections rapidly turned to the worship of a golden calf. From this scene, we have a sad commentary that all are utterly incapable of keeping the Law.

Now compare this to the first fruits of the New Testament Pentecost at the base of a new mountain in Jerusalem known as Mount Zion.[118] We see the reverse happens. Shortly after the coming of the Holy Spirit,[119] Peter stood before his brethren and said, "They that gladly received his word were baptized: and the same day there were added unto them about three thousand souls." (Acts 2:41).

From the two separate events under the two different administrations, we can see a harvest reaped. The Law reaps death, while the Spirit reaps life. Let us take careful note of this sobering fact, Israel failed to continue to produce faith shortly after the Feast of Pentecost of Acts 2. It was out of the uncircumcised, Gentile field that the Christian Church arose thereafter so that the harvesting of the earth could continue uninterrupted. Israel, as the *Church in the Wilderness*, was, once again, left wandering off the prophetic time clock.

The Harvest of Life, Not Death

Unquestionably, this old Pentecostal comparison with the new Pentecostal experience of Acts 2 exists for our learning. Again, we see how the *fruit* of the Law is unequivocally death, but the *fruit* of the Spirit is always life. Typologically speaking, this is the reason why Elijah and Enoch did not experience physical death—because they both lived by the Spirit in their respective periods, and neither were under Law.

Even though Elijah lived in the post-judged and post-law age, he chose to live a life by faith and not like the majority who remained faithful to the Law

---

[118] Mt. Zion is the place where the fortress of the City of David once stood (root meaning "landmark, fortress") and is located in Israel's capital city Jerusalem and has both historical and religious significance to the Jews as well as to the Christians. Historically, this is where the Jebusite fortress once stood and was conquered by King David. According to prophecy, Mount Zion is set as a landmark where the "remnant of Jacob" or God's chosen ones are gathered to a "refuge" before the "Great Day of the Lord" and his final judgment. Mt. Zion is still viewed as a city otherwise called "The City of the Righteous," as written in the book of Isaiah. Great significance is placed on this mountain as "The Mount of the Lord" and as "His Holy Hill."

[119] **Acts 2:1-4:** And when the day of Pentecost was fully come, they were all with one accord in one place. And suddenly there came a sound from heaven as of a rushing mighty wind, and it filled all the house where they were sitting. And there appeared unto them cloven tongues like as of fire, and it sat upon each of them. And they were all filled with the Holy Ghost, and began to speak with other tongues, as the Spirit gave them utterance.

and Judaism. Therefore, Elijah represents a remnant, being a small portion of Israel who believes Christ is the Son of God and the promised Messiah. Moses represents the remaining house of Israel stuck "working" under the Law.

If it were not for Christianity, the harvesting of the earth that began (as described in Acts 2) would have come to a screeching halt due to Israel's unbelief and their resulting scattered state. This, in turn, gave rise to the "body of Christ"—wrought from all nations of the earth, not just one— as one spiritually "born" body.

The world is simply incapable of seeing spiritual things, much less comprehending them. But rest assured, just as Christ is the "younger brother" to Israel, so too is His "spiritual body." They are the first "body" to be caught up due to their mystical nature and unmarked timeline, which occurs sometime before the coming judgment just like Enoch. That leaves Firstborn Israel as the public "body of God," which is once again "known of God" on the world's stage at that time to be caught up in a "chariot of fire" like Elijah on the day of judgment just as Noah's flood and placement on the Christ-line represents.

Enoch's placement as the seventh member on the Christ-line looks to the harvest phase of the Garden Program, which is also known as the "Grace Age." The "open invitation" portion of the harvest phase is equal to "Paul's gospel,"[120] which primarily addresses the uncircumcised nations due to Israel's rejection. The next chapter on Lamech will make this clear.

For now, we are to understand that those saved by Paul's teaching are saved by grace through faith and are not under the law.[121] As such, they do not face judgment because, like Enoch, their standing position before God is "pre-law" and "pre-judgment." By this example, the Christian Church aligns with Enoch. The Christian Church, just like Enoch, will be "caught up" to escape judgment and not undergo wrath.[122]

The exclusion of the Christian Church from wrath is opposite to Firstborn National Israel's destiny. Being a national body, they are on a marked and public timeline, still working in the outer field. Once the Christian Church is "caught up," it is Firstborn National Israel's destiny and calling to lead a joyous jubilee among the nations as the Cain-line summary statement suggests. Their journey is a legalistic pilgrimage, which must continue until they have "overcome" in the final hour set to occur in the last age.[123]

---

[120] 1 Cor. 11:1; Rom. 2:16, 16:25; Eph. 3:1-13; Gal. 1:8-9; 2 Tim. 2:8.

[121] Eph. 2:8-9; Rom. 5:13, 7:3-4; Gal. 2:16; 3:11; 5:4.

[122] **1 Thes. 5:9:** For God has not appointed us to wrath, but to obtain salvation by our Lord Jesus Christ.

[123] 1 Jn. 5:4-5; Rev. 2:7, 11, 17, 26.

The New Covenant Finds New Ground to Give New Life

The New Covenant, as foretold by Jeremiah,[124] crossed new ground under Paul's ministry to the Gentiles. As discussed previously, the practice of circumcision and Passover found spiritual application under Paul's teaching. Unlike Israel, Paul's Gentile converts were not to undergo physical circumcision. Paul taught, "But he is a Jew, which is one inwardly; and circumcision is that of the heart, in the spirit, and not in the letter [of the Law]; whose praise is not of men, but of God." (Rom. 2:29). Jesus confirmed that His blood is the new Covenant, which was shed for many (Mk. 14:24), and if anyone eats of His flesh and drinks His blood has eternal life. (Jn. 6:54).

Likewise, the Christian equivalent to Israel's Passover Seder is Communion. The model is the Last Supper as performed by Jesus as the mediator of the New Covenant.[125] Unlike the annual Seder dinner, Christians observe Communion as "oft" as you eat the bread (His body broken for you) and drink of the cup (His blood shed for you). By this act, Paul teaches his converts the act of Communion symbolizes the individual's "proclamation of His death till He come."[126]

True to form, we continue to see how the approach of the two lost lines of man boils down to how they view the sin-offering differently. Israel, as the older brother, was only willing to drink of the water flowing from the *Rock* in the wilderness.[127] Jesus came to bring a new cup filled with the fresh, new drink of the "New Covenant" This "new cup" with a "new drink" expectation explains why His first miracle sign was turning water into wine at the wedding in Galilee[128] because both water and wine are "types and shadows" of the Holy Spirit. However, Israel could not see anything good coming from Nazareth of Galilee[129] and refused the offer given to them.

With that, the Christian Church, as the younger brother, becomes the first to wholeheartedly drink from the New Covenant's "cup of the Spirit." Undeniably, our findings so far offer interesting insight as to how the two lost

---

[124] **Jer. 31:31:** Behold, the days come, saith Lord, that I will make a new covenant with the house of Israel, and with the house of Judah.

[125] Mt. 26:17-29; Mk. 14:12-25; Lk. 22:7-38.

[126] **1 Cor. 11:24-26:** And when he had given thanks, he brake *it*, and said, Take, eat: this is my body, which is broken for you: this do in remembrance of me. After the same manner also *he took* the cup, when he had supped, saying, This cup is the new testament in my blood: this do ye, as oft as ye drink *it*, in remembrance of me. For as often as ye eat this bread, and drink this cup, ye do shew the Lord's death till he come.

[127] **Ex. 17:6:** Behold, I will stand before thee there upon the rock in Horeb; and thou shalt smite the rock, and there shall come water out of it, that the people may drink. And Moses did so in the sight of the elders of Israel.

[128] Jn. 2:1-11.

[129] Jn. 1:46, 7:41-43, 52.

family lines of fallen Adam view and apply the teaching about the "Blessed God" very differently. The younger brother, who is placed last within the family, continues to be the first to readily accept the sin-offering as typified by Abel and the Christian Church.

Israel, on the other hand, holds the first position of the family, like Cain, and continues to reject the sin-offering, which is Christ's own body and blood under the New Covenant. Like before, they are left wondering for another proverbial 40-year cycle among the nations. Again, the Lord waits until the appointed time when they step back onto the world's stage. At that time, they come on the scene, once again, as the *Church in the Wilderness* (Acts 7:38), to face their final trial, which is also called the day of Jacob's Trouble, as foretold by Jeremiah:

> **Jer. 30:7-14:** "Alas! for that day is great, so that none is like it: it is even the *time of Jacob's trouble; but he shall be saved out of it.* For it shall come to pass *in that day, saith the LORD of hosts, that I will break his yoke from off thy neck*, and will burst thy bonds, and strangers shall no more serve themselves of him: But *they shall serve the LORD their God, and David their king, whom I will raise up unto them.* Therefore fear thou not, O my servant Jacob, saith the LORD; neither be dismayed, O Israel: for, lo, I will save thee from afar, and thy seed from the land of their captivity; and Jacob shall return, and shall be in rest, and be quiet, and none shall make him afraid. For I am with thee, saith the LORD, to save thee: though I make a full end of all nations whither I have scattered thee, yet will I not make a full end of thee: but I will correct thee in measure, and will not leave thee altogether unpunished. For thus saith the LORD, Thy bruise is incurable, and thy wound is grievous. There is none to plead thy cause, that thou mayest be bound up: thou hast no healing medicines. All thy lovers have forgotten thee; they seek thee not; for I have wounded thee with the wound of an enemy, with the chastisement of a cruel one, for the multitude of thine iniquity; because thy sins were increased [emphasis added]."

Jer. 30:17: "For I will restore health unto thee, and I will heal thee of thy wounds, saith the LORD; because they called thee an Outcast, saying, *This is Zion*, whom no man seeketh after [emphasis added]."

Jer. 30:22-24: "And ye shall be my people, and I will be your God. Behold, the whirlwind of the LORD goeth forth with fury, a continuing whirlwind: it shall fall with pain upon the head of the wicked. The fierce anger of the LORD shall not return, until he have done it, and until he have performed the intents of his heart: in the *latter days* ye shall consider it [emphasis added]."

From these passages written by the Prophet Jeremiah, we learn Jehovah has some unfinished business with His firstborn nation. Jehovah promises to resolve their legal issues in the day of Jacob's Trouble, and "he, [Jacob/Israel] will be saved out of it." The promise is—Israel's yoke from the Law will finally break. They shall serve the Lord their God and David their king, whom the Lord shall raise-up in the last day, which is Christ. They will eventually find their rest, and the Lord shall make a full end of the nations, which He scattered them. Nevertheless, He will not make a "full end" of His firstborn nation.

As far as the Christ-line is concerned, the time of Jacob's Trouble represents Noah's day at the end of the age. Until such time, the days of Methuselah and Lamech must run their course as the next two chapters will present. The contributions of these next two generations will forever change the course of human history. These changes turn both Cain and the Christ-line into prophetic timelines to reveal the Garden Program's harvest/restoration plan or rescue plan of the ages. This plan is about to take some surprising twists and turns, as we soon will see.

CHAPTER 9 – METHUSELAH
"Christ's Death Shall Bring"

Extending the Invitation

In the previous chapter, we discovered Enoch's prophetic teaching office about the "Blessed God," and how the two lost lines of man (Adam) view and apply that teaching. This chapter will outline the foresight of Methuselah's father, Enoch, who purposely pinned a prophecy upon his son's name. The curious meaning of Methuselah's name treats his lifespan as if it was a stopwatch. All will become clear in a moment.

First, we need to understand the context of Enoch's reasoning for naming his son, "his death shall bring." Such an odd and depressing name is the literal translation for the Hebrew word Methuselah. To get the New Testament's background as to why Enoch named his son as he did, we look to another parable taught by Christ.

Matthew records Jesus' wedding feast parable. (Mt. 22:1-14). In this account, Jesus tells how a king's original invitees to his son's wedding feast were unworthy. The invitation was then indiscriminately offered to anyone willing to come. The typological points of the parable are:

- National Israel is the original invitee to the wedding feast of the king's son.[130]
- The wedding invitation was extended to all, outside of Israel, due to Israel's refusal to come (vs. 3, 8-10).
- The invitation is valid up to, and including, the time of the wedding for those with the proper "covering" (vs. 12-14).

When we combine the foregoing typological aspects from the parable to the Methuselah context, the picture widens considerably. For starters, besides the peculiar meaning of his name, Methuselah is the oldest man who ever lived. Genesis tells us he was 969 years old when he died (Gen. 5:27). John Gill's commentary explains further:

---

[130] See, *JFB Commentary* (1871) *and Gill's Commentary* (1748-63) on Matthew 22:2-24.

"And all the days of Methuselah were nine hundred and sixty nine years, and he died...This was the oldest man that ever lived... His name carried in it a prediction of the time of the flood, which was to be quickly after his death, as has been observed" (Gill, *Exposition of the Bible*, Gen. 5:21).

With Gill's insights added to the mix, we are now able to fine-tune the typological picture for further understanding. Remember, Methuselah's name means, "his death shall bring." Enoch's intent when naming his son was to leave a cultural legacy as a warning of the coming judgment, which was to occur at the time of his son's death.

Since Scripture ascribes Methuselah as the oldest man who ever lived, the span of his life covers the last four generations[131] in the preflood world. The Christ-line uses the span of his life as a prophetic fulfillment of the coming judgment,[132] and the teaching about the "Blessed God" to the whole world during the harvest phase of the Garden Program. Methuselah's unusually long life demonstrates the long-suffering of Jehovah-God not wanting any to perish.[133]

Enoch Models the Church Age Harvest

Just as Enoch is the first to escape before the coming wrath by being "caught up," Noah and "his house" will be the last to escape judgment due to the safety of the Ark and sailing through the judgment waters. We know this from the Genesis record. From the known sequence of events, we can presume there is a portion of the Despairing that is "removed" before the coming judgment and a second group of the Despairing that goes through the coming judgment.[134]

---

[131] Using the Masoretic text as the standard and assuming there are no copy errors in the text, Enoch was 65 years old at the time Methuselah, his son, was born (Gen. 5:21). At 365 years old, Enoch was "caught up" and was no more (Gen. 5:23-24). Methuselah was 187 years when he fathered his son, Lamech (Gen. 5:25), who fathered Noah at 182 years old (Gen. 5:28). Noah was 500 years old when he gave birth to his sons (Gen. 5:32). After that, Noah was instructed to build the Ark, which took another 100 years because the record shows he was 600 years old when the floodwaters came (Gen. 7:6). Now add the 187 years when Methuselah gave birth to Lamech and the 182 years when Lamech gave birth to Noah and the 500 years when Noah gave birth to his sons and the final 100 years for him and his family to build the Ark, makes (187+182+500+100)=969 years, the age Methuselah died (Gen. 5:27). As we can see, Methuselah's life covered a span of four generations.

[132] "Some say he [Methuselah] died in the year of the flood; others, fourteen years after, and was in the garden of Eden with his father, in the days of the flood, and then returned to the world (a); but the eastern writers are unanimous that he died before the flood: the Arabic writers (b) are very particular as to the time in which he died; they say he died in the six hundredth year of Noah, on a Friday, about noon, on the twenty first day of Elul, which is Thout; and Noah and Shem buried him, embalmed in spices, in the double cave, and mourned for him forty days: and some of the Jewish writers say he died but seven days before the flood came, which they gather from Gen. 7:10 "after seven days"; that is, as they interpret it, after seven days of mourning for Methuselah: he died A. M. 1656, the same year the flood came, according to Bishop Usher." (Gill, *Exposition of the Bible*, Gen. 5:21).

[133] Mt. 18:14; 2 Pet. 3:9.

[134] **Isa. 63:4:** For the day of vengeance *is* in mine heart, and the year of my redeemed is come.

Concerning the first group of the Despairing as represented by Enoch, we look to the Apostle Paul's converts who model the idea that their destiny is to meet the Lord in the air:

> **1 Cor. 15:51-52:** "Behold, I tell you a mystery: We all shall not sleep, but we shall all be changed, in a moment, in the twinkling of an eye, at the last trump: for the trumpet shall sound, and the dead shall be raised incorruptible, and we shall be changed."

> **1 Thes. 4:16-17:** "For the Lord himself shall descend from heaven with a shout, with the voice of the archangel, and with the trump of God: and the dead in Christ shall rise first: Then we which are alive and remain shall be caught up together with them in the clouds, to meet the Lord in the air: and so shall we ever be with the Lord."

> **I Thes. 5:9**: "For God hath not appointed us to wrath, but to obtain salvation by our Lord Jesus Christ."

From these passages, Paul speaks of a mystery, which relates to the "mystery" of Christ and His Church, not Israel. Paul is careful to keep those "in Christ" apart from judgment as he writes new details about the mystery to the Thessalonians. Note how the mystery of those in Christ meeting the Lord in the air aligns with Enoch's same pre-law and pre-judgment position of standing and method of escape. Again, the emphasis is on how all share the same salvation status before the "Blessed God." So, like Enoch, the Christian Church will be caught up in the air. All who remain on the earth must face the day of judgment[135] when Methuselah dies, as the meaning of his name indicates.

If Enoch's salvation model is equal to the "open invitation" within the Grace Age, then by deduction, Elijah's salvation model, as we learned in the last chapter, is equal to Noah's day on the Christ-line, which is a time of judgment under the Law. Being such a small group, the eight members in Noah's household naturally prefigure National Israel reduced to the remnant saved in the Ark.

---

[135] **Joel 2:31:** The sun shall be turned into darkness, and the moon into blood, before the great and terrible day of the LORD come.

Appropriately, the unbelieving nations along with Israel share the same fate of end-time judgment, while Abel, Enoch, and the Christian Church as the spiritual "body of Christ" all escape it. The Divine treatment of these three prominent figures in Scripture who escape God's wrath exemplifies the promise made to Abraham that his "seed" will also enjoy the same righteous credit by faith (Rom. 4:3-8) that avoids the fate of the wicked like Sodom and Gomorrah in his day.

The grand takeaway for us today is that the members on the Christ-line represent a global prophetic cycle of events that begins at the coming of the "Blessed God" in the last generation of humankind. This is the Divine plan as revealed through the bloodline of Christ in the pre-flood generation. A plan we like to call the "Garden Program" because it all began in the Garden of Eden, which was created with the intent to produce an eternal harvest. It is a plan that puts the post-flood world on notice that judgment is coming just like before. As soon as the "open invitation" of the harvest phase of the Garden Program is over, which is represented by Methuselah's passing, the day of judgment begins as represented in Noah's day.

Methuselah's Generational Reach

From our observations so far, we can see how the Christ-line uses Enoch, who holds the seventh position, as a sacred trigger point to unleash the teaching about the "Blessed God" and the hope of escape. Again, the method of escape is either before judgment, like Enoch, or going through judgment, like Noah in the Ark.

With Enoch, the count of the remaining members on the Christ-line is precisely four. Only Methuselah has the privilege of living a lifespan that reaches all four generations who receive the warning of the coming judgment and the hope of escape. His reach illustrates Jehovah not wanting any to perish because of the use of the number four with its global implications according to our number chart.

Curiously, four is also the count at the beginning of this pre-flood age as represented by the first family. At this juncture, it becomes clear that due to the placement and the contributions of each member on the Christ-line, we have a true prophetic timeline as illustrated by Chart 7.

The Christ-Line's Harvest-Escape Plan

Chart 7 is an alternate view of the Christ-line chart. Just by organizing the Christ-line horizontally instead of vertically, a timeline is created. The timeline naturally divides into three sections. The first section is formed by the first four generations of Adam who represent all born in "mortal sorrow." Next is Christ's first coming, which leaves the last section to represent the harvesting of the earth due to the planting of the good "seed" of Christ in the hearts of men to produce a harvest. (Mt. 13:37-38).

By design, the mortal sorrow issue of Adam's first four generations are balanced-out by the last four generations. The Christ-centered configuration of the chart is key to correcting humanity's death sentence. The timeline makes it easy to see how the curse finds its correction *after* the coming of the "Blessed God," and proceeds to serve as a timeline of the Garden Program's harvest phase or escape plan.

Firstfruits of the Season

After Christ's ascension, Paul was traveling on the road to Damascus and finally saw "The Light," the risen Christ, face-to-face, and was saved.[136] In this vision, the Lord Jesus commissioned Paul to take the gospel to the children of Israel, kings, and the uncircumcised Gentiles.[137] A few years later, the growing tension between Paul and the Jewish council grew into a heated debate. Finally, Peter and the Jerusalem leaders settled the issue by agreeing that they would exclusively shepherd circumcised Israel. In turn, Paul accepted exclusive Apostleship over the uncircumcised Gentiles.[138]

Under Divine inspiration, Paul wrote letters to the uncircumcised congregations to give the "open invitation" outside of what was considered exclusive only to Israel. This vision of the extended invitation is what Jesus foresaw, as alluded to in His wedding feast parable. Remember, the open invitation was due to the unworthiness of the original invitees, Israel. The whole Jewish field was, clearly, not ready.

To the Corinthians, Paul taught that despite Israel's rejection of their Messiah, the "fruit" of the King's invitation did not go in vain and had a fixed "seasonal" order:

---

[136] **Acts 9:3-4:** And as he journeyed, he came near Damascus: and suddenly there shined round about him a light from heaven: And he fell to the earth, and heard a voice saying unto him, Saul, Saul, why persecutest thou me?

[137] **Acts 9:15:** But the Lord said unto him, Go thy way: for he is a chosen vessel unto me, to bear my name before the Gentiles, and kings, and the children of Israel.

[138] **Gal. 2:7:** But contrariwise, when they saw that the gospel of the uncircumcision was committed unto me, as the gospel of the circumcision was unto Peter.

The Christ-Line Harvest Timeline Chart

1	2	3	4
Adam (1st)	Seth (2nd)	Enosh (3rd)	Kenan (4th)
Man	Appointed	Mortal	Sorrow

SECTION 1

This section represents the effects of the Garden Curse

All families of the earth born in "mortal sorrow" with no hope of their eternal inheritance of life and dominion of the earth.

Christ's 1st Advent

Mahalaleel (5th)	Jared (6th)
The Blessed God	Shall Come Down

SECTION 2

This section represents The Garden Promise

The Garden Promise Christ comes as the "Seed of the Woman" To be sown in the earth at His death. (Jn. 12:24) to produce a harvest.

— Methuselah's Reach —
Grace Age Harvest Period

1	2	3	4
Enoch (7th)	Methuselah (8th)	Lamech (9th)	Noah (10th)
Teaching	His Death Shall Bring	Despairing	Rest

SECTION 3

This section represents The Garden Restoration Plan or Harvesting of the Earth

All those within the Despairing category find rest due to the death of Christ as the "Blessed God." Entry into His rest begins at Christ's 2nd Advent, which is after the 7-yr. Tribulation (represented by Noah's Day), then the Millennium Kingdom begins.

Chart 7 – The Christ-Line Harvest Timeline Chart

1 Cor. 15:20, 22-23a: "But now Christ is risen from the dead and become the firstfruits of them that slept…For as in Adam all die, even so in Christ shall all be made alive. But every man in his own order."

The concept of firstfruits is the product of seedtime and harvest. The Feast of Firstfruits is one of the Lord of the Harvest's "set times" on His prophetic calendar of Leviticus 23. Firstfruits required the gathering of two bundles from the field to present to the priest, and two loaves of bread made of "new meal" were baked to represent the coming crops of the harvest to come.[139]

The next "set time" is Pentecost, which is called the "Feast of Harvest." As we learned earlier, the Holy Spirit's public arrival described in Acts 2 was precisely on the Feast of Pentecost to indicate the official arrival of the harvest season of the earth. This time is also known as the *Feast of Weeks*[140] because fifty weeks must pass after Passover.[141] The root word in Greek, "pente," means fifty to signify that the harvest is the 50th part of a thing, or the 50th in order or a cycle.

The number fifty should ring a bell to us by now. As far as God's calculations are concerned, fifty is equal to the number five (grace) increased to the 10th power, launching grace to perform on a global platform. For this reason, the number fifty signifies Jubilee and deliverance on the number chart. When we apply fifty within the context of Pentecost during Methuselah's watch, we instantly recognize how the harvest season is also an invitation of salvation (deliverance) by grace to the world.

Acts 2:1 states: "And when the day of Pentecost was fully come, they were all with one accord in one place." Albert Barnes explains, "Pentecost was now to be completed, and refers, not to the day itself, but to the completion of the interval, which was to pass before its arrival."[142]

The strange wording of this passage in Acts alerts the reader that the time of Pentecost (the main harvest season of the earth) is fully arrived

---

[139] Lev. 23:10-11, 17, 20; Num. 28:26-31.

[140] This Feast day (or "set time" which is the Hebrew meaning of the word "feast") was reckoned from the 16th day of the month Abib (or April) or the second day of the Passover. The paschal lamb was slain on the 14th of the month at evening, and the 15th day of the month was a holy convocation being the proper beginning of the feast. On the day after the next regular Sabbath was the offering of the firstfruits of harvest, and from that day they were to reckon seven weeks, 49 days, to the feast called the Feast of Pentecost, so that it occurred 50 days after the first day of the Feast of the Passover.

[141] Ex. 34:22; Num. 28:26; Deut. 16:10.

[142] Albert Barnes quoting Olshausen. (Barnes, *Notes on the Bible*, Acts 2:1). Also see, Luke 9:51. Compare Mark 1:15 to Luke 1:57.

to account for the events that occurred afterward. Barnes helps us to understand how the Holy Spirit's public arrival on the first day of the Feast of Harvest was the Garden Program's plan all along. The long-awaited harvest season is here just as Methuselah's Day on the Christ-line represents.

Incorruptible Seed for the Harvest

Jesus saw that the harvest was ready when He said, "Behold, I say unto you, Lift up your eyes, and look on the fields, that they are white already unto harvest." (Jn. 4:35). As we can see, the Garden Program anticipates a harvest from all peoples of the earth. What Jesus saw ready for the picking in His day was those Gentile fields, which were afforded the open invitation due to Israel rejecting Him.

From our modern-day perspective, when we think of seedtime and harvest, we usually think of dirt and plants growing from the ground and not in terms of people. However, Jehovah's Garden occurs on higher ground. This idea, once again, relates directly to the formation of Adam and Eve. Remember, Adam is from the substance of the earth, which was later cursed. Eve, on the other hand, was formed before the fall, from Adam's pierced side while he slept, thereby becoming a "refined ground."

Since we know Adam is a type of Christ, typology points to the woman being "formed" because of Christ's death. Moreover, by His death, her ground is redeemed by His substitute death for her, which instantly becomes a purified territory and has the unique ability to produce life. With this understanding, Adam named her Eve because he understood, "she was to be the mother of all living."[143] Unfortunately, because of the fall, the seed of Adam could only produce corruption, but by the woman, there remained the potential for life on new ground.

By using the refined ground analogy, the holy planting of another seed on redeemed ground was sure to produce a hybrid. This combination had the potential to generate a life separate and apart from the old seedbed of incurably corrupt ground such as fallen flesh. As a hybrid, Christ could have remained on this earth indefinitely in that weak and imperfect earthen vessel. However, why would He? He left the eternal, limitless realm to come down to live within the confines of a weak, earthen body to do the will of the Father. It was out of His complete love and obedience that He willingly

---

[143] **Gen 3:20:** And Adam called his wife's name Eve; because she was the mother of all living.

82

came in the first place only to lay His earthly life down for His friends[144] to produce more life.

Just as a plant lives and dies carrying seed, so we apply this idea to the hybrid vessel of Christ. His body, according to the Gospel records, was laid to rest in the clay bottom tomb, which represents a fallen seed sown in the earth. (Jn. 12:24). Just like a farmer who plants seeds in his field, new life springs forth. So too, is a picture of the resurrected, born-again life.

From an agricultural stance, Christ's resurrected life germinated from the sowing of "the seed of the woman" in the ground after three days. Such a process explains why Christ taught Nicodemus the importance that all must be "born anew" to live in eternity. (Jn. 3:5-7). As we can see, the Garden Program's foresight to use Christ as the incorruptible seed to produce an everlasting harvest of the earth was the Divine plan all along.

"Faith to Faith" Harvest

The harvest season is about the harvesting of faith found on the earth.[145] Paul taught "faith cometh by hearing, and hearing by the word of God." (Rom. 10:17). As discussed in Chapter 6,[146] the Word of God is the "seed" sown in the hearts of men. As such, the fruit of "faith" becomes the desired crop in every generation in every age. Paul wrote it another way:

> **Rom. 1:16-18:** "For I am not ashamed of the gospel of Christ: for it is the power of God unto salvation to everyone that believeth [everyone who has faith]; to the Jew first, and also to the Greek. *For therein is the righteousness of God revealed from faith to faith: as it is written, the just shall live by faith* [emphasis added]."

Here, Paul claims the power to save comes from the good news of the risen Christ, which is rooted in the principle of the sin-offering initiated in Adam's day under the Old Testament's types and shadows format (Heb. 1:1-2). Paul then quotes the prophet Habakkuk (2:4) to confirm that the "righteousness of God" is revealed "from faith" to "faith." True to form,

---

[144] **Jn. 10:17-18:** Therefore doth my Father love me, because I lay down my life, that I might take it again. No man taketh it from me, but I lay it down of myself. I have power to lay it down, and I have power to take it again. This commandment have I received of my Father.

[145] **Lk. 18:8:** I tell you that he (Christ) will avenge them speedily. Nevertheless when the Son of man cometh, shall he find faith on the earth?

[146] See Section, *What is Purity of Race* in Chapter 6.

the Old Testament quote is strangely cryptic. However, it still carries the idea of advancement from one faith position to another. By this "righteous" equation, the object of faith (Christ as the sin-offering) remains the same, but the process of application changes.

Israel models this application change perfectly because they were "born" into "one body" on a national platform by external means (circumcision and blood of the Passover Lamb applied on the doorposts). They will always maintain their "firstborn" status in the family of God (Ex. 4:22; Deut. 21:15-17), but due to the disjointed nature of the individuals within this group, a new "body" fit for eternity was always the goal. Hence the reason we see in Paul's day, the process of salvation turned inward on an "individual platform" (Rom. 2:24-29). Because true "saving faith" has always been "hidden" within the hearts of men that prove them "righteous" before God in any age.

So, while the whole nation of Israel proved willing to drink of the water flowing from the Rock (1Co. 10:2-4), only a few went forward to receive the "new drink" of the New Covenant given by that same Rock, Christ, as the chief cornerstone, whom the builders rejected (Eph. 2:20). Paul's only hope for Israel in his day was that "his gospel" might become a "stepping-stone" for them on an individual basis instead of a "stumbling block" for the whole.

The "First will be Last" Harvest Order Principle

Jesus tells of another parable about a man who hires laborers to harvest his vineyard at various times during the day yet paid everyone the same amount. He then asked, "Is it not lawful for me to do what I wish with what is my own? Or is your eye envious because I am generous? So the last shall be first, and the first last." (Mt. 20:15-16). His final statement marks a fundamental principle concerning the reward of the laborers who work the harvest.

This statement, "the first will be last, and the last will be first," directly correlates to a specific order as it relates to "Christ's own." Since the Christian Church is last, they will be first, and since Israel is the firstborn, they will be last. Even Israel's own harvesting rules reflect this same requirement.

The "First will be Last" Principle was first introduced through practical means after Israel entered the Promised Land under the leadership of Joshua. Possession of the land allowed farming, as dictated by the *Law of Firstfruits and Harvest*. This practice allowed Israel to become thoroughly acquainted by experiencing the doctrines built into their religious calendar.[147] By this method, Jehovah was teaching the times and the seasons of the spiritual harvest of the world.

The concept of Firstfruits and Harvest was somewhat evident within the practice of the first family. We know this from Genesis 4:3-4 as rendered by the New Living Translation, which states: "When it was time for the harvest, Cain presented some of his crops as a gift to the LORD." (NLT). Even though we know Jehovah was not able to accept the firstfruits of the cursed ground, which Cain offered during the prescribed season, the concept of Firstfruits and Harvest was always a part of the Garden Program's expectation. This expectation could only be possible by the power of the Holy Spirit on new ground with a new incorruptible seed.

Elijah Heralds a Harvest for Israel

As we have seen so far, Enoch's prophetic forerunner role curiously resembles the "Spirit of Elijah" requirement. Enoch, like Elijah in his day, warns of the coming judgment to his audience, except Enoch does it by preserving the prophecy within the meaning of his own son's name. Ironically, we do not learn about the "Elijah" forerunner office until we get to the very last book of the Old Testament. There, Malachi writes, "Behold; I will send you Elijah the prophet before the coming of the great and dreadful day of the LORD. And he shall turn the heart of the fathers to the children, and the heart of the children to their fathers, lest I come and smite the earth with a curse." (Mal. 4:5-6).

Malachi was a prophet living about one hundred years after Israel returned to their homeland following the Babylonian exile. His book completes the Old Testament literature and roughly four hundred years later, starting with the birth of our Lord, the New Testament breaks on the scene. Malachi reveals Jehovah's plans to purge Israel of their corruption and unbelief to fulfill their calling as a witness to the nations and to lead a joyous jubilee into the Kingdom, as the Cain-line summary statement suggests.

Amidst Malachi's judgment theme that was aimed at Israel, there resides the curious Spirit of Elijah requirement, which is critical to Israel's

---

[147] **Lev. 23: 9-10:** And the LORD spake unto Moses, saying Speak unto the children of Israel, and say unto them, When ye be come into the land which I give unto you, and shall reap the harvest thereof, then ye shall bring a sheaf of the firstfruits of your harvest unto the priest.

prophetic timeline. The reason is simple. Restoration and reconciliation became the prescription for a fractured and dispersed house. Since Malachi is the last book of the Old Testament, Jehovah not only promised His elect nation judgment by "atonement through affliction,"[148] but He also promised to make them a "whole" house again.

Furthermore, Jehovah provided Elijah as a sign on their public timeline. The Jews did not recognize Jesus as the Messiah because they were looking for the *person* of Elijah, and not the *spirit* of Elijah. They expected and taught the same Elijah, who rode away in the sky in a chariot of fire, would come back in the same way. There is even a cup reserved for Elijah at the Seder dinner held on the eve of Passover. So, when John the Baptist said he was not Elijah,[149] it was true. John was *not* Elijah. However, that did not mean John's "spirit and ministry" was not in the likeness to Elijah's spirit and ministry. Jesus confirmed John the Baptist as the one who came in the Spirit of Elijah.[150] The subject is settled by Christ, but it also serves as an object lesson, in type.

Unquestionably, there is a Spirit of Elijah prerequisite, which becomes an established pattern, that must occur before the coming judgment at the end of a judgment cycle. It requires a designated forerunner to assist with the harvest preparations in its prescribed order. In terms of the pre-flood and pre-law period, Enoch is the precursor of this sign. In the context of Christ's first advent, it was John the Baptist. Concerning the last days, we will soon see how this prerequisite will once again come in the form of another who comes to prepare those who will participate in the final harvest efforts of the ages.

No Escaping the Harvest

The method of escape or the harvesting, as we have noted previously, directly correlates to both Enoch and Elijah's process of being "caught up" and escaping death. Both prophets had such a blessed fate because of their faith connection. Enoch, remember, lived in a time that was outside the Law and judgment. His timeframe naturally makes him the "escape model" for the mysterious or secret rapture of the Christian Church.

By comparison, Elijah lived and served within the age of Law and judgment, where there was an active choice given—to live by faith or by Law.

---

[148] Lev. 23:26-32; Dan. 9:24; Mt. 24:9.

[149] **Jn. 1:21:** And they asked him, What then? Art thou Elias? And he saith, I am not. Art thou that prophet? And he answered, No.

[150] **Mt. 17:11:** And Jesus answered and said unto them, Elias truly shall first come, and restore all things.

Elijah's escape model aligns with the remnant of Israel, who must choose wisely as they go through the Divine judicial process. Notice how Scripture describes Enoch's departure with no details other than, "Enoch was caught up and was no more." Elijah's departure, however, was a known event, as recorded in 2 Kings:

> **2 Ki. 2:11:** "And it happened, as they were going on and speaking, behold, a chariot of fire and horses of fire came. And they separated between them both, and Elijah went up in a tempest to Heaven." (LITV).

From the above snapshot, it is evident how Elijah's being caught up, was publicly witnessed by Elisha, who becomes a direct benefactor because of the occasion. Such an occurrence was not the case for Enoch, who appears to have no witnesses and no warning of his departure. Notice the promise given to Elisha. His receipt of the double portion was conditional and not freely given. It required an active choice. This active choice represents Israel's continual charge to keep watch, overcome, and choose wisely even up to the end. So, it will be for those who remain faithful within the marked line of National Israel on their marked timeline at the end of the ages.

It is Elijah's ministry that forces Israel off the fence to choose wisely but only in the context of challenging the false religion of the day to determine who is the one true God. This occasion repeats in the 7-year tribulation period of Revelation. Second Kings Chapter 18 gives the account of Elijah's showdown between the false gods and Jehovah. The story prefigures how Elijah's forerunner office prepares Israel to make the right choice in the judgment period of tribulation. The heat is turned up to the highest degree during the last half of the tribulation period in hopes that Israel, as one national body, chooses wisely to overcome by faith. Thus, Jehovah's stern warning comes to mind:

> **Mal. 3:1-2:** "Behold, I will send my messenger, and he shall prepare the way before me: and the Lord, whom ye seek, shall suddenly come to his temple, even the messenger of the covenant, whom ye delight in: behold, he shall come, saith the LORD of hosts. But who may

abide the day of his coming? and who shall stand when he appeareth? for he *is* like a refiner's fire, and like fullers' soap."

As we can see, the last book of the Old Testament continues to portray Jehovah's anger against Israel as an apostate nation and the surety of their judgment. Yet, they have this hope, "Then shall ye return, and discern between the righteous and the wicked, between him that serveth God and him that serveth him not." (Mal. 3:18).

Israel's choice involves their whole heart as one national body of believers. They must choose Jehovah or the world once and for all. We pieced this puzzle together simply by comparing the two prophets who escaped death within their respective dispensations. In terms of our two bloodline statements, it becomes clear how both groups of the Despairing automatically fall within their own divisions and order of escape.

Rules for Harvesting the Soil

As we have learned so far, the Feast of Pentecost in Acts 2 (also called the Feast of Harvest) points to the Garden Program's harvest phase. The harvest also underscores Methuselah because his life span reaches the last four members in the Christ-line. It is with these associations that both Enoch and Elijah come to prepare their respective generations for the escape as dictated within their specific administrations. Again, we must look to Israel's system of harvesting, which continues to put everything in its proper perspective.

In Palestine, the first crop of the harvest season is from the barley fields in the spring. According to their harvest rules,[151] each Israelite family was to go into their field, which was about 15 acres square, while it was still green. You could see yellow heads of grain sprinkled throughout the area. The yellow heads reflect the few that had ripened in the field first. Some of these stems were collected to form a bundle, called a sheaf. The bundle was then brought to the priest as a wave-offering on the Feast of Firstfruits. Matthew's Gospel includes a tiny detail in his account of Jesus' own resurrection that compares to this wave-offering typology:

---

[151] **Lev. 23:9-10:** And the Lord spake unto Moses, saying, Speak unto the children of Israel, and say unto them, When ye be come into the land which I give unto you, and shall reap the harvest thereof, then ye shall bring a sheaf [bundle] of the first fruits of your harvest unto the priest.

Mt. 27:51-53: "And, behold, the veil of the temple was rent in twain [torn in two] from the top to the bottom; and the earth did quake, and the rocks rent [break]... And the graves [in Jerusalem] were opened [not all of them] and many bodies of the saints which slept arose, and came out of the graves *after his resurrection* [emphasis added]."

This verse in Matthew is significant because it confirms a literal wave-offering was given to Jehovah in heaven after Christ's own resurrection. Christ is the first to have been resurrected from the dead. He, therefore, completes the plural of the term firstfruits. Had Christ come alone, then the feast would be called the firstfruit of the resurrection, which would be an expression in the singular. Instead, it is in the plural because Firstfruits required to take not just one stem of grain but several as a sampling of the crop to come. This scene pictures Jesus and the risen saints as a sampling of the whole earth as the field. Once the rest of the stems ripened within the field, the harvest is ready. Leviticus Chapter 19 provides the remaining instructions as to how they were to proceed:

Lev. 19:9-10: "And when ye reap the harvest of your land, thou shalt not wholly reap the corners of thy field, neither shalt thou gather the gleanings of thy harvest... thou shalt leave them [the corners] for the poor and stranger."

This passage outlines the method of harvesting. Note how the four corners of the field and the droppings are a specially reserved portion of the harvest. The meaning of this will find its context shortly. First, we must zero-in on this one point. The harvest has rules, order, and is a type of resurrection.

Paul's teaching is consistent with the Israelite's harvesting system as a model of the resurrections (plural). Paul said that every man, lost or saved, will proceed *in his own order.*[152] The Greek word for "order" is the idea of a company as in a military chain of command. The smallest company in the military is about 100-120 men. The next group is more sub-

---

[152] **1 Cor. 15:23:** But every man in his own order: Christ the firstfruits; afterward they that are Christ's at his coming.

stantial, called a battalion, then a regiment. Paul chose to use this word company to convey the same idea as a military organizational system for God's eternal harvest of the earth.

Of all the people who have ever lived and died, *all* are one day going to be resurrected in their own order and with their own specific company. There is not just one resurrection on the last day, as Martha thought when she confessed to Jesus. Raised by Judaic customs and the Law, she knew Lazarus would be raised again on the last day.[153] She only knew of one resurrection as taught by the Rabbis and the prophets of old. Even though the annual feast days were a part of everyday life for the typical Israelite family, the understanding of the spiritual harvest was still unknown.

Due to Israel's spiritual blindness, they were unaware that just as they annually applied the Leviticus 23 Feast-Day cycle for the "harvesting of the soil" in the promised land, so too, the Lord would apply once, on the stage of human history, for the harvesting of souls on the earth. Therefore, the Feasts of the Lord become the map that provides the details of the Garden Program's "seed of the woman" plan to successfully achieve its long-awaited harvest, because it failed to do so in Adam's day due to sin.

Rules for Harvesting Souls

Unquestionably, the rules for harvesting the souls of the earth comply with the Israelite Harvesting System, except it operates on a scale of human history. Its season runs in three courses: spring, summer, and fall.

The order of the harvest never changes, but the duration of the courses is a different matter. For example, when we compare the extended life of Methuselah of 969 years old (who largely exemplifies the spring and summer portions of the harvest), with the 7-year tribulation period (which signifies the fall portion of the harvest), it is easy to conclude how the "end' is dramatically cut short. Mark tells us it is by design and said it this way:

> **Mk. 13:20:** "And except that the Lord had shortened those days, no flesh should be saved: but for *the elect's sake, whom he hath chosen,* he hath shortened the days [emphasis added]."

---

[153] **Jn. 11:24:** Martha saith unto him, I know that he shall rise again in the resurrection at the last day.

In Mark's passage, we can learn a great deal about the end of the age and its level of intensity. Israel, in this instance, is the elect, *whom he hath chosen*. Jehovah made Israel an everlasting people and His elect.[154]

In the context of the Cain-line summary statement, and due to Cain's firstborn legal status, he and his line are "the elect" (or ear-marked) to walk on a fixed and public timeline. Cain and Israel's first-born position is reserved to be *last* by the "First will be Last" Principle (Mt. 20:16).

The end of days as Daniel foretold unquestionably qualifies as last. As that time draws near, Daniel's book shall once again open with new revelation and insights. Daniel and his lot are chosen in the beginning to be preserved and dealt with in the end. During the last days, Israel's choice will be to lead a joyous jubilee or to face wrath and judgment.

Methuselah Suffers Long for the Harvest

In this chapter, we established how Methuselah's day on the Christ-line represents three themes as it relates to prophecy. First, because Methuselah was alive during the last four generations of Adam in the pre-flood genera-tion, his reach represents the entire harvest period of the Garden Program. Second, the meaning of his name serves as a warning of the coming judg-ment. Third, his legendary long life is synonymous with the patience and grace of Jehovah, as evident by the open invitation extended to the Gentile nations due to the rejection of Israel. Once we saw the fuller ramifications of these themes, we then realized that the Christ-line also doubles as an outline of these prophetic events, as Chart 7 displays.

As we continued to work out the dynamics of the Christ-line as a pro-phetic timeline, we also learned that our present-day represents what Jesus saw ready for harvest on the horizon (Jn. 4:35). It began in power by the Holy Spirit, who was sent as a rushing, mighty wind on the Day of Pentecost as described in Acts 2. The Acts 2 event begins the harvesting of the earth, while the close of the tribulation period concludes the harvest.

Next, we learned how the reaping of this planet takes its model from the Israelite harvest system. A model that pictures the escape plan, or the

---

[154] E. W. Bullinger refers to Israel as an everlasting nation, and states: "The nation of Israel is everlasting, like the Covenant. The nations which oppressed Israel (Egypt, Assyria, Babylon, Rome) have passed away; but Israel remains, and, when re-stored, will remain for ever. Note and compare the nine everlasting things in Isaiah: (1) covenant (Isa. 55:3; Isa. 61:8; com-pare note on Gen. 9:16); (2) kindness (Isa. 54:8); (3) salvation (Isa. 45:17); (4) excellency (Isa. 60:15); (5) joy (Isa. 51:11); (6) name (Isa. 56:5); (7) light (Isa. 60:19, Isa. 60:20); (8) sign (Isa. 55:13); and (9) as the pledge of all, "the everlasting God" (Isa. 40:28; Isa. 63:12)." (Bullinger, *The Companion Bible*, Isa. 44:7). Re: Israel's elect and chosen position, see Deut. 32:6, Jer. 31:3; Isa. 44:7-8, 21; Rom. 11:7, 28-29.

resurrection of all the saints of God in three stages: Firstfruits, Pentecost, and the Feast of the Tabernacles or In-Gathering, which is the late gleaning of the leftovers from the four corners of the earth's field.

The harvest intimately involves the Garden Prophecy's "seed of the woman" (Gen. 3:15). Christ is that "seed," who came as the "Blessed God" born of a virgin, only to die and be raised to defeat sin, hell, and the grave and offer rest to the Despairing. The Despairing, as we have learned, is the meaning of Lamech's name. We will discover his extraordinary contributions in the next chapter.

CHAPTER 10 – LAMECH
"Christ's Despairing"

The Twist of the Despairing Tale

This chapter is all about "the Despairing," as suggested by the meaning of Lamech's name. By now, we have come to understand that the Despairing is a subset of all who are born in mortal sorrow, who find rest from it. We also know that the Despairing is divided into two family lines of the redeemed. We have identified the two lines as Firstborn Israel and the Christian Church, as the younger brother. Both lines have been placed on two separate paths with two separate fates due to their birth order and application of the sin-offering that was provided by the "Blessed God" who came down.

In the last chapter, we reviewed a prophetic timeline of the "fate" of the world as depicted by Chart 7. The timeline revealed the Garden Program's basic harvest plan. We also learned that the "First will be Last" Principle,[155] governs the harvesting order of the two lines of the Despairing. Even though Chart 7 was a pleasant surprise, it did not show the harvest order that transpires within the last four generations on the Christ-line's Harvest Timeline. This is the twist of the Despairing tale, as we are about to see.

The Master Harvest-Escape Plan According to Both Lines

Now that we are in the day of the Despairing, we must include both sides of the family. To do that, we must insert the Cain-line into the mix to make a new chart. As we saw on Chart 7, the Christ-line will continue in its horizontal position, except in this chapter, the Cain-line will now be included directly below in like manner. When both lines are combined horizontally, a complete overview of the ages is produced. This new timeline, illustrated by Chart 8, reveals the fate of Israel, the Christian Church, and the world at large as it relates to the Garden Program's harvest-rescue plan.

---

[155] Mt. 19:30, 20:16; Mk. 9:35, 10:31; Lk. 13:30.

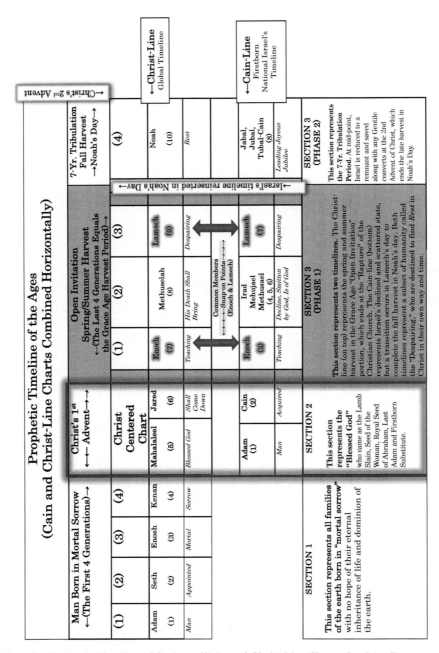

Chart 8 - Prophetic Timeline of the Ages (Cain and Christ-Line Charts Combined)

Notice how the Christ-line and the Cain-line in Chart 8 "snap" together at their common-counter members, Enoch and Lamech. As we can see, the harvest timeline of Chart 7 is still in full view. Except now, it appears in two separate phases. The first and longest phase (Phase 1, Section 3 of Chart 8) serves as the "Open Invitation" to the nations, where Israel declines into a scattered state. Their timeline resumes back on a global stage in Noah's day or the "7-Year Tribulation Period," when the final phase or "gleanings" of the "Grace Age Harvest Period" is conducted. This will be explained further as we continue our review.

Chart 8 is a true representation of the fixed timeline for all those born in "mortal sorrow," as it relates to the Garden Program's harvest plan or the Messianic plan of redemption. The success of this plan, as the chart shows, solely relies on Christ. Notice how His first coming on the chart rests between the first and the last four generations of the family of man, which is appropriately labeled as "Christ's 1st Advent." This positioning is not by accident. It makes Christ central to the plan because He was elected in eternity as the "Lamb slain from the foundation of the world." Therefore, His blood was already shed before the world was formed.

Since eternity must work within the realm of time and space where mortal men live, Chart 8 illustrates how time has a beginning and an end as far as mortality and this world is concerned. Scripture clearly teaches that mortality began at the fall of Adam and our current world system ends at the second coming of Christ.

Paul taught that Christ came in the "fulness of time" to be born under the Law[156] in the likeness of sinful men to redeem. Backed by His eternal election as the Lamb Slain, the moment Christ was crucified on this earth, on and as the Passover, His blood instantly substantiated every animal sacrifice that was ever offered in time.

The Passover in Egypt looks forward to Christ's finished work on the cross. Due to His eternal election, the blood applied to the doorposts of every household who desired to save their firstborn as well as their family in that day, was equally, His blood. The blood of animals served as a placeholder. This explains why Passover is equal to Christ's first advent, which, again, is appropriately labeled in Chart 8.

Moreover, note how the Cain-line's first two members, Adam and Cain, (shown directly under the Christ-line) collectively mean, "man acquired." The

[156] **Gal. 4:4-5:** But when the fulness of the time was come, God sent forth his Son, made of a woman, made under the law, To redeem them that were under the law, that we might receive the adoption of sons.

significance of this vertical alignment between the two-family lines accurately reflects the "acquisition" of the redeemed by Christ who died for the whole world as the "Blessed God" who came down in the form of the babe born of the virgin Mary.

By default, the two shared members from both lines (Enoch and Lamech) represent the spring and summer harvest. This portion is labeled "Open Invitation" on the chart because this section represents the open invitation portion (or "Phase 1") of the Grace Age Harvest Period. The summer harvest concludes once the Christian Church is raptured, and we cannot forget, when Methuselah dies, as his name indicates, the judgment waters of Noah begin to flow.

The Cain-line's lower horizontal insertion, at the shared members' connection points within Chart 8, naturally represents the fallout of Israel's timeline in Enoch's day. This causes the unmarked timeline of the Christian Church to become mainline on the Christ-line. According to Daniel, when Messiah is "cut-off" (Dan. 9:26), which we know is on the cross at His first coming, Israel's public timeline is set to transition out of view being disbursed among the nations.

This transition gives way for the hidden timeline of the Christian Church to emerge and to accept the open invitation, which continues the harvest uninterrupted. As soon as the Christian Church is caught up to meet the Lord in the air, Chart 8 then depicts Israel's timeline transitioning back into the mainline, as represented by Noah's day ("Phase 2" of the Grace Age Harvest Period) to conclude the harvest and fulfill their destiny as the Cain-line summary statement suggests.

Who could have imagined that the two lines of Adam in the pre-flood period had the power to expand into a Prophetic Timeline of the Ages? Such a wonder! We can only attribute it to supernatural engineering. With such a discovery, we now have the complete picture of the Bible's epic tapestry in view as it relates to what Christ seeks to save, which was lost. As we bring our final chapters to a conclusion, from this point on, Chart 8 will serve as a visual tool to show how all the prophetic puzzle pieces fit according to the sum of His image.

The Despairing Way

Just as we learned how Enoch's contributions are essential to the Christian Church's teaching and preparations, so we will see how Lamech is as equally important to the Jewish congregations in like manner. Lamech, as noted earlier, is known as the first polygamist in biblical history. From this insight, in addition to his "murderous and cursed line" heritage, Orthodox teaching has done much to ruin anything left of Lamech's reputation and dignity. However, just as we saw with Cain, we will soon see there is more to Lamech than meets the eye. His story begins in Genesis 4 from a strange incident:

> **Gen. 4:23-24:** "And Lamech said unto his wives, Adah and Zillah, Hear my voice; ye wives of Lamech, hearken unto my speech: for I have slain a man to my wounding, and a young man to my hurt. If Cain shall be avenged sevenfold, truly Lamech seventy and sevenfold."

From this passage, Lamech is claiming a right of 70 times that of the claim of his famous ancestor, Cain, who received a mere 7-year period. It appears Lamech desired to surpass the curse of Cain and claim total restoration and forgiveness for him and his family line. The difference between Lamech and Cain is that Cain's killing was deliberate. The punishment for Cain's crime was to be visited upon him in the seventh generation.[157] Therefore, Cain, whether in defiance or if he genuinely believed he could work his way back into Jehovah's graces, refused to become a vagabond (wanderer) and settled in the land of Nod, and even became a builder of cities.

The first city he called Enoch. He named this city after his son. According to legend, Cain experienced a measure of joy around the time of the birth of his firstborn. He also founded six other cities. According to the classic book, *The Legends of the Jews*, by Louis Ginzberg, this building of cities was a godless enterprise, "for he surrounded them with a wall, forcing his family to remain within. All his other activities were equally profane."

As the story goes, Cain passed in the seventh generation of men. As irony would have it, the infliction of Cain's demise was by the hand of his 3rd-great-grandson, Lamech. The classic Jewish book continues to enrich its readers with the background of Lamech's accidental killing of Cain. At that time, Father Lamech was blind. He needed his youngest son to go hunting with him to be his eyes. Lamech would then shoot the subject with his bow and arrow upon the cue of Tubal Cain.

---

[157] Interpretation according to the collation of the Haggada--the traditions which have grown up surrounding the biblical narrative. These stories and bits of layered detail are scattered throughout the Talmud and the Midrash, and other sources, including oral. In the 19th century Louis Ginzberg undertook the task of arranging the Haggada into chronological order, and in a series of volumes entitled, *The Legend of the Jews* (1938).

"One day," Ginzberg continues, "Lamech's son discerned something "horned" in the distance. He naturally took it to be a beast of one kind or another, and he told his blind father to let his arrow fly. The aim was good, and the quarry dropped to the ground." The Jewish legend concludes:

> "Lamech knew at once what had happened—he had killed his ancestor Cain, who had been marked by God with a horn. In despair he smote his hands together, inadvertently killing his son as he clasped them. Misfortune still followed upon misfortune. The earth opened her mouth and swallowed up the four generations sprung from Cain—Enoch, Irad, Mehujael, and Methushael. Lamech, sightless as he was, could not go home; he had to remain by the side of Cain's corpse and his son's. Toward evening, his wives, seeking him, found him there. When they heard what he had done, they wanted to separate from him, all the more as they knew that whoever was descended from Cain was doomed to annihilation. But Lamech argued, "If Cain, who committed murder of malice aforethought [on purpose], was punished only in the seventh generation, then I, who had no intention of killing a human being, may hope that retribution will be averted for seventy and seven generations." With his wives, Lamech repaired to Adam, who heard both parties, and decided the case in favor of Lamech." (Ginzberg, *The Legends of the Jews Vol. 1*, Ch. III).

Although this tale is not a biblical account, it is part of the Rabbinical literature and serves as background to at least trace the thought process of Lamech's reasoning and right to claim forgiveness 70 times that of Cain's 7-year right (Gen. 4:15). We do not have to accept the embellishments provided in the Jewish story, especially as it relates to the physical appearance of Cain. However, if we can take from the story the general principle of forgiveness of crimes committed, whether intentional or unintentional, then the Jewish tradition has done its job. To cross-check this on biblical ground, confirmation of this "70 times 7" forgiveness principle was also validated by Christ:

Mt. 18:21-22: "Then came Peter and said to him, Lord, how oft shall my brother sin against me, and I forgive him? until seven times? Jesus saith unto him, I say not unto thee, Until seven times; but, *Until seventy times seven* [emphasis added]."

From this account, notice how Peter just assumed that seven times (7x) was the standard time to forgive. From a Jewish standpoint, Peter undoubtedly was using the seventh generational visitation curse of Cain as a model to forgive others. However, Jesus corrected Peter's misinterpretation of the forgiveness model and validated Lamech as the true model of forgiveness by referencing Lamech's 70 x 7 extension request.

In His response to Peter, Jesus applied the extended forgiveness formula within the context of the parable of the head servant (Mt. 18:23-35), who was forgiven of a substantial debt that he could never repay. In turn, the head servant could not forgive others who owed considerably smaller amounts than him. By his actions, the head servant proved to be hypocritical, which serves as the perfect portrait of Israel's own attitude and actions. How they so readily receive acquittal and mercy from their Lord, yet they continue to refuse "to do unto others as it has been done to them."

In due course, the Lord scolded his head servant and judged him wicked. The servant was ultimately turned over to tormentors until the debt was satisfied. Notice how the man was not imprisoned or put to death but tormented until payment was received. Since Cain represents that portion of Jewish Israel stuck under the Law, it would be reasonable to assume that Christ would teach His Jewish disciples the model of forgiveness in terms of the Jewish ideology. After all, Cain was the ultimate example of forgiveness by Jehovah, or so the Jews thought.

However, Jesus knew that Cain's 7-year model fell short, so He corrected Peter to recognize Lamech's 70 x 7 model as the new standard. The granting of Lamech's extension request not only represents the debt-forgiveness plan, but it also becomes the judicial remedy to all of Israel's legal problems, as we will soon see.

Lamech's Motion for Extension Saves the Family

We need to examine the joint-influences that each counter-Lamech has and how each contributes to the fuller story of *HIS-Story*. In the context of

Lamech in the Christ-line, he is the 9th generation (remember 9 is the number for the Holy Spirit), who lives to a ripe old age of 777 years old.[158] So typologically speaking, his triple-seven lifespan represents the amplified power of the Godhead, which fuels the extended forgiveness model.

By comparison, Lamech on the Cain-line represents the 7th generation on the firstborn line. As Jewish legend has it, Cain's initial 7-year right (Gen 4:15) was extended 70 times due to Lamech's petition before Father Adam, which was upheld by Christ to Peter. We cannot ignore the strong number association and how the number "7-times," and its multiples "77-times," and "70 times 7" are also commonly used in association with the firstborn-line of the family, no matter if it is Cain or if we are speaking of Firstborn National Israel. In the case of Israel, their prophetic timeline is foretold by Daniel, which curiously reflects Lamech's forgiveness extension formula:

> **Dan. 9:24-28:** "*Seventy weeks* [literal translation "Seventy weeks of Sevens" represents the expanded prophetic timeline of Israel uninterrupted in "weeks" of years] are decreed as to *your people*, and as to *your holy city*, to finish the transgression, and to make an end of sins, and to make atonement for iniquity, and to bring in everlasting righteousness, and to seal up the vision and prophecy, and to anoint the Most Holy. Know, then, and understand that from the going out of a word to restore and to rebuild Jerusalem, to Messiah the Prince, shall be *seven weeks* [1st Part of Israel's expanded marked timeline], *and sixty-two weeks* [2nd Part of Israel's expanded marked timeline]; The street shall be built again, and the wall, even in times of affliction. *And after sixty two weeks, Messiah shall be cut* off [3rd part is the interruption of Israel's timeline to insert the Grace Age Timeline], but not *for* Himself. And the people of a coming ruler [Prince of Darkness, Antichrist] shall destroy the city and the sanctuary. And its end *shall be* with the flood, and ruins are determined, and war *shall be* until *the* end. And he [Antichrist] shall confirm a covenant with the many *for one week*. [last and final week

---

[158] **Gen. 5:31:** And all the days of Lamech were seven hundred seventy and seven years: and he died.

100

of Israel's marked timeline], And in the middle of the week he [Antichrist] shall cause the sacrifice and the offering to cease. And on a corner *of the altar will be* abominations *that* desolate, even until *the* end. And that which was decreed shall pour out on the desolator [emphasis added]." (LITV).

This prophecy reveals the allotted timeline of the holy city (Jerusalem) and Daniel's people (Israel). The 70 weeks of years equate to the following mathematical formula 70 x 7 = 490 years total. The prophecy further breaks down the 490 years into three separate intervals on Israel's marked timeline. Anything outside of those years reflects an "unmarked timeline" when Jehovah is dealing with the Gentile nations as the "open invitation" portion of the harvesting of the earth as illustrated by this next chart:

**70 x 7 WEEK OF YEARS BREAKDOWN EQUATION CHART
DANIEL 9:24-27**

I.   **7 weeks** (7x7 = 49 yrs. to rebuild; Neh. 3-6)

II.   **62 weeks** (62x7=434 yrs. to the Messiah)

= **69 weeks total** (*Messiah cut-off. Unmarked Timeline Begins*)

III. **1 week** (7x1 yrs. Last Week - Israel's Timeline Reinserted)

= 70 weeks or 70 x 7 = 490 weeks of years

Chart 9 – The Breakdown of the 70x7 Week of Years Equation Chart

Chart 9 provides a breakdown of Israel's Prophetic Timeline according to Daniel.[159] His prophecy breaks down Israel's timeline into three known parts (7 weeks + 62 weeks [= 69 weeks] + 1 week = 70 total). What is not known, nor revealed, is the "unmarked timeline," which begins once the Messiah is cut-off at the 69th week and ends just before the last week begins. Notice how Daniel's 70 weeks of years emulate Lamech's extension

---

[159] Chart 9 represents Israel's fixed-prophetic timeline according to Daniel 9:24-27. The 7-year tribulation period is equivalent to the last week or 7-year period and is broken down into two halves. Each 3.5 years are then further broken down to 1290 days. The 1290 days in Daniel directly correlate to 1260 days mentioned in Revelation, which excludes a month's time because the figure in Revelation is calculated from a 360-year prophetic standard (3.5 yrs. x 360).

of 70 x 7. More importantly, note how the two expressions produce the same product— 490 years, which is Israel's marked timeline! Daniel continues:

> **Dan. 9:26:** "And after threescore and two weeks shall Messiah be cut off, *but not for himself:* and the people of the prince that shall come shall destroy the city and the sanctuary; and the end thereof *shall be* with a flood, and unto the end of the war desolations are determined [emphasis added]."

Between the last week of Daniel and the point in time when the Messiah was cut-off, some scholars refer to this as a "gap of time" because it is not explicitly called-out in Daniel's prophecy. In hindsight, especially seen from our present age, this gap is none other than a placement marker to represent the unmarked time or the open invitation to the nations. However, for Israel, this gap represents a missed opportunity to enter the Promised Land only to face another 40-year generational cycle of wandering among the heathen.

Daniel's prophecy saw the fulfillment of the 69th week, the moment Christ was crucified. The unmarked timeline of the harvest began on Pentecost of Acts 2. Shortly thereafter, the Romans destroyed the Temple in 70 A.D. as Jesus predicted, and the Jewish diaspora continued. Desolate of their ability to worship in their Temple in Jerusalem, still even to this day, we see the cause of their "despairing" state.

The upside to this is that Christianity has a chance to root and grow among the Gentile population. We also see evidence of this within the Christ-line. For example, if the prophetic timeline of Israel was not interrupted, there would have been no effectual power of grace to insert the unmarked timeline, which includes the invitation to both the circumcised and uncircumcised nations of the world as illustrated in this next chart:

The 7-Year Marked Timeline
(Without Lamech's 70 x 7 Extension)

1	2	3	4	5	6	7
				Christ's 1st Advent		
Adam	Seth	Enosh	Kenan	Mahalaleel	Jared	Noah
Man	Appointed	Mortal	Sorrow	The Blessed God	Shall Come Down	Rest
Garden Curse: All families of the earth born in "mortal sorrow," without hope of their eternal inheritance of life and dominion of the earth.				The Garden Promise: Christ comes as the "Seed of the Woman" to be sown in the earth at His death. (Jn. 12:24) to produce a harvest.		7 yr. Tribulation/ Coming Kingdom

"Messiah cut-off"

Chart 10 – The 7-Year Marked Timeline (Without Lamech's 70 x 7 Extension)

Chart 10 shows how the "unmarked timeline" of the harvest (as represented by Enoch, Methuselah, and Lamech) is eliminated entirely from the ten-member Christ-line. The once global timeline instantly reverts to Daniel's condensed version that reflects how the last week is to immediately occur once the Messiah is cut-off, without any interruptions.

By reducing the count to 7 members, Chart 10 curiously reflects the same generational measure used for Cain. His 7-year allowance was based on Jehovah's Sabbatical standard. But due to the cost of sin, Jehovah's finished 7-day work week of creation model fell short. This required a new model based on Christ's finished work of re-creation, which Lamech's 70 x 7 forgiveness formula represents. By this example, the need for a worldwide "Grace" extension goes without question.

Israel's Bankruptcy and Blindness

For Israel, their view of end-times concerns the coming of the Kingdom and their Messiah as the king. They are bankrupt of faith and have no understanding about a suffering Messiah who had to come and die for their redemption first before He could come as their king.

Due to the right of their firstborn position, Israel's faith solely relies upon the strong-arm of the Law, just like Cain. Their legal claim to the birthright was an automatic guarantee, or so they thought. They are blind to the fact that the very Law they look to can only condemn. All the tantrums in the world could not correct this predicament without the appropriate application of the sin-offering.

In addition to their misguided legal notions, they also had misinterpretations of the prophecies that concerned them. Such errors indoctrinated the whole Jewish belief system just as a little leaven would when mixed with dough. The result is the puffing up of their pride before their fall.

Even the most earnest Jew, like Paul, fell victim to the leaven of the Jewish theology by zealously butchering his own fellow Jews who claimed Jesus as their Messiah. However, perhaps the best example is from Jesus' disciples in an incident that occurred right before His final hour as recorded by Luke:

> **Lk. 18:31-34:** "Then he took unto him the twelve, and said unto them, Behold, we go up to Jerusalem, and all things that are written by the prophets concerning the Son of man

shall be accomplished. For he shall be delivered unto the Gentiles, and shall be mocked, and spitefully entreated, and spitted on: And they shall scourge him, and put him to death: and the third day he shall rise again. And they *understood none of these things: and this saying was hid from them, neither knew they the things which were spoken* [emphasis added]."

Luke's passage states how Jesus revealed precisely what was about to happen to Him, yet His own did not have a clue. Christ knew why He had to die, but His own disciples could not comprehend. This lack of spiritual discernment explains why the closest of His disciples slept while Jesus stayed up all night and prayed alone in the garden of Gethsemane[160] just before the morning of His kiss of betrayal by Judas.

Since we know sleep is a type of death where Scripture is concerned, the three closest disciples of Jesus, as willing and as well-intentioned as they were, were still spiritually dead to the Messianic prophecies, which were now upon them.

From Saul of Tarsus (before he became Paul at his conversion) and Christ's own disciples, we learn even the best of the best of the Jewish field has no understanding of Christ as the suffering Messiah and the need to die first before He can be king. However, Israel's blind condition was not without purpose. We must always remember, "for had they known it, they would not have crucified the Lord of glory." (1 Cor. 2:8).

Israel's Legal Problems

Again, we are back to the subject of the firstborn (as represented by Cain) in his blind and bankrupt condition. Cain and his firstborn line's ability to interpret prophecy about Christ's finished work on the cross was, and still is (in terms of the Jewish portion of Israel), significantly impaired. Jehovah made provisions for him and his line, which extends to all generations. With Jesus confirming Lamech's extended forgiveness formula of 70 x 7, Jehovah has compensated for the crime of Cain and his firstborn house, and their problem is solved—right?

Unfortunately, Israel's deficiencies are still at issue, and this is due to free will and the right of individual choice. The freedom of choice is an

---

[160] Mt. 26:36-46.

area that is respected and protected by the Almighty. Even the angels can choose. Evidence of this is in Revelation, where we read one-third of the angels fell to follow Satan,[161] while Genesis 6 speaks of angels who left their first estate for their own degenerate purposes. From these examples, we see how choice is a fundamental God-given right enjoyed by all His creation.

Similarly, choice is evident in the Garden of Eden in the form of *the tree of the knowledge of good and evil.* (Gen. 2:17). Jehovah's warning "not to eat from the tree as they would surely die," was the Law of the day. Once Adam and Eve chose against God's word by believing a lie, no amount of mercy could cure their act of disobedience except by way of restitution and redemption. If the debt was not paid, which Paul tells us the wages for sin is death, then all that remains is judgment. So, Jesus taught His twelve this sobering truth:

> **Lk. 12:10**: "And whosoever shall speak a word against the Son of man, it shall be forgiven him: but unto him that blasphemeth against the Holy Ghost it shall not be forgiven."

Jesus' teaching here is in the context of the leaven of the Pharisees, which produces hypocrisy.[162] Luke ends the chapter with Jesus' summary on the matter, "a hypocrite cannot judge what is right." (Lk. 12:56-57). This summation curiously falls within the context of the unpardonable sin.

The unpardonable sin (or blaspheme against the Holy Spirit) is a sin against the Holy Spirit, which directly involves the heart's confession in terms of belief or unbelief. Blasphemy of the Holy Spirit means more than just what we say, it intimately involves the true intent of the heart, "But those things which proceed out of the mouth come forth from the heart; and they defile the man." (Mt. 15:18-19).

Remember, the Holy Spirit's official role in the harvesting of the earth is to convict the world concerning righteousness and sin, then judgment.[163] Here, we are at the very heart of the issue and the very heart of Cain, Israel, and Judaism's problem. Although the Holy Spirit may be the last person of the Godhead, His is the power unto judgment. If a heart refuses to profess

---

[161] **Rev. 12:4:** And his tail drew the third part of the stars of heaven, and did cast them to the earth: and the dragon stood before the woman which was ready to be delivered, for to devour her child as soon as it was born.

[162] **Lk. 12:1:** In the meantime, when there were gathered together an innumerable multitude of people, insomuch that they trode one upon another, he began to say unto his disciples first of all, Beware ye of the leaven of the Pharisees, which is hypocrisy.

[163] **Jn. 16:8:** And when he is come, he will reprove the world of sin, and of righteousness, and of judgment.

faith in Christ and accept His blood sacrifice, then there is no more remission of sin.

Christ paid it all. The work of the Holy Spirit in the Garden Program is to lead *all* to drink of the fountain of Christ, who is the living water turned into the New Covenant wine to celebrate the joyous union. Yet, no one will ever be forced to drink if it is against the will of the individual.

Christ's disgust with Israel's inability to produce fruit in the form of faith is graphically portrayed when He cursed the fig tree.[164] The reason Jesus assumed that the fig tree had fruit is that fig trees in that region produce fruit first, then leaves. So, like the fig tree, Israel appeared to have a form of "fruitfulness," which proved to be false.

Christ's false assumption is the reason why He called Israel's religious leaders phonies and whitewashed tombs. They were beautiful on the outside but dead on the inside because on "the outside you appear righteous, but on the inside, you are full of hypocrisy and wickedness."[165]

Divine Due Process

Israel is the textbook example for all to learn and understand the consequence of unbelief. The book of Hebrews uses the story of Israel's refusal to go into the Promised Land as the object lesson. The place was Kadesh Barnea, which stood as the gateway to the Promised Land. The time was at the end of their forty-year wandering in the wilderness.

The majority proposed to send out spies to determine the status of the land. Their proposal was made despite Jehovah's instructions, "Go in and take the land, and I'll send in hornets ahead of you and drive the people out."

Because Israel could not take Jehovah for His word, they got their way. Out of the twelve spies, ten came back and said all Israel were like grasshoppers in the sight of the Canaanites, and they were no match for such men. From this point, the book of Hebrews sums up the issue and gives us the moral to the story:

> **Heb. 3:15-19:** "While it is said, 'Today if ye will hear his voice, harden not your hearts, as in the *provocation* [Israel's

---

[164] See, Mt. 21:19; Mk. 11:12-14; Lk. 13:7 as it concerns Jesus' teaching of cursing and cutting down the fig tree, which represents Israel and their inability to produce a crop of faith as one united body.

[165] **Mt. 23:27-28:** Woe unto you, scribes and Pharisees, hypocrites! for ye are like unto whited sepulchres, which indeed appear beautiful outward, but are within full of dead *men's* bones, and of all uncleanness. Even so ye also outwardly appear righteous unto men, but within ye are full of hypocrisy and iniquity.

trial in the wilderness]. For some, when they had heard, did *provoke*: howbeit not all that came out of Egypt by Moses. But with whom was he [God] grieved forty years? Was it not with them that had sinned, whose carcasses fell in the wilderness? And to whom sware he that they should not enter into his rest [the Promised Land], but to them that believed not?' So we see that they could not enter in because of unbelief [emphasis added]."

Here, we learn how Israel's wilderness journey started as a "Provocation Proceeding." By their acts of provoking, Israel turned it into a time of putting Jehovah on trial instead of the reverse. For forty years, that generation refused to trust Jehovah, which is key to yielding a crop of faith in this Jewish field.

All the power of God and His Son cannot save an unbelieving heart against their will, so the Hebrew writer leaves us with this sobering thought, "So we see that they [Israel] could not enter in [His rest] because of unbelief." (Heb. 3:19). Because of the unpardonable sin of unbelief, the record shows how that generation did not enter the Promised Land, which Jehovah refers to as His rest (Ps. 95:9-11).

The Israelites had to wait for the following generation (another forty years) before they were allowed entry. This example shows the consequences of unbelief. Hebrews goes on to sum it up this way: "But without faith it is impossible to please Him." (Heb. 11:6). While left wandering another forty years in the wilderness, that unbelieving generation still experienced mercy and every opportunity to accept the sin-offering.

From these examples, we can see Jehovah's use of the forty years as a generational cycle. Since forty is the number of judgment and trial, it was also His way of establishing a legal system of due process[166] for His elect and chosen nation before an eternal court of Divine Law. Ezekiel gives us further insight on the subject:

Eze. 20:5-10: "Thus saith the Lord Jehovah: In the day when I chose Israel, and sware unto the seed of the house

---

[166] Due process in a court of law is, "The principle that an individual cannot be deprived of life, liberty, or property without appropriate legal procedures and safeguards. The Bill of Rights and the Fourteenth Amendment to the Constitution guarantee that any person accused of a crime must be informed of the charges, be provided with legal counsel, be given a speedy and public trial, enjoy equal protection of the laws, and not be subjected to cruel and unusual punishment, unreasonable searches and seizures, double jeopardy, or self-incrimination." (*The New Dictionary of Cultural Literacy, 3rd Edition*).

of Jacob, and made myself known unto them in the land of Egypt, when I sware unto them, saying, I am Jehovah your God; in that day I sware unto them, to bring them forth out of the land of Egypt into a land that I had searched out for them, flowing with milk and honey, which is the glory of all lands. And I said unto them, Cast ye away every man the abominations of his eyes, and defile not yourselves with the idols of Egypt; I am Jehovah your God. But they rebelled against me, and would not hearken unto me; they did not every man cast away the abominations of their eyes; neither did they forsake the idols of Egypt. Then I said I would pour out my wrath upon them, to accomplish my anger against them in the midst of the land of Egypt. But I wrought for my name's sake, that it should not be profaned in the sight of the nations, among which they were, in whose sight I made myself known unto them, in bringing them forth out of the land of Egypt. *So I caused them to go forth out of the land of Egypt, and brought them into the wilderness* [emphasis added]." (ASV).

Eze. 20:21: "But the children rebelled against me; they walked not in my statutes, neither kept mine ordinances to do them, which if a man do, he shall live in them; they profaned my sabbaths. *Then I said I would pour out my wrath upon them, to accomplish my anger against them in the wilderness* [emphasis added]." (ASV).

Eze. 20:23-24: "*I lifted up mine hand unto them also in the wilderness,* that I would scatter them among the heathen, and disperse them through the countries; Because they had not executed my judgments, but had despised my statutes, and had polluted my sabbaths, and their eyes were after their fathers' idols [emphasis added]." (ASV).

From these passages, we get the sense that Jehovah established a due process system by way of the wilderness. Besides providing a place for testing and trials, the way of the wilderness accomplished two additional purposes: (1) For Jehovah to save face before the nations while providing a place to deal privately with Israel, and (2) in subsequent years, the wilderness becomes a time-out period of Israel dispersed among the heathen.

In Hebrews, we learned how the Provocation Proceeding (or Israel's trial), was initially scheduled to occur upon their passing through the Red Sea, which Paul calls this the "baptism unto Moses" (1 Cor. 10:1-5), as they watched the Egyptian army drown in its wake. (Ps. 78:40-43). However, because the first generation proved bankrupt in faith, the Provocation Proceeding was rescheduled for a later time. Ezekiel reveals Jehovah's timing:

> **Eze. 20:33-38:** "As I live, saith the Lord Jehovah, surely with a mighty hand, and with an outstretched arm, and with wrath poured out, will I be king over you: *and I will bring you out from the peoples, and will gather you out of the countries wherein ye are scattered*, with a mighty hand, and with an outstretched arm, and with wrath poured out; *and I will bring you into the wilderness of the peoples, and there will I enter into judgment with you face to face.* Like as I entered into judgment with your fathers in the wilderness of the land of Egypt, so will I enter into judgment with you [again in a future time], saith the Lord Jehovah. *And I will cause you to pass under the rod* [judgment language], *and I will bring you into the bond of the covenant* [wedding language]; *and I will purge out from among you the rebels, and them that transgress against me* [emphasis added]." (ASV).

This little-known truth about Israel's future Provocation Trial Proceeding in the wilderness is picked up by Peter. He correctly addresses Israel in the New Testament as the *Church in the Wilderness*.[167] By the use of this strange title, the legal process of dealing with Israel's unfinished business concerning their hypocrisy, bankruptcy, blindness, rebellious, and murderous heart is unquestionably identified and marked.

---

[167] **Acts 7:38:** This is he, that was in the Church in the Wilderness with the angel which spake to him in the mount Sina, and with our fathers: who received the lively oracles to give unto us.

Through the prophet Malachi, Jehovah promised, "Then the offering of Judah and Jerusalem will be pleasing to the Lord, as in days gone by, and as in past years. And I will come near to you for judging." (Mal. 3:4-5; BBE). Again, we see these verses indicate Israel's future Provocation Trial is scheduled to occur during the time of Christ's second coming, as the "Messenger of the Covenant," who comes to refine and purify, as noted by the last book of the Old Testament:

> **Mal. 3:1:** "Behold, I will send my messenger, and he shall prepare the way before me: and the Lord, whom ye seek, shall suddenly come to his temple, even the messenger of the covenant, whom ye delight in: behold, he shall come, saith the LORD of hosts. But who may abide the day of his coming? and who shall stand when he appeareth? for he is like a refiner's fire, and like fullers' soap."

The timeframe here correlates with Daniel's last week and Revelation's 7-year tribulation period. Remember, from the Jewish standpoint, both advents of Christ are viewed as one continuous Divine undertaking and not as two separate events on their timeline. However, others in the Jewish faith still stubbornly hold to the belief that there are two different Messiahs known as *Messiah ben Joseph* and *Messiah ben David*.

Bankruptcy Stay

Despite Divine handholding, Israel, on a national level, remains spiritually dead and bankrupt of faith. Because of this, they would continue to wander in the wilderness indefinitely if it were not for the appointed set times of the Lord and Daniel's prophecy that used Lamech's 70 x 7 forgiveness formula as Israel's fixed-prophetic timeline. Now with the New Covenant established in our day, Divine intervention comes from the third person of the Godhead, being the Holy Spirit and His contributions to ensure a successful harvest.

With the Holy Spirit's involvement, so brings the issue of the unpardonable sin. Jesus said all can be forgiven concerning the Father and the Son,[168] but when it comes to the Holy Spirit— the buck stops there! To illustrate, we again turn to the book of Acts:

---

[168] **Mt. 12:31-32:** Wherefore I say unto you, All manner of sin and blasphemy shall be forgiven unto men: but the blasphemy *against* the *Holy* Ghost shall not be forgiven unto men. And whosoever speaketh a word against the Son of man, it shall be forgiven him: but whosoever speaketh against the Holy Ghost, it shall not be forgiven him, neither in this world, neither in the world to come.

Acts 6:3, 5, 15: "Wherefore, brethren, look ye out among you seven men of honest report, full of the Holy Ghost and wisdom, whom we may appoint over this business....And the saying pleased the whole multitude: and they chose Stephen, a man full of faith and of the Holy Ghost... And all that sat in the council, looking steadfastly on him, saw his face as it had been the face of an angel."

Stephen *glowed* with the presence of the Holy Spirit. The Holy Spirit was so powerfully upon him that his physical appearance changed to the face of an angel. Later, Stephen, still overflowing with the Holy Spirit, confronted the unbelieving Jewish leaders just like Jesus did, except this time Stephen spoke for the third person of the trinity. He goes on to summarize Israel's whole rebellious history under Divine inspiration and judgment, in which the entire unbelieving Jewish congregation violently reacted:

Acts 7:54-56, 58-60: "And when they [the Jews] heard these things, they were cut to the heart, and they gnashed on him with their teeth. But he, being full of the Holy Ghost looked up steadfastly into heaven, and saw the glory of God, and Jesus [not sitting but rather] standing on the right hand of God....And cast him out [Stephen] of the city, and stoned him: and the witnesses laid down their clothes at a young man's feet, whose name was Saul. And they stoned Stephen, calling upon God, and saying, `Lord Jesus, receive my spirit.' And he kneeled down, and cried with a loud voice, `Lord, lay not this sin to their charge. And when he had said this, he fell asleep'* [emphasis added]."

It is not by accident Stephen utters almost the same words of Jesus committing His spirit on the cross. The difference here is how Stephen committed his spirit to his resurrected Lord and not to the Father as Jesus did on the cross. From that point on, as the nation of Israel began to scatter abroad, their influence began to fade while Christianity moved to the forefront on the stage of world history.

The stoning of Stephen reveals the true heart of Israel. It was a violent, sinful act of unbelief. After they rejected and killed the Son as Jesus predicted in His parable (Mt. 21:33-46), their rejection turned into outrage, which was against the Holy Spirit, who shone so gloriously in the face of another innocent victim being Stephen.

With National Israel's inability to trust Jehovah to deliver them into the Promise Land, the rejection of the Son, and ultimately the Holy Spirit, the unpardonable sin is complete. Another forty-year generational cycle ensues. Our present-day Grace Age finds Israel scattered among the nations desolate of their Temple in Jerusalem and faith. Again, we see how the Divine judicial process works for His chosen stuck "working" under the Law.

From all appearances, Jehovah's legal proceedings are remarkably like our own Bankruptcy Court System here in the United States. Both systems impose an automatic stay on all other civil actions filed by creditors until the resolution of the bankruptcy action is complete. Israel is utterly bankrupt in faith. Because they refuse the sin-offering that "lieth continually at their door," they will never be able to pay the eternal debt.

With Jehovah's automatic stay in place that allows the harvesting of the uncircumcised nations to run its course, Israel's Provocation Trial Proceeding in the wilderness is pushed back to a later time. For almost two thousand years, Israel's prophetic clock has stopped right before Daniel's final week is scheduled to commence. Until such time, the Jewish congregations will continue the *status quo*.

After the stoning of Stephen, Saul of Tarsus (Paul) steps on the scene and is dramatically saved by "The Light" from a face-to-face vision with the risen Lord Jesus (Acts 9). Even though Peter will go to the house of Cornelius after Paul's conversion (Acts 10), Peter is mentioned only in three more chapters (Acts 11, 12, 15), then is completely ignored for the rest of the book of Acts.

From then on, the book turns to the humble beginnings of Paul's ministry, which ends on a sour note due to the prosecution and rejection of the Jewish leaders who represent the whole nation of Israel (Acts 28:16-29). With that, we have a good indication that Israel's clock has once again stopped only to resume at the appointed time.[169]

---

[169] **Dan. 10:14:** Now I have come to give you knowledge of the fate of your people in the later days; for there is still a vision for the days. (BBE).

Seven Marks the Time and the Timeline

Israel's timeline begins exactly as marked, with the number 7 marking that spot. This statement should not come as a surprise. The number 7 has been a consistent factor in terms of the firstborn position. Initially, Cain received a 7-year generational allowance. In the 7th generation of Cain, Lamech, his descendant, pleaded for an extension of Cain's initial years by requesting an additional 70 years, which Jesus confirmed as the forgiveness model.

Consequently, that same 70 x 7 equation was implemented by Daniel as the fixed-prophetic timeline for his people (Daniel's people are those practicing Judaism). By following Daniel's 70 x 7 weeks of years prediction, the last 7-years on Israel's timeline picks back up as soon as the 7-year tribulation of Revelation begins.

The book of Revelation is full of sevens and marks the spot for those who are looking. For example, there are 7 churches,[170] 7 spirits,[171] 7 candlesticks,[172] 7 stars,[173] 7 lamps or torches of fire,[174] 7 seals,[175] 7 horns,[176] 7 trumpets,[177] and so forth.

Furthermore, there are specific topics in the book of Revelation having a sequence of sevens such as Christ's blood,[178] Christ's name,[179] the book of life,[180] and judgments,[181] just to name a few. Even Jesus stated 7-times that he will come quickly.[182] Some think it is impossible to count all the sequences of "sevens" within the book. From those examples alone, we realize how the last book of the Bible speaks in the language of sevens, which screams of Israel's marked 7-fold timeline.

This number 7 association is not true for the Christian Church. They are on an unmarked timeline. They have no placement in the tribulation period because they are "not appointed unto wrath" (1 Thes. 5:9), and their

---

[170] Rev. 1:4, 11, 20.

[171] Rev. 1:4, 3:1, 4:5, 5:6.

[172] Rev. 1:12, 2:1, 13, 20.

[173] Rev. 1:16, 2:1, 3:1, 20.

[174] Rev. 4:5.

[175] Rev. 5:1, 5.

[176] Rev. 5:6.

[177] Rev. 8:2, 6.

[178] Rev. 1:5, 5-14, 12:11, 13:8.

[179] Rev. 2:13, 3:8, 12, 13, 16, 19:12, 22:4.

[180] Rev. 3:5, 13:8, 15, 17:8, 20:12, 21:27, 22:19.

[181] Rev. 14:7, 15:4, 16:7, 17:1, 18:10, 19:2, 20:4.

[182] Rev. 2:5, 3:11, 11:14, 12, 16, 20, 22:7.

"citizenship is in Heaven (Phil. 3:20). Christianity's appointed Apostle is Paul (formerly Saul of Tarsus) as commissioned by the Lord on the road to Damascus and confirmed later by Peter and the Jerusalem leaders.[183] His converts come mostly from the uncircumcised, Gentile nations.

Israel's rejecting the Messiah and the Holy Spirit triggered a new course of action. As a nation, they committed the unpardonable sin. Their actions invoked a new and mysterious timeline as represented by the open invitation to the uncircumcised nations, which is the Christian Church.

This explains one of the reasons for the appointment of the Apostle Paul. From his ministry, we learn about the mysteries of the body of Christ, His Church, in preparation for the coming harvest. These mysteries were never disclosed until Paul, nor even known by the Old Testament prophets.

When we discern that Christ and His disciples are ministers to the circumcised nation,[184] and Paul as the Apostle to the uncircumcised nations, we immediately see two different gospels for two different groups on two vastly different timelines. Once we understand this, the message of the whole Bible comes into agreement.

Jesus used parables because He was ministering under the Law. Just as the Old Testament is dimly veiled, so too, Jesus spoke in parables to maintain the same format.[185] The time to unveil the fuller mysteries of Christ is after the Acts 2 Pentecost is *fully come*, which is the set time of the Holy Spirit's arrival for the harvesting of the earth.

The Acts 2 Pentecostal event was contingent upon Christ's ability to become the literal fulfillment of the spring feasts, which are Passover, Unleavened Bread, and Firstfruits. (Lev. 23). Once He died as the Lamb of God (Passover), was raised from the dead (Unleavened Bread), and went to the Father (Firstfruits),[186] the Holy Spirit that summer was able to come in full force and power at Pentecost.

With that, the complete understanding of the mysteries of Christ under a New Covenant economy through Paul's ministry would later come. However, until such time, the Old Testament economy was still the model. By law,

---

[183] **Gal. 2:7:** But contrariwise, when they saw that the gospel of the circumcision was committed unto me [Paul], as the gospel of the circumcision was unto Peter.

[184] **Rom. 15: 8:** Now I say that Jesus Christ was a minister of the circumcision for the truth of God, to confirm the promises *made* unto the fathers.

[185] **Mk. 4:11-12:** And he said unto them, Unto you it is given to know the mystery of the kingdom of God: but unto them that are without, all these things are done in parables: That seeing they may see, and not perceive; and hearing they may hear, and not understand; lest at any time they should be converted, and their sins should be forgiven them.

[186] **Jn. 20:17:** Jesus saith unto her, Touch me not; for I am not yet ascended to my Father: but go to my brethren, and say unto them, I ascend unto my Father, and your Father; and *to* my God, and your God.

Jesus' earthly ministry had to maintain the Old Testament format because He came to fulfill the Law and bring it to rest.[187]

The Timeline Postponed

Matthew 23 gives an excellent example of the coming cultural shift on Israel's prophetic timeline. On this occasion, Jesus spoke in an area within the Temple that prohibited Gentile attendance. He was addressing Israel's leaders and cultural influencers, which were the Pharisees, the Sadducees, and the Herodians,[188] and was pointing out their issue of self-righteousness and hypocrisy. Since Passover was fast approaching, crowds of Jewish worshipers came worldwide to gather in Jerusalem in the Temple to meet their requirements of the Law. It was in that atmosphere, Christ said:

> **Mt. 23:37:** "O Jerusalem, Jerusalem, thou that killest the prophets, and stonest them which are sent unto thee, how often would I have gathered thy children together, even as a hen gathereth her chickens under her wings, and ye would not!"

From this account, we see the heart of the Father speaking through the Son, His true desire for His chosen nation. Throughout their history, Jehovah had been protecting them as a hen would her chicks. He had been watching and shielding them and supplying all their needs in miraculous ways.

However, Israel remained blind and bankrupt in faith, just like the generation in the wilderness before, which indicates another proverbial forty-year generational cycle was about to begin. As the Messiah stood and observed this scene, His heart broke. He knew that because of their continued unbelief, their promised Kingdom would once again have to wait. Israel's unbelief was confirmed scriptually. This led to their cultural reasoning, ...Can anything good come out of Nazareth [speaking of Jesus]? Let His blood be on us and on our children."[189]

---

[187] **Mt. 5:17-18:** Think not that I am come to destroy the law, or the prophets: I am not come to destroy, but to fulfil. For verily I say unto you, Till heaven and earth pass, one jot or one tittle shall in no wise pass from the law, till all be fulfilled.

[188] The Pharisees, the Herodians, and the Sadducees all held positions of authority and power over the people. There were other groups such as the Sanhedrin, the scribes, and the lawyers; each of these groups held power in either religious or political matters. The Herodians held political power, and most scholars believe that they were a political party that supported King Herod Antipas, the Roman Empire's ruler over much of the land of the Jews from 4 B.C. to A.D. 39.

[189] Jn. 1:46; Mt. 27:25.

When Jesus was speaking about how He desired to gather Israel as a hen gathers her chicks, He concludes, "Behold, your house [the Temple] is left unto you desolate."[190] Notice He said, "your" house. After departing ancient Egypt as a newborn nation, Jehovah called them *My people*. However, after they became stiff-necked and disobedient, He told Moses they were *thy people* like He did with Daniel as he penned the prophecy about their prophetic timeline of forgiveness and deliverance.[191]

Jesus is doing the same thing here because it has become evident that Israel was not accepting Him right before the close of His earthly ministry. It is in this context that He refers to the Temple as *your* house. Just like it was in Moses and Daniel's time, now generations later, Jesus once again confirms the Father's withdrawal from their Temple of vipers and their faithless hearts.

The Father's withdrawal from Israel was not the case at the beginning of His ministry when Jesus said, "unto them that sold doves. Take these things hence make not my Father's house [the Temple at Jerusalem] a house of merchandise." (Jn. 2:16). In this context, the Temple was still considered God's house. Sadly, the attitude of unbelief forced the Father to withdraw from *their* house at the end of Jesus' ministry. We are left with Jesus' definitive conclusion on the matter, "Behold, your house is left unto you desolate." (Mt. 23:38).

Here, we see the fulfillment of Psalm 118:22. Israel, as the original builders of the Church,[192] rejected Christ, "the Rock," as the chief component. Jesus warned of the consequence of this action, just two chapters before, "The kingdom of God shall be taken from you, and given to a nation bringing forth the fruits thereof (Mt. 21:43). The "nation" that will bring forth fruit due to Israel's failure to produce is what Scripture refers to as the fullness of the Gentiles, which we are about to learn in its full context.

The Timeline Reset

After Jesus concluded Israel's house is left desolate, He further pronounced, "For I say unto you, Ye shall not see me henceforth, *till* ye shall say Blessed is he that cometh in the name of the Lord [emphasis added]." (Mt. 23:39). As it turns out, there are a total of three distinct *until* time-periods

---

[190] Mt. 23:38; Lk. 13:35.

[191] Dan. 9:24-27.

[192] **Mt. 16:18:** And I say also unto thee, That thou art Peter, and upon this rock I will build my church; and the gates of hell shall not prevail against it.

that must occur, which concern both groups of the Despairing being Israel and the Christian Church. At the end of His ministry, Jesus gave two of the three "until predictions," which referred to a future generation of Israel[193] who would consider themselves blessed to see His return.[194]

The second of the three *until* periods is in Luke, where Jesus again uses the same *until* theme. He is foretelling the destruction of Israel's Temple and their city, Jerusalem, as recorded by Luke:

> **Lk. 21:24:** "And they [in Jerusalem] shall fall by the edge of the sword, and shall be led away captive into all nations [this is a major clue because Israel will not be led away captive during tribulation at Armageddon. They were led captive for the last time in 70 A.D.]: and Jerusalem shall be trodden down of the Gentiles *until* [this is a time factor, a certain time in the future] the times of the Gentiles be fulfilled [emphasis added]."

In this account, Jesus predicts the desolation of the Temple. It starts with "Jerusalem shall be trodden down of the Gentiles," which began in 70 A.D., at the hand of the Romans. Christ incorporates this same "until" timeframe as part of the harvest of the earth. He spoke in parables on the subject and its interpretation is recorded in Matthew 13:39-49.

Jesus labeled the late portion of the earth's harvest as "the end of the world." The original text makes this clear. The word "end" is *suntelia* in the Greek. It means "consummation," and the Greek word for "world" is *aion*, which means "unbroken age, universe." In other words, the full spectrum of the "harvesting of the earth" encompasses all seasons of the harvest that concludes at the end of the age.

The Body of Christ or the Christian Church is raptured before the tribulation as the summer harvest, and the remnant of Israel, along with any surviving converts, are saved as the late harvest, which closes the tribulation period that occurs at the end of the age.

---

[193] Jesus' *until* prediction refers to a future final generation of Israel that is reduced to a remnant. "The end" concludes the harvesting of the earth when the remnant is saved at the end of the 7-year tribulation period. Key verse: **Mt.10:22:** And you will be hated by all for my name's sake. But the one who endures to the *end* [Greek word is *telos*, which means final act, conclusion] will be saved.

[194] The harvesting of the earth is considered the "end of the world" which begin at Pentecost of Acts 2 and ends when the remnant of Israel is saved at the end of the 7-year tribulation period but the sorting of the harvest concludes at the Great White Throne Judgment. Key verse: **Mt.13:39:** The enemy that sowed them is the devil; the harvest is the **end** of the world [Greek word for "end" in this verse is *suntelia*, which means consummation]; and the reapers are the angels.

The sorting of the "wheat" and "tares," also called "sheep and goats" (Mt. 13:25-30; 25:32-33), is simply a function of completing the harvest. The sorting process of the harvest concludes at the Great White Throne Judgment, which is after the Millennial Kingdom.[195] We know this because Jesus uses the phrase "the end of the world." (Mt. 13:39).

The phrase "the end of the world" is not to be confused with "the end." The phrase "the end" addresses a future generation of Israel that Christ warned, "but he that endureth [*hupomeno* means remain][196] to the end [*telos* means conclusion, goal].[197] The use of these two Greek words (*hupomeno* and *telos*) by Christ is key. We are to understand that those who endure, suffer, persist, and remain to the end, or *telos*, concludes the purpose or goal, which is to complete the harvesting of the earth.

The last of the three *untils* is specified by Paul, who speaks of the day that Israel's timeline is re-inserted, and the Gentile's time ends:

> **Rom. 11:25-27:** "For I would not, brethren, that ye should be ignorant of this mystery lest ye should be wise in your own conceits; that blindness in part [not forever, a portion of time] is happened to Israel, until the *fulness of the Gentiles be come in. And* so all Israel shall be saved: as it is written, There shall come out of Sion the Deliverer, and shall turn away ungodliness from Jacob: this is my covenant unto them, when I shall take away their sins [emphasis added]."

The *fullness of the Gentiles* in modern terms is the fullness of the "Body of Christ." When "His spiritual body" is finally complete, and the last person included, the Christian Church, which is mostly those saved out from the Gentile population, will be translated (or "caught up") like Enoch. However, before the rapture happens, a transitioning will take place as represented in Lamech's day on the Christ-line. After the *fullness*

---

[195] The Great White Throne Judgment is described in Rev. 20:11-15, which concludes the process of sorting the wheat and tares or sheep and goats by the casting into the lake of fire. According to Rev. 20:7-15, this judgment will take place after the Millennium and after Satan is thrown into the lake of fire where the beast and the false prophet are (Rev. 19:19-20, 20:7-10).

[196] "1) To remain: 1a) to tarry behind. 2) to remain, i.e. abide, not recede or flee. 2a) to preserve: under misfortunes and trials to hold fast to one's faith in Christ. 2b) to endure, bear bravely and calmly: ill treatments." (*Thayer's Greek Definitions*).

[197] "Primary form is *tello* (to set out for a definite point or goal). Translated in the English as "end," as in termination, the limit at which a thing ceases to be (always of the end of some act or state, but not of the end of a period of time)." (*Thayer's Greek Definitions*).

of the Gentiles, Israel's timeline will be re-inserted as the mainline, which is portrayed by Noah's day on the Christ-line.

Noah's day is the time Jehovah fulfills His covenant to Israel. During that time, He will cause Israel to pass under the rod and bring them into the bond of the covenant [wedding language] and purge out the rebels who transgress against Him.[198] He will then take away their sins by "sending the Deliverer of Zion to turn away ungodliness from Jacob."[199]

Plainly stated, two of the *until* periods are satisfied when Christ returns at His second coming. The last *until* period concerns the removal of the Christian Church, which causes Lamech's day to transition into Noah's day on the Christ-line's timeline. Jesus continues:

> **Mt. 24:9-14:** "Then [the beginning of Tribulation] shall they deliver you [Jewish National Israel] up to be afflicted, and shall kill you: and ye shall be hated of all nations for my name's sake. And then shall many be offended, and shall betray one another, and shall hate one another. And many false prophets shall rise, and shall deceive many, and because iniquity shall abound, the love of many shall wax cold. But he that shall endure unto the end [Greek word: telos, means final act, conclusion, the end goal], the same shall be saved. And this gospel of the kingdom [not Paul's gospel of grace] shall be preached in all the world for a witness unto all nations; and then shall the end [telos] come."

Again, Jesus is speaking about the future generation of Israel as typified in Noah's day. In that day, Israel will circumnavigate the globe to preach the Kingdom Gospel. Their message is about the coming King and the Kingdom. Their message is not the same gospel of grace because the Christian Church will be caught up from this world, thereby completing the fullness of the Gentiles requirement. At that point, the dispensation will change to suit Israel's timeline reinserted as the mainline and their anticipation of the coming King and His Kingdom on earth (Rev. 5:5).

---

[198] Eze. 20:37-38.

[199] Rom. 11:26-27; Ps. 14:7; Isa. 59:20.

Double Sevens Doubles the Blessings for Lamech, His Two Wives, and the Two-Family Lines

As we can see, the granting of Lamech's petition extended his firstborn family's timeline onto a perfect platform to find "grace," which becomes a powerful legal weapon in Jehovah's justice system. Because both Jesus and Daniel's prophecy[200] confirmed Lamech's 70 x 7 forgiveness extension as a model for Israel. Cain's 7-year right was postponed to the end.

Now that we solved that mystery, we turn to another, which concerns Lamech being the first recorded polygamist in the Bible. There is a Jewish tradition preserved in the Talmud and the Book of Jasher,[201] which claims the two wives of Lamech, Adah, and Zillah, were descendants of the patriarch Seth, and they were taken in marriage by Lamech, from the Cain-line. The account in Jasher reads:

> "And Enosh [the son of Seth] lived ninety years and he begat Cainan...And when Cainan was seventy years old, he begat three sons and two daughters. And these are the names of the children of Cainan; the name of the first born Mahalalel, the second Enan, and the third Mered, and *their sisters were* Adah and Zillah; these are the five children of Cainan that were born to him. And Lamech, the son of Methushael [the descendant of Cain], became related to Cainan [Kenan, a descendant of Seth of the Christ-line] by marriage, and he [Lamech of the Cain-Line] took his two daughters [of the Christ-line] for his wives." (*The Book of Jasher*, 2:10, 15-17).

Here, we see the joining of the two lines of the Christ-line (Kenan's two daughters) and the Cain-line (married Lamech). This marriage is said to have taken place in Mahalaleel's generation,[202] and specifically within Adam's lifetime. While the book of Jasher provides a contextual view, the two wives draw our attention to the double-portion blessing of the Cain-line clan. The joining of the two houses (Cain and the Christ-line through Seth) are now back under the original house of Adam, their father.

---

[200] Dan. 9:24-27.

[201] The book of Jasher is a biblically recognized source and is quoted in Joshua 10:13 and 2 Samuel 1:18.

[202] **Gen. 5:12:** When Kenan [alternate spelling "Cainan"] had lived seventy years, he became the father of Mahalalel. (BBE).

Tradition also claims Lamech of the cursed line (being the Cain-line) had a total of 77 children from his two wives who were from the blessed-line of Seth, the third son of Adam. The implications of the Cain-line finally merging with the Christ-line looks forward to the in-gathering of the whole house of Israel from the four corners of the earth back into Father Jehovah's house, as one national body:

> **Isa. 11:11-12:** "And it shall come to pass in that day, that the Lord shall set his hand again the second time to recover the remnant of his people, which shall be left, from Assyria, and from Egypt, and from Pathros, and from Cush, and from Elam, and from Shinar, and from Hamath, and from the islands of the sea. And he shall set up an ensign for the nations, and shall assemble the outcasts of Israel, and gather together the dispersed of Judah from the four corners of the earth." (Also see, Deut. 30:1-5; Jer. 29:14; and Eze. 20:41-42).

In terms of the general timeline as represented by the Christ-line, Methuselah's long life allowed Noah to build the Ark. His extended lifespan affords the gathering of the firstborn nation back unto the Father in Lamech's day, as represented by the Cain-line's lower horizontal position on Chart 8. Israel will, once again, be in the public eye and will be recognized nationally as "of God" in Noah's day, as the Cain-line's summary statement suggests.

According to Daniel Chapter 9, Israel's official timeline of deliverance begins at the last week of the 70 x 7 fixed-prophetic timeline. This last week, according to the meaning of Noah's name, is supposed to be a time of rest. In the next chapter on Noah, we will discover how the fiery waters of the tribulation period, as described by the book of Revelation, come to rest due to the execution of Lamech's extension request.

CHAPTER 11 – NOAH
"Christ's Rest"

The Days of Noah

We are now at the tenth and final member of the Christ-line. Noah's day represents the marked timeline of the older brother, Israel. Just as it was in Noah's day, the coming judgment in the last days will also come as a "flood," except now, we will view it in terms of prophetic themes and concepts.

The Prophetic Timeline of the Ages Chart, as presented in the last chapter as Chart 8, will continue to serve as a visual guide. Our primary focus going forward will be to navigate through the fiery floodwaters of Revelation as it relates to Israel's marked timeline and their Divine destiny within the context of the bloodline statements.

The chapters on Methuselah and Lamech set the stage for this final chapter on Noah. In those chapters, we learned that the span of Methuselah's life prefigures the harvest season of the earth by the grace of the Lord, not wanting any to perish. Once we rearranged the Cain and the Christ-line charts horizontally and aligned them at their shared snap-on points, which are Enoch and Lamech, instantly, the two family lines in their horizontal positions became one complete chart projecting the Prophetic Timeline of the Ages (Chart 8).

As an expanded chart, Chart 8 cleverly uses the two line's common counter-members (Enoch and Lamech) as an internal border to provide details about the hidden and public timelines of the Despairing. With the internal border in mind, Enoch's day represents the hidden timeline of the Christian Church, and Lamech's day represents a gradual transition back to the marked or Israel's public timeline, which ends at the death of Methuselah.

Again, Methuselah's name means "his death shall bring." His name puts all on notice that the coming judgment at the end of the age begins when he dies. This judgment will erupt on the scene like a flood as represented on the far right of Chart 8 in Noah's day.

Noah's day is equivalent to Revelation's 7-year tribulation period and Daniel's final week of years. Both Matthew and Luke quote Jesus saying,

"And as it was in the days of Noah, so shall it be also in the days of "The Son of Man."[203] While one could argue the days of Noah began at his birth, from Peter, we learn the beginning of his ministry was, "when once the longsuffering of God waited in the days of Noah, while the ark was a preparing, wherein few, that is, eight souls were saved by water." (1 Pet. 3:20).

The Tenth and Perfect Generational Judgment Cycle

Noah's day falls within the tenth generation of Adam on the Christ-line. His day represents the end of a global judgment cycle, as well as a new beginning. The primary reason is that the curse will be resolved in the tenth generation by judgment. Scripture consistently uses the base-ten model to illustrate a global, or more specifically, a world's system reference. With number typology aside, the idea that the tenth generation is the end of a judgment cycle comes from the verses:

> **Deut. 23:2:** "An illegitimate child shall not enter into the assembly of Jehovah, even to the tenth generation none of his shall enter into the assembly of Jehovah." (LITV).

> **Gen. 3:17:** "And unto Adam he said, Because thou hast hearkened unto the voice of thy wife, and hast eaten of the tree, of which I commanded thee, saying, Thou shalt not eat of it: cursed is the ground for thy sake; in sorrow shalt thou eat of it all the days of thy life."

> **Gen. 5:29:** "And he called his name Noah [10th generation], saying, This same shall comfort us concerning our work and toil of our hands, because of the ground which the LORD hath cursed."

> **Gen. 6:8-9:** "But Noah [10th generation] found grace in the eyes of the LORD...Noah was a just [righteous] man and perfect [complete] in his generations, and Noah walked with God."

---

[203] Mt. 24:37; Lk. 17:26.

The verses above may appear random at first, but they surprisingly provide an understanding of why the tenth generation of Adam is so instrumental to the Garden Program. The key verse is Deuteronomy 23:2, which speaks oddly about the punishment of allowing illegitimate children within the Lord's assembly.

The illegitimate issue is not so odd, especially when viewed within the realm of eternity. From Jehovah's standpoint, His assembly is born of the Spirit. They stand on new ground. They have nothing to do with flesh, which stands on the old, cursed ground.

When we apply this perspective to Cain and his firstborn line, which remains stuck "working" on the old, cursed ground, their failure to get with the "Garden Program" becomes quite clear. However, with dispersed Israel now gathered back together as one house in Lamech's day, Noah's day is not only set to occur at the end, which is the tenth generational judgment cycle, to begin anew.

Besides this being the first mention of grace, which was due to his faith,[204] Jehovah also pronounced Noah "perfect in his generations." (Gen. 6:9). This extra-special status had nothing to do with Noah being genetically pure. This point is made clear in Genesis 6:12, "And God looked upon the earth, and, behold, it was corrupt; for all flesh had corrupted his way upon the earth." The phrase "all flesh" includes the flesh of Noah. For he too was a direct descendant of fallen Adam, whom the "Blessed God" came down to seek and to save.

The Hebrew word for "perfect" found in the phrase "perfect in his generations" (Gen. 6:9) is tamýym ("tawmeem") and means blameless, complete,[205] while the Hebrew word for "generations" is dor ("dore"), which refers to a revolution of time such as age or generation.[206] To make things even more confusing, note how the King James Version of the Bible uses the word "generations" for two completely different Hebrew words in this one verse:

Gen. 6:9: "These are the **generations** [tôledâh, plural only, means descent, that is, family; (figuratively) history]

---

[204] **Heb. 11:7:** By faith Noah, being warned of God of things not seen as yet, moved with fear, prepared an ark to the saving of his house; by the which he condemned the world, and became heir of the righteousness which is by faith.

[205] **tâmîym:** An adjective meaning blameless, complete. In over half of its occurrences, it describes an animal to be sacrificed to the Lord, whether a ram, a bull, or a lamb (Ex. 29:1; Lev. 4:3; Lev. 14:10). With respect to time, the term is used to refer to a complete day, a complete seven Sabbaths, and a complete year (Lev. 23:15; Lev. 25:30; Jos. 10:13)." (Baker, *The Complete Word Study Dictionary*, Gen. 6:9).

[206] **dôr:** A masculine noun meaning generation, period of time, posterity, age, time, setting of life." (Baker, *The Complete Word Study Dictionary*, Gen. 6:9).

of Noah: Noah was a just man and **perfect** [tâmîym, means without blemish] in his **generations**, [dôr, means revolution of time, that is, an age or generation] and Noah walked with God."

The foregoing examination helps to convey how this peculiar phrase "perfect in his generations" stresses the *age*, which confirms Noah's birth was in a perfect or complete cycle. This phrase has nothing to do with Noah being *genetically* perfect. Jehovah was referring to a revolution of time.

The "end of a cycle" concept automatically pushes Noah's day to the end of the age of which the Prophetic Timeline Chart of the Ages (Chart 8) brilliantly displays. While Noah's position is the tenth generation, Peter goes on to describe him as the eighth member of his family rescued in the Ark:

> **2 Pet. 2:5:** "And spared not the old world, but saved Noah the eighth person, a preacher of righteousness, bringing in the flood upon the world of the ungodly."

We see how the numbers ten and eight have a big influence on Noah's life in terms of typology. Both numbers should have a familiar ring since Cain, and his firstborn family tree also has a ten-to-eight structure. Recall how the Cain-line consists of ten members yet stopped at the eighth generation.

Scripture uses the ten-to-eight structure to link Cain and Noah together to indicate they are an extension of the firstborn line on a public or known timeline. The numerical associations help to trace the older brother, who is the elect and the "marked" of God.[207]

Even more impressive is how the last age ends in exactly seven years. Seven years not only speaks of Daniel's final week as it relates to the book of Revelation, but it also associates with Cain's 7-year right (Gen. 4:15). This period, as we learned in the previous chapter, was earmarked for Israel as the firstborn line to face their last Provocation Trial.

With the addition of Noah and his household, we are to understand that together they represent Israel as the remnant saved in the 7-year tribulation period. During that time, the remnant of Israel, as one house, must produce a crop of faith to "overcome" as they sail through the judgment waters in the tenth and final generation of Adam.

---

[207] Used of Israel. Isa. 41:9, 43:20, 45:4. Compare the verb in Isa. 41:8 and Deut. 7:6-7.

Set Times Show the Way by Wilderness

From an Old Testament standpoint, Israel's future Provocation Trial is virtually a repeat of Israel's deliverance from ancient Egypt by way of the wilderness. Just as it was in that day, Israel will again become a *Church in the Wilderness*. Like before, their last exodus journey will take its cue according to the annual set times of the Lord as specified in Leviticus 23.

Their religious calendar is a memorial of the original Passover in Egypt. Because of that one event, Israel's year now begins in the spring,[208] which previously was in the fall. This change was so significant that it gave cause for the nation's use of two separate calendars, one civil and the other religious.

The Jewish civil calendar focuses on three main seasons of the harvest, which is not only interrupted but interpreted by the Jewish religious calendar. The next chart is a comparison of the two Hebrew calendars and the corresponding feasts or harvest times. While reviewing Chart 11, notice the first month of Abib (Nisan) is the first month on the religious calendar but is the seventh month on the civil calendar.

Due to the addition of the religious calendar, the Feast of Passover now becomes the first nationally recognized event of the year, which pushes the Jewish New Year, Rosh Hashanah, to fall on the first day of the seventh month (Tishri), which is also the Feast of Trumpets.[209] This Divine shift caused Israel's New Year to occur within the fall feast days, which looks forward to the set time when National Israel (as one body) is finally atoned of their sin and is gathered back unto the Father's house.

The religious calendar forced the set times of the harvest to occur in three months based on a 7-month cycle and not on a 12-month cycle as before. This observation comes into full view only when we compare Israel's two calendars together, as illustrated by Chart 11 above. From this view, we can immediately see the timing of the set times and its effects.

Israel's Calendar Comparison Chart (Chart 11) makes it clear. There are only three months out of the year that all the set times of the Lord occur. Notice how Passover, Unleavened Bread, and Firstfruits begin in springtime and represent the early harvest. Next, observe how Pentecost more closely

---

[208] **Ex. 12:1-2:** And the Lord spake unto Moses and Aaron in the land of Egypt saying, This month shall be unto you the beginning of months: it shall be the first month of the year to you.

[209] **Lev. 23:24-25:** Speak unto the children of Israel, saying, in the seventh month, in the first day of the month, shall ye have a sabbath, a memorial of blowing of trumpets, an holy convocation. Ye shall do no servile work therein: but ye shall offer an offering made by fire unto the Lord.

Israel's Religious and Civil Calendar Year

Month	Religious Year	Civil Year	Gegorian Calendar	The Lord's Feast Days and Israel's 3 Pilgrimage Journeys
Abib (Nisan)	1st Month	7th Month	March/April	(1st Feast) 14th day - Passover (1st Pilgrimage)
				(2nd Feast) 15-21st - Unleaven Bread
				(3rd Feast) Firstfruits - 1st Sunday after the week of Unleaven Bread - Barley /Flax Harvest
Ziv (Iyyar)	2nd Month	8th Month	April/May	
Sivan	3rd Month	9th Month	May/June	(4th Feast) Pentecost (2nd Pilgrimage) Or Feast of 7 weeks or 50 days from Firstfruits; wheat harvest, dry winds, early fig harvest, grapes ripen
Tammuz	4th Month	10th Month	June/July	
Ab	5th Month	11th Month	July/Aug.	
Elul	6th Month	12th Month	Aug./Sept.	
Tishri	7th Month	1st Month	Sept./Oct.	(5th Feast) 1st day - Feast of Trumpets (6th Feast) 10th Day - Day of Atonement (7th Feast) 15-21st - Tabernacles (3rd Pilgrimage) Feast of ingathering or Feast of Booths - 1st Sunday - Holy convocation
Heshvan	8th Month	2nd Month	Oct./Nov.	
Chislev	9th Month	3rd Month	Nov./Dec.	
Tebeth	10th Month	4th Month	Dec./Jan.	
Sebat	11th Month	5th Month	Jan./Feb.	
Adar	12th Month	6th Month	Feb./March	

Seven annual feasts of the Lord is Christ's responsibility (Ex 12:1-28; 43-51; 13:1-10; Lev 23:5-44; Num 28:16-39) of which Israel is to make three Pilgrimage journeys in the spring, summer, and fall (Ex. 23:14-17; 34:22-23).

Chart 11 – Israel's Religious and Civil Calendar Year

128

represents the main harvest of the field in the summer. The last of the set times, which are Trumpets, Atonement, and Tabernacles, represent the fall harvest, with the Feast of Tabernacles signifying the final "In-Gathering" of the four corners of the field.

Typologically speaking, each harvest season represents a push-point to help Israel in their journey to the promised rest as represented by their homeland. Just as Israel's civil calendar was central to the harvesting of the soil, so we see how Jehovah's religious calendar is central to the harvesting of souls. By comparing Israel's two calendars, it becomes evident how the three seasons complete the annual harvest within a 7-month period, which falls on Israel's New Year (Rosh Hashanah) to represent a new beginning.

Again, we cannot ignore all the strong associations as it relates to Israel's 7-scale cycle of reckoning. Since the last 7-years of Daniel marks the final hour on Israel's timeline, they have one last chance to be "born as legitimate sons" into one united house as required by Deuteronomy 23:2. As soon as this legality is satisfied, grace finds the tenth generation of Adam. By grace, this generation is deemed "righteous" through faith. This perspective, as we learned earlier, is represented by Jehovah's righteous view of Noah, who was "perfect in his generations." (Gen. 6:9).

Judging Pilgrim's Progress

As noted previously, the feast days are actual set times performed in succession by Christ as the Messiah and "begotten" Firstborn of the Father. As far as National Israel was concerned, they, too, had a duty to perform in succession as a firstborn representative to the nations. Every year all Israelite males[210] were required to travel to the Temple in Jerusalem for the Feast of Passover and Unleavened Bread in the spring, Pentecost in the summer, and the Feast of Tabernacles in the fall known as the three annual Pilgrimage Feasts.[211]

The first mention of the three annual journeys[212] was after Jehovah delivered His people at the Red Sea from the Egyptian army by the way in the

---

[210] Ex. 23:15, 34:23; Deut. 16:16.

[211] The set times of the Lord (Lev. 23) represents the annual harvest cycle broken down into three sections: the beginning, the progression, and the completion. The harvest's three divisions correspond to Israel's three annual Pilgrimage Feasts. The harvest cycle moves from the Feast of Passover (that celebrates Israel's deliverance from slavery to sin and the evil world system as represented by Egypt) and ends with the Feast of Tabernacles (to celebrate Israel's future arrival to their homeland as represented by Zion).

[212] **Ex. 23:14-17:** Three times thou shalt keep a feast unto me in the year. Thou shalt keep the feast of unleavened bread: (thou shalt eat unleavened bread seven days, as I commanded thee, in the time appointed of the month Abib; for in it thou camest out from Egypt: and none shall appear before me empty:) And the feast of harvest, the firstfruits of thy labours, which thou hast sown in the field: and the feast of ingathering, which is in the end of the year, when thou hast gathered in thy labours out of the field. Three times in the year all thy males shall appear before the Lord God. Also see, Ex.34:22-23.

wilderness. The second mention of these three yearly journeys was at the giving of the second set of stone tablets just after Israel's worship of the golden calf. Israel's excuse for such lewd acts—Moses abandoned them. His absence turned out to be forty days and forty nights.[213]

Again, we see the number forty come into play by representing a time of testing, trials, and judgment. The typological meaning of the number forty explains why the duration of the flood equals forty days and forty nights.[214] Likewise, Scripture measures Israel's wanderings in the wilderness in terms of forty-year increments. Even Christ, in His day, was tested in the wilderness for forty days.[215] Such events represent a time of trial and judgment for those who operate under the Law, including their leaders. Not only does the number forty apply to Firstborn National Israel and Christ, as their firstborn replacement, but it also applies to Moses due to his leadership role under the Law, which demands judgment.

Since Moses' life also divides into three forty-year segments,[216] it appears we have a pattern that concerns three sets of judgment or trial periods, which applies to those who are under the Law. What is most striking is how both Moses and National Israel did not enter the Promised Land as planned. Therefore, the three forty-year intervals must relate to the intended destiny of those who are stuck "working" under the Law and to their progress to find rest, as it was promised.

Like Moses, National Israel also has three trial segments, with the exception that their testing comes in the form of the successful completion of their three pilgrimages back to the homeland. Again, the three required pilgrimages occur on Passover, Feast of Weeks (Pentecost), and Feast of Tabernacles (or the Feast of the In-Gathering).

Jehovah established the Passover in Egypt as Israel's first successful pilgrimage journey of the spiritual harvest season. The other two pilgrimage journeys could not be pursued because of two main factors. The first

---

[213] **Ex. 24:18:** And Moses went into the midst of the cloud, and gat him up into the mount: and Moses was in the mount forty days and forty nights.

[214] **Gen. 7:17:** And the flood was forty days upon the earth; and the waters increased, and bare up the ark, and it was lift up above the earth.

[215] **Mk. 1:13** And he [Christ] was there in the wilderness forty days, tempted of Satan; and was with the wild beasts; and the angels ministered unto him.

[216] In Moses' first forty years, he was adopted into Egyptian royalty and trained as a public servant. Due to his misapplication of Jehovah's redemption plan, he became exiled because he killed an Egyptian task master (Acts 7:22-24). At midpoint, he began his next forty years (Acts 7:29-30) by starting a family and becoming a lowly shepherd over his father-in-law's sheep (Ex. 2:14-22; 4:19-20) all used by Jehovah to develop a servant's heart. In his mature years, Moses had finally learned to trust in Jehovah's ways over his own. He was instructed to go back to Egypt (Acts 7:34) to perform his public service, this time in exact accordance with Jehovah's plan (Ex. 7:8-13). He died forty years later at the age of 120 years old, yet he did not enter the Promised Land (Deut. 34:7-12).

factor concerned the Law. As we discovered previously, it was given and accepted that summer, on the first Feast of Pentecost, only to produce a crop of death.

The second factor concerned the first Feast of Tabernacles that fall. The journey could not go forward because the Tabernacle was not yet constructed. Once their forty-year judgment cycle in the wilderness ended, Jehovah instructed Israel to change the location of their Passover sacrifices to occur "in a place where He will choose to place His Name there." (Deut. 16:2, 6). The change in location sets the scene to move the site of their pilgrimage sacrificial worship from the Tabernacle to the Temple in Jerusalem (Ps. 78:67-68).

Israel's second judgment cycle occurred in Jesus' day. In the spring of that year, Jesus became the literal Passover Lamb, Unleavened Bread, and Firstfruits. That summer, the Holy Spirit came fifty days later, precisely as scheduled—on the Feast of Pentecost as recorded in Acts 2. But, come fall, their successive pilgrimage journey was interrupted due to their rejection of Christ as their Messiah who is the literal Tabernacle (meeting place) of God (Amo. 9:11; Rev. 21:3). Once again, the stage is set for one more judgment cycle for Israel to complete all three pilgrimage journeys as one national body.

Trials and Tribulation in the Way of Rest

In ancient times, Jews far and wide would journey back to the homeland to bring their sacrifices in gratitude, along with their prayers for a continued abundance throughout the year. Today, our Jewish brethren continue to commemorate their traditions but without their Temple. No Temple means they are unable to complete their pilgrimage journey in the wilderness. No Temple also means Daniel's prophetic time clock has stopped.

Once Temple-worship returns in Jerusalem as before, Daniel's final week for Israel will begin (Dan. 9:27), and so another opportunity to complete their pilgrimage journey back to the homeland. Therefore, the practice of sacrificial worship in Israel's newly restored Temple in Jerusalem is a critical sign we must watch for in our present day.

While the three annual pilgrimages are meant to map-out Firstborn National Israel's three-stage redemption journey by way of the wilderness, its purpose is two-fold. The first is to highlight the importance of an expected harvest from this group as one united body of believers. The second purpose is to highlight the expectation that they are to complete all three journeys at the appointed time[217] and place where Jehovah had chosen to place His name.[218]

The book of Hebrews makes it clear that the whole nation of Israel did not pass their first trial (test) in the wilderness:

> **Heb. 4:7-8** "Therefore, since it remains for some to enter into it [the Promised Land/Rest], and those who formerly had the gospel preached did not enter in on account of disobedience, *He again marks out a certain day*, saying in David, Today (after so long a time, according as He has said), "Today, if you hear His voice, do not harden your hearts." For if Joshua gave them rest, then He would not have afterwards spoken about another day [emphasis added]." (LITV).

Again, the Hebrew writer continues to use Israel's initial failure to enter the Promised Land as an object lesson. Note how the Promised Land is the same as entering God's rest.[219] What is more remarkable is the fact that "there remains a certain day that has been marked out." This statement relates exclusively to Israel and their proper entry into His rest as one complete national body at their appointed time.

So, just as the Christian Church is taken *spiritually* in the air as one complete believing body in Christ, so too, Israel is taken *physically* as one believing body by Christ at His second coming at the end of the age. Note how the Hebrew passage confirms that the first trial period for Israel looks back to their first exodus-wilderness experience. Yet, we are assured there remains a future "marked" time. This means by default, Israel's second trial period occurred in Jesus' day. We know this because at the end of His ministry, Israel, as one national body, stood judged due to their rejection of Him as their Messiah and King. (Lk. 13:35; Acts 28:27-28).

We can also conclude that the "place where He will choose to place His Name there" (Deut. 16:2, 6), is the Temple in Jerusalem (Ps. 78:67-68), which must be reinstituted before the Provocation Trial can begin. In that future time, Passover and Pentecost will run their course as before, but

---

[217] **Ex. 34:22-23:** And thou shalt observe the feast of weeks, of the firstfruits of wheat harvest, and the feast of ingathering at the year's end. Thrice in the year shall all your men children appear before the Lord God, the God of Israel.

[218] **Deut. 16:2b:** In a place where He will choose to place His Name there.

[219] Heb. 3:16-19. Also see, LXX, Ps. 94:11-14; Ps. 95:10-11.

come fall, Israel, as one house, must produce a crop of faith as the late harvest, which the last pilgrimage journey represents.

Israel's final journey of the season occurs on the Feast of Tabernacles. It is also known as the Feast of the In-Gathering. Its purpose is to signify how Israel will be delivered at the end of the ages, which is by way of the wilderness.

The Tenth Generation Faces One More Week of Trials

Noah's day on our Prophetic Timeline of the Ages Chart (Chart 8), represents the final week (7 years) of Daniel's 70 x 7 timeline for Israel. Once the Church Age ends, Israel's last 7-years on their timeline will be reinserted as the mainline and will run its course during the 7-year tribulation period as represented by Cain's 7-year right (Gen. 4:15).

The granting of Lamech's motion for extension of time for his firstborn family line pushed back Cain's 7-years of reckoning to occur in the tenth generation of Adam in Noah's day. Amazingly, Lamech's petition suddenly becomes Jehovah's extension plan that moved the tenth generation of Adam into a legally sufficient position (remember, ten signifies the end of a global judgment cycle) to satisfy the illegitimacy issue of Deuteronomy.[220]

The Deuteronomy illegitimacy issue helps to explain why Noah was "perfect in his generations." It also helps to explain why Lamech from the Christ-line named his son Noah rest.[221] Lamech understood that the illegitimacy issue was a direct consequence of the curse pronounced in the Garden. Noah's father had his hope in Jehovah's extension plan because he said in his heart as he named his son, "This one [Noah] will comfort us concerning our work and the toil of our hands, because of the ground which the Lord has cursed."

Peter, in his second letter, tells us that "a thousand years is like one day to the Lord" (2 Pet. 3:8). This statement is a direct link to "The Day of the Lord" (Mal. 4:5; Rev. 1:10), which is followed by the Millennial Reign. However, in terms of Israel's religious calendar, the Sabbath, with its seven feast days, brings the total count of the Leviticus set times of the Lord to eight, not seven. The purpose of the number eight indicates a new beginning, as well as the beginning of a new cycle. From the "new beginning" context, the placement of the tenth generation is just where it should be. Its place, by default, speaks of the end of a cycle to begin anew.

---

[220] **Deut. 23:2:** An illegitimate child shall not enter into the assembly of Jehovah, even to the tenth generation none of his shall enter into the assembly of Jehovah. (LITV).

[221] **Gen. 5:29:** And he [Noah's father, Lamech] called his name Noah, saying, This same shall comfort us concerning our work and toil of our hands, because of the ground which the LORD hath cursed.

Tracing the Tracks

As we begin to track National Israel's steps during their last annual pilgrimage journey, it is helpful to know that the book of Revelation is like the rest of the Bible—it is not in chronological order. The most straightforward approach is to categorize events that happen in the beginning, midway, and at the end of the 7-years, then fill in the gaps. This categorized approach is also the same approach Daniel applied in his prophecies, in addition to his use of symbolism that helps to interpret the symbolism in Revelation.

When Israel's timeline is reinserted, the 7-year tribulation period will begin. Once again, supernatural occurrences will be common-day experiences, just as it was in the first exodus-wilderness experience of old. Except in this future day, the plagues and cosmic disturbances will affect the whole world, not just one localized area, as it was in ancient Egypt and with the Israelite's forty-year wonderings.

The very first supernatural act by the Almighty will be subtle, but it is the catalyst of which all subsequent events will ensue. This initial supernatural act will bring all the nations of the world together in agreement and alliance with one up and coming world leader, the Antichrist. Otherwise, this period will never occur because it will take a miracle to bring the nations together under a one-world government. Once again, we look to Daniel's prophecies to supply a wide-lens view of the 7-year tribulation period as it applies to the Revelation story:

> **Dan. 9:26-27:** "Then after the sixty-two weeks [sixty-two "sevens"] Messiah will be cut off but not for Himself. And the people of a coming ruler [the Prince of Darkness/Antichrist] shall destroy the city [Jerusalem] and the sanctuary [the Temple]. And its end shall be with the flood, and ruins are determined, and war shall be until the end. And he [Satan as the Antichrist] shall confirm a covenant with the many for one week. And in the middle of the week he shall cause the sacrifice and the offering to cease [in the Jerusalem Temple]. And on a corner of the altar will be abominations that desolate, even until the end. And that which was decreed shall pour out on the desolator." (LITV).

Here, we see the "Prince of Darkness" or the Antichrist's primary goal in this 7-year tribulation period is to destroy Jerusalem, its temple worship, and the nation of Israel. In other words, the Antichrist's primary goal is to ultimately become the object of worship by all the nations of the world. Daniel informs his readers, "all will come to an end with a flood of wars and desolations." Note the added emphasis on the word flood, which should strike a mental picture of Noah's flood that brought judgment in his day, and in the last age of which Daniel's prophecy is describing.

Daniel's prophecy reveals that Antichrist's first order of business is to make a 7-year covenant with the nations. Some call it a peace treaty. National Israel will agree to this peace treaty, along with the other nations. However, according to Daniel's prophecy, the Antichrist will break his agreement with Israel at mid-tribulation by putting a stop to their temple sacrifices by committing an "abomination of desolation." Daniel continues to outline the Antichrist's plan:

> **Dan. 8:23-25:** "And in the latter time of their kingdom, when the transgressors have come to the full, a king, strong of face and skilled at intrigues, shall stand up. And his power shall be mighty, but not by his own power. And he shall destroy wondrously, and he shall prosper, and work, and destroy the mighty, and the holy people. And also through his skill he will make deceit succeed in his land. And he will lift himself up in his heart, and be at ease; he shall destroy many. He shall also stand up against the Ruler of rulers [Christ], but he shall be shattered without a hand." (LITV).

> **Dan. 11:30-35:** "For those who go out from the west will come against him, and he will be in fear and will go back, full of wrath against the holy agreement; and he will do his pleasure: and he will go back and be united with those who have given up the holy agreement. And armies sent by him will take up their position and they will make unclean the holy place, even the strong place, and take away the regular burned offering and put in its place an unclean thing causing fear. And those who do evil against the agreement will

be turned to sin by his fair words: but the people who have knowledge of their God will be strong and do well. And those who are wise among the people will be the teachers of the mass of the people: but they will come to their downfall by the sword and by the flame, being made prisoners and undergoing loss for a long time. Now at the time of their downfall they will have a little help, but numbers will be joined to them in the town, and in their separate heritages. And some of those who are wise will have wisdom in testing themselves and making themselves clean, till the time of the end: for it is still for the fixed time." (BBE).

Here, Daniel gives further details of how this king and "Prince of Darkness" is a man of great deception. He comes in peace and with flatteries to a world primed and ready for his message. His charisma draws them in like a moth to a flame.

From Daniel, we see how the 7-year peace agreement is readily agreed to by all. His prophecy implies that Israel will once again offer the daily sacrifices under the Mosaic Law in the Temple at Jerusalem. Yet, an alliance is made with the dark forces to "do evil against the agreement and turn to sin." Thus, giving us a clear sign that Israel's prophetic time clock will be restarted the moment Daniel's final week materializes onto the stage of world history.

Elijah's National Battle Call

Once the peace treaty begins, Israel's two witnesses come to Jerusalem in supernatural power. Through their ministry, the 144,000 young Jewish men (12,000 from each tribe of Israel) will be "sealed" to preach the Kingdom Gospel.[222] This understanding aligns with Jesus' statement:

> **Mt. 24:14:** "And this gospel of the kingdom shall [at a future time] be preached in all the world for a witness unto all nations; and then shall the end come."

Jesus' description from this passage indicates how the 7-year tribulation like Noah's day is divided into two categories: preaching and

---

[222] **Rev. 7:3-4:** Don't harm the earth or the sea or any tree! Wait until I have marked the foreheads of the servants of our God. Then I heard how many people had been marked on the forehead. There were one hundred forty-four thousand, and they came from every tribe of Israel. (CEV).

judgment. From that model, the two witnesses and the 144,000 naturally represent Noah preaching to the then known world while building the Ark (2 Pet. 2:5). Once the flood came, only Noah and his little house are sealed in the Ark to sail through the judgment waters, just like the remnant of Israel in Revelation (Rev. 12:17). Here we have a picture of how things will dramatically change in the second half of the 7-year tribulation period, as we shall soon discover.

Before we move on, again, we would like to stress how the "gospel of the kingdom," which will be preached by Jewish National Israel during the 7-year tribulation period, is not the same as Paul's gospel. Jesus was a "minister of the circumcision" at His first coming. In that capacity, He could only "confirm the promises made unto the fathers."[223] When Peter said to Jesus, "Thou art the Christ, the Son of the living God,"[224] it was a confession of faith unto salvation, as only a blood-born Jewish Israelite could express.

Jesus validated Peter's confession of faith as foundational for the whole house of Israel, when He said, "Blessed art thou, Simon Barjona: for flesh and blood hath not revealed *it* unto thee, but my Father which is in heaven. And I say also unto thee, That thou art Peter, and upon this rock I will build my church; and the gates of hell shall not prevail against it." (Mt. 16:17-18).

In the same way, because the seven churches in Revelation represent Jewish National Israel's timeline reinserted, Christ will expect them, at that time, to "overcome."[225] Such an expectation is appropriate for the Kingdom Gospel. John understood this and defined how to "overcome." It is merely "belief" that Jesus is the Son of God. Note, in his confession of faith, which is Israel's standard way to overcome, there is no mention of Christ's death and resurrection:

> **1 Jn. 5:4-5:** "For whatsoever is born of God overcometh the world: and this is the victory that overcometh the world, *even* our faith. Who is he that overcometh the world, but he that believeth that Jesus is the Son of God?"

---

[223] **Rom. 15:8:** Now I say that Jesus Christ was a minister of the circumcision for the truth of God, to confirm the promises *made* unto the fathers.

[224] **Mt. 16:16:** And Simon Peter answered and said, Thou art the Christ, the Son of the living God.

[225] Rev. 2:7, 11, 17.

Once the 7-year tribulation period begins, it is Jewish National Israel's time to bring the "good news" to the world and lead a joyous jubilee into the Kingdom. John informs us that the requirement to "overcome" is to believe that Jesus is the Son of God. The Divine plan to accomplish Israel's mission includes the two witnesses and the 144,000 sealed from each of the 12 tribes of Israel. Revelation continues about Israel's two witnesses:

> **Rev. 11:4-6:** "These are the two olive trees, and the two candlesticks standing before the God of the earth. And if any man would hurt them, fire proceedeth out of their mouth, and devoureth their enemies: and if any man will hurt them, he must in this manner be killed. These have power to shut heaven, that it rain not in the days of their prophecy; and have power over waters to turn them to blood, and to smite the earth with all plagues, as often as they will."

This passage tells how the two witnesses will have the power to kill their enemies with their mouths, and they will have the authority to turn bodies of water into blood and to strike the earth with plagues. They will also be able to shut the rains from heaven. The first two supernatural powers are reminiscent of Moses as the deliverer of the Israelites in Egypt, and the last is reminiscent of Elijah when he stood against Queen Jezebel and her spiritually bankrupt husband and king, Ahab.

Scripture does not tell us who the two witnesses are, even though we know this is according to the Spirit of Elijah requirement. Some commentators think Moses and Elijah because they both appeared before Jesus at His transfiguration (Mt. 17:1-3), who provided adequate testimony from the Law (Moses) and the Prophets (Elijah) of which Israel's timeline aligns.

Others think the two witnesses could be Elijah and Enoch because both of their offices are like the Holy Spirit in power and faith. Still, it could be two completely new people. No matter who the two witnesses are, their presence will signify that the Spirit of Elijah's office will be operating in full force and effect, which provides the essential battle and harvest preparations for this time-period as foretold by Malachi.

Note the description of the two witnesses who are said to be "the two olive trees and the two candlesticks standing before the God of the earth."

This imagery takes us back to the fifth vision of Zechariah (Zec. 4:1-14) to highlight Jewish National Israel's mission in Revelation[226] as the channel of blessing to the nations due to an abundant supply of the Spirit of God.[227]

Supernatural Battleground

In Elijah's day, Israel lost their salt, their light, and their way. It was Elijah's job to prepare them for the coming showdown between God Almighty and the gods of the nations, in hopes that they would choose wisely. As before, the battle will re-emerge again, as depicted in Revelation. This time Elijah's spirit will rest on the two witnesses. After three and a half years, they will have finished their testimony in hopes of Israel's successful pilgrimage to the homeland at the appointed time as represented by the fall feast. Their story continues:

> **Rev. 11:7-10:** "And when they shall have finished their testimony [the two witnesses], the beast that ascendeth out of the bottomless pit shall make war against them, (this is the first appearance of Satan as the person of the Antichrist) and shall overcome them, and [finally] kill them. [This ends the first three and a half years.] And their dead bodies shall lie in the street of the great city, which spiritually is called Sodom and Egypt, where also our Lord was crucified. And they of the people and kindreds and tongues and nations shall see their dead bodies three days and a half, and shall not suffer their dead bodies to be put in graves. And they that dwell upon the earth shall rejoice over them, and make merry, and shall send gifts one to another; because these two prophets tormented them that dwelt on the earth."

Thanks to our modern-day technology, we now understand how everyone around the world will personally have an opportunity to witness the two dead prophets on the streets of Jerusalem for three days. For the

---

[226] Rev. 2:17, 11:3-4, 26-29.

[227] **Zec. 4:2-6:** And said unto me, What seest thou? And I said, I have looked, and behold a candlestick all *of* gold, with a bowl upon the top of it, and his seven lamps thereon, and seven pipes to the seven lamps, which *are* upon the top thereof: And two olive trees by it, one upon the right *side* of the bowl, and the other upon the left *side* thereof. So I answered and spake to the angel that talked with me, saying, What *are* these, my lord? Then the angel that talked with me answered and said unto me, Knowest thou not what these be? And I said, No, my lord. Then he answered and spake unto me, saying, This *is* the word of the LORD unto Zerubbabel, saying, Not by might, nor by power, but by my spirit, saith the LORD of hosts.

first three and a half years, the Antichrist will blame all the world's sorrows on these two men because of their supernatural torments upon the earth (Rev. 11:10) and as the leaders of the 144,000 sealed warriors that have been sent to the ends of the earth. Once killed and their dead bodies put on public display, we can only imagine how the Antichrist will proudly present his victory speech and the universal celebration that will erupt from such an event.

As we think about how the world and the "Prince of Darkness" will, in this future time, dance their victory dance and exchange their gifts with one another, we are reminded of this same type of attitude at the foot of the cross in Jesus' day. Rev. 11:8 curiously links the death of the two witnesses with Christ's death by stating, "And their dead bodies shall lie in the street of the great city, which spiritually is called Sodom and Egypt [both are types of the world under judgment], where also our Lord was crucified." However, to both the Antichrist and the world's surprise, the two witnesses, just like Christ, will not remain dead for long because Revelation reveals:

> **Rev. 11:11-12:** "After three days and a half the Spirit of life from God entered into them, and they stood upon their feet; and great fear fell upon them who saw them. And they heard a great voice from heaven saying unto them, Come up hither. And they ascended up to heaven in a cloud; and their enemies beheld them."

In helpless amazement, the world will watch the two witnesses ascend to heaven in a cloud, just as Christ did in His ascension. Because the death and resurrection of the two witnesses curiously identify with their Lord's, JFB offers this insight:

> "His [Jesus] prophetic life lasted three and a half years; the very time in which "the saints are given into the hand" of Antichrist (Dan. 7:25). Three and a half does not, like ten, designate the power of the world in its fullness, but (while opposed to the Divine, expressed by seven) broken and defeated in its seeming triumph; for immediately after the three and a half times, judgment falls on the victorious world powers (Dan. 7:25-26). So Jesus' death seemed the

140

triumph of the world, but was really its defeat (Joh. 12:31)." (*JFB Commentary*, Dan. 9:27).

JFB presents a compelling perspective about the death and resurrection of the two witnesses as it compares to Christ's public crucifixion. Like Christ, the two also publicly experience rejection and death by the forces of evil. Except in the apocalypse, that evil is seen in the face of Antichrist and his army of nations. And, like Calvary, Satan and the evil world-system will, once again, celebrate the death of God's anointed as a victory, but in truth, it is their defeat.

Crossing Battle Lines to Make the Pilgrimage Journey to Home
At this point, we will begin tracing Israel's final pilgrimage journey to the homeland, as provided by the Revelation narrative. Although there is no indication in the text that the two witnesses will be killed exactly on Passover, we cannot ignore all the other direct associations that are before us (Rev. 11:8). For instance, if these two witnesses answer to our Lord's death and resurrection, then this event in Revelation 11 is a direct link to Israel's first Pilgrimage Journey in the spring representing the Feast of Passover, Unleavened Bread, and Firstfruits.

This association reminds us of the very meaning of Passover, which is the shed blood of the Lamb that provides redemption. According to the Jewish religious calendar, we know that the day after Passover is the Feast of Unleavened Bread.

The Feast of Unleavened Bread points back to the day when Firstborn National Israel walked through the Red Sea as a type of baptism[228] and ate the bread with no yeast, which represents without sin. This began their unfinished journey as the Church in the Wilderness.

The book of Exodus tells of how the Egyptians were plundered by the children of Israel just before they traveled from Rameses to Succoth (Ex. 12:35-39). John Darby provides further insight:

> "The people, their loins girded, having eaten in haste, with
> the bitter herbs of repentance, begin their journey; but
> they do so in Egypt: yet now God can be, and He is, with

---

[228] **1 Cor. 10:1-4:** Moreover, brethren, I would not that ye should be ignorant, how that all our fathers were under the cloud, and all passed through the sea; And were all baptized unto Moses in the cloud and in the sea; And did all eat the same spiritual meat; And did all drink the same spiritual drink: for they drank of that spiritual Rock that followed them: and that Rock was Christ.

them. Here it is well to distinguish these two judgments, that of the firstborn, and that of the Red Sea. As matters of chastisement, the one was the firstfruits of the other, and ought to have deterred Pharaoh from his rash pursuit. But the blood, which kept the people from God's judgment, meant something far deeper and far more serious than even the Red Sea, though judgment was executed there too. What happened at the Red Sea was, it is true, the manifestation of the illustrious power of God, who destroyed with the breath of His mouth the enemy who stood in rebellion against Him-final and destructive judgment in its character, no doubt, and which effected the deliverance of His people by His power. But the blood signified the moral judgment of God, and the full and entire satisfaction of all that was in His being. God, such as He was, in His justice, His holiness, and His truth, could not touch those who were sheltered by that blood." (Darby, *Synopsis of the Bible*, Ex. 12:1-51).

From Darby, we see Israel's deliverance was from bondage (type of slavery to sin) in Egypt (a type of the world) under the heavy hand of Pharaoh (a type of Antichrist). Note the two judgments that occurred in this one event. The first was the judgment of Firstborn National Israel. Second, the enemies of the redeemed were judged. The Lamb slain at Passover proved its power unto Israel's deliverance, just as it will again, as we are about to learn from the Revelation narrative.

Even at Calvary, the Gospel letters are careful to point out there was an immediate earthquake upon Christ's last breath, which caused the veil in the Temple to tear from top to bottom. (Mt. 27:51). In like manner, we read about an even greater earthquake, which occurs just after the death and resurrection of the two witnesses in Revelation.

> **Rev. 11:13:** "And the same hour [just after the ascent of the two witnesses at mid-tribulation] there was a great earthquake,[in the area of Jerusalem] and the tenth part of the city fell, and in the earthquake were slain of men seven thousand: and the remnant were affrighted, and gave glory to the God of heaven."

142

Just as the veil was torn to represent direct access to God upon the death of His son, so too, this new future earthquake will tear Israel into a remnant that will be primed and ready to gain that access. The ministry of the two witnesses are considered the firstfruits of the resurrection redeemed by the Lamb Slain at Passover. Only by Christ's finished work on the cross, can He be the *seed* sown in death that makes the coming Pentecostal harvest even possible. Therefore, the Passover becomes the Garden Program's ultimate weapon in this cosmic warfare.

Surprisingly, Revelation stays consistent with the pilgrimage pattern. The second Pilgrimage Feast in the summer occurs sometime after the seventh trumpet blows and in-between the second and third woes (Rev. 11:14-15). In this brief interlude, we learn that the 144,000 are "redeemed from among men, being the firstfruits unto God and to the Lamb" (Rev. 14:3-5). Here, speaks of the Pentecostal harvest. John Gill eloquently portrays it this way:

> "As the converted Jews received the firstfruits of the Spirit, on the day of Pentecost, and at other times, so these will receive the firstfruits of the far greater pouring forth of the Spirit in the latter day, which will begin, and usher in the kingdom of Christ." (Gill, *Exposition of the Bible*, Rev. 14:4).

After the 144,000 are deemed the firstfruits of the Spirit of Life, as typified by the coming of the Holy Spirit on the day of Pentecost in Acts 2, several angels come forth. One will bring the gospel to preach to the earth. (Rev. 14:6). Another will announce the fall of Babylon. (Rev. 14:8).

A third angel will warn of taking the mark of the beast (Rev. 14:9), while the remaining will pronounce, "the hour to reap has come because the harvest of the earth is ripe." (Rev. 14:15-20). This last section undoubtedly speaks of the final act of the late harvest in the fall, which occurs on the Feast of Tabernacles. Then, seven more angels will appear with seven plagues, which are the last because in them the wrath of God is finished. (Rev. 15:1).

The Nation Reduced to a Remnant

From Zechariah, we learned how one-third of Israel will survive to face the second half of this 7-year tribulation period:

> **Zec. 13:9:** "And I will bring the third part [the remnant of Israel] through the fire, and will refine them as silver is refined, and will try them as gold is tried: they shall call on my name, and I will hear them: I will say, It is my people: and they shall say, The LORD is my God."

Zechariah sees Israel split into thirds, which the remnant represents one portion of that split. From Ezekiel, we learn Israel's "face to face" trial is scheduled to occur in the wilderness at this same time Zachariah saw the third part of Israel going through the fire, which represents the last half of the 7-year tribulation period.

> **Eze. 20:35:** "And I will bring you into the wilderness of the peoples, and I will be judging face to face there with you." (LITV).

Both passages help to widen the Revelation lens, especially concerning Rev. 11:12-13, which informs us that just after the resurrection of the two witnesses, at mid-tribulation, a tenth part of the city of Jerusalem will fall due to a sudden earthquake. These verses also speak of the remnant for the first time, who will be viewed as one united body. They will look to Jehovah to lead them out of a desperate and frightening situation. Even though at this point, they will not have a full understanding of Christ as their Messiah, they are ready to humbly follow Jehovah, as their Shepherd, as before in the wilderness days of old.

Here, the remnant represents Noah and his little family sealed in the Ark, which denotes a place of safety, to *sail* through the fiery waters of the wrath of God. This period also correlates to Matthew 24, where Jesus encourages Israel to flee from Jerusalem due to a terrible earthquake. It is in this context Jesus warns of the coming Great Tribulation:

> **Mt. 24:15-22:** "When ye therefore shall see the abomination of desolation [at mid-tribulation], spoken of by Daniel the prophet, stand in the holy place, (whoso readeth, let him understand); Then let them which be in Judaea flee into the mountains: Let him which is on the housetop not come down to take anything out of his

house: Neither let him which is in the field return back to take his clothes. And woe unto them that are with child, and to them that give suck in those days! But pray ye that your flight be not in the winter, neither on the sabbath day: For then shall be great tribulation, such as was not since the beginning of the world to this time, no, nor ever shall be. And except those days should be shortened, there should no flesh be saved: but for the elect's sake those days shall be shortened."

In this account, Jesus spoke of an incident He called, the "abomination of desolation." This phrase refers us back to Daniel 9:27 and Daniel 12:11, which describes an event that is to occur at mid-tribulation, where Antichrist is going to go into Israel's newly restored Temple in Jerusalem and defile it. He is going to shut it down and turn on the Nation of Israel as no persecutor has ever done. The worse global tyrant known to man will be a picnic compared to the Antichrist.

It is at this point and time that Satan will appear as the great red dragon (Rev. 12:3), who will begin to chase the woman (Israel), who had the man child (Christ). Through Satan's influence, the Antichrist is also going to convince the nations to go against Israel. The remnant (remember, which is one-third of Israel due to the earthquake that will occur once the two witnesses are resurrected) will then be supernaturally taken out of the city to a place of safety. Revelation continues:

Rev. 12:6: "And the woman [the remnant of Israel] fled in the wilderness, where she hath a place prepared of God that they should feed her there a thousand two hundred and threescore days [at mid-tribulation]."

Rev. 12:14: "And to the woman [the fleeing remnant] were given two wings of a great eagle, that she might fly into the wilderness, into her place, where she is nourished for a time [one year] and times [plural for two years] and half a time [three and a half years, which is the last half of the tribulation period] from the face of the serpent."

Note how these passages refer to Israel in the feminine, instead of in the masculine. This association helps us to readily accept the birth, and the bride analogies, which John uses in his final chapters of the book of Revelation. This female association also agrees with the "deliverance by travail" analogy used by Christ and Isaiah as we will learn in the next three sections.

For the last three and a half years, the fleeing remnant of Israel will be under the protection of Jehovah, as it was in the first exodus from ancient Egypt. It is in this instance that we can see how Jehovah will, once again, afford His people one final opportunity to trust Him with their whole heart to enter His rest and complete their journey to the homeland. This final choice is their last chance to overcome by faith, as one complete national body of born-again believers.

We must also note how, in Matthew 24, Jesus called the remnant's place of safety, "mountains." Some scholars think the mountains will be the mountains of Moab or probably the ancient city of Petra, but Scripture does not say specifically. All we know is they will be under the protection of the Almighty for this last half of the 7-year tribulation period.

With Jesus' teaching in Matthew 24 and John giving us the secret as to how to overcome, we can piece together just as soon as the remnant flees from the Temple in Jerusalem, "two wings of a great eagle are given, that she might fly into the wilderness." (Rev. 12:14). Again, John uses another familiar inference from Israel's historical deliverance from Egypt with the use of the phrase "eagles' wings."

Ex. 19:4: "Ye have seen what I did unto the Egyptians, and how I bare you on eagles' wings, and brought you unto myself."

This recount certainly falls within the context of Israel's ability to flee as it concerns certain situations, such as annihilation. The Egyptian threat serves as our textbook example. Jehovah specifically said, "I bare you on eagles' wings to myself." However, being such a massive body of people, the record clearly shows that they walked. The peculiar phrase used by Jehovah infers how Israel was supernaturally delivered and will be again in her final hour. Except, it will be the Antichrist and his army who will stand against the remnant of Israel instead of Pharaoh and his army.

Birth Pains for a Born-Again Nation

Once the remnant flees from Jerusalem to the mountains, they will stay safe from the perils of the last half of the now Great Tribulation holocaust. Just like before, Jehovah will, once again, direct the plagues upon the enemy, while protecting the Israelite territory:

> **Ex. 8:22:** "And at that time I will make a division between your land and the land of Goshen where my people are, and no flies will be there; so that you may see that I am the Lord over all the earth." (BBE).

This scene illustrates how Jehovah protected His people as the great plagues were dispensed upon the Egyptians. In that day, 10 plagues were sent because it relates to a worldwide deliverance, in type. However, in Revelation, we have a total of 7 plagues, and that is because it relates to Israel's 7-scale cycle, in type. In Matthew 24, Jesus calls this time as "the beginning of sorrows."

> **Mt. 24:3-9:** "And as he [Jesus] sat upon the mount of Olives, the disciples came unto him privately, saying, Tell us, when shall these things be? and what shall be the sign of thy coming, and of the end of the world? And Jesus answered and said unto them, Take heed that no man deceive you. For many shall come in my name, saying, I am Christ; and shall deceive many. And ye shall hear of wars and rumours of wars: see that ye be not troubled: for all these things must come to pass, but the end is not yet. For nation shall rise against nation, and kingdom against kingdom: and there shall be famines, and pestilences, and earthquakes, in divers places. All these are the *beginning of sorrows*. Then shall they deliver you up to be afflicted, and shall kill you: and ye shall be hated of all nations for my name's sake [emphasis added]."

In verse eight from Matthew's account, Jesus said the coming of the end of the age is the beginning of "sorrows." The word sorrow in this passage means travail because it intentionally conveys the idea of birth pains.

Jesus intended His listeners to view the process of the tribulation period like a woman about to deliver her newborn. At first, her birth pains start gently and far apart, but the closer she comes to the hour of delivery, the faster and more intense are her contractions. When applying this theme to the book of Revelation, notice the intensity of the story increases as it progresses along.

As the last three and one-half years draw near, the plagues and the cosmic disturbances become so unbearable death will run rampant. The horrible events will begin to stack on top of each other and will occur almost instantaneously until Christ physically appears as the Great Deliverer to deliver Firstborn National Israel.

However, at the mid-tribulation point, the remnant will flee to the mountains because the Antichrist breaks his peace treaty with Israel, commits the "abomination of desolation," and begins his rule from the Temple in Jerusalem. At that instance, the birth pains intensify even more. In the final hour, Antichrist's war campaign will climax as the nations of the world assemble at his side with the sole purpose of annihilating the little nation of Israel, now reduced to a remnant, once and for all.

It is at this point, all of Israel's enemies have surrounded her at every turn. Once again, we see Israel trapped just like she was between the Red Sea and Pharaoh's army. Except now, in this final hour, the salvation of the Lord will come by Christ's literal return with His heavenly host, including His spiritual body, the Christian Church.[229] Revelation 14-16 describes this scene, which culminates at the battle of Armageddon.

Battlefield Armageddon

The word Armageddon comes from a village by the name of Megiddo. In ancient times, Megiddo was an ideal place to build a city. It had good food production, water, and natural defenses. It sat right on the edge of the Plain of Esdraelon, which is just a flat floor valley at the base of Megiddo. The Plain of Esdraelon is several square miles of open area. The armies of the ancients fought battle after battle there. Revelation indicates that in this same ancient valley, all the nations of the world will pack their armies in one collective effort for the sole purpose of obliterating national Israel. Revelation 14 tells us their fate from the perspective of heaven:

---

[229] Jude 1:14-15; 1 Thes. 3:13; and Zec. 14:5 tells us that Christ will return with saints. Mt. 25:31 tells us that Christ will return with angels. Because there are no contradictions in the word of God, both are true.

Rev. 14:14-19: "And I looked and behold a white cloud, and upon the cloud one sat like unto the son of man, having on his head a golden crown, and in his hand a sharp sickle. And another angel came out of the temple, crying with a loud voice to him that sat on the cloud, 'Thrust in thy sickle and reap, for the time is come for thee to reap; for the harvest of the Earth is ripe. So he that sat on the cloud, thrust in his sickle on the earth; and the earth was reaped."

This scene surprisingly describes the conclusion of the fall harvest, being the last pilgrimage journey of the season. Christ, as "The Son of Man," which is His glorified title at His second coming, leads the final harvest efforts. The Greek uses a stronger word for "ripe" in this verse. It implies that the crop in the field is more than ripe, or it is almost past harvest time. Thus, placing Israel (and whosoever will come at that time) as the last gleanings of this fall season in compliance with the Israelite harvest program.

It is here, in that final moment, those that remain under Satan and the Antichrist's influence will be gathered in one spot, like a cluster of grapes as Revelation describes it, and reaped (harvested) along with Israel.[230] Just like the ancients gathered their grapes and put them into a huge wine vat and walked on them until the juice ran out, so we have this same association with the final harvesting of the earth. Even more, just as the final plague killed the Egyptian firstborn, and ultimately, Pharaoh and his army in the Red Sea, so too, the battle of Armageddon is associated with Israel's deliverance from Ancient Egypt. Revelation 16 tells us the fate of the nations at the battle of Armageddon from our perspective:

Rev. 16:16, 19, 21: "And He assembled them in the place having been called in Hebrew, Armageddon... And the great city came to be into three parts, and the cities of the nations fell. And Babylon the great was remembered before God, to give to her the cup of the wine of the anger of His wrath... And a great hail, as the size of a talent, came down out of the heaven upon men. And men blasphemed God from the plague of the hail, because its plague is exceedingly great." (LITV).

---

[230] **Hos. 9:10:** I found Israel like grapes in the wilderness. I saw your fathers as the firstfruits in the fig tree at her first time. They came to Baal-peor and set themselves apart to a shameful thing. (LITV).

From this account, Babylon represents the world's system as a modern form of captivity over Israel (Rev. 12-19), just like Pharaoh did in Egypt who ruled and enslaved them. Once again, Israel must flee from sin and slavery, except this time it is from Babylon. (Rev. 18:1-6). As the judgments culminate within that final hour of the apocalypse, the global community will, once again, unite in a worldwide rebellion, like before at the tower of Babel.

The seven plagues that will be poured out (Rev. 16) represent, in part, a repetition of the plagues poured upon Egypt (sores on bodies, water turned into blood, supernatural darkness), and the last two plagues reflect the historical fall of Babylon. So, just as ancient Babylon fell due to the source drying up or diverting of its Euphrates' waters by King Cyrus, so too, apocalyptic Babylon will fall by another drying up of its Euphrates' waters caused by Kings who come from the East.[231]

As the events in Revelation continue to mirror Jehovah's breaking of the evil power over Israel from Ancient Egypt, the reason for the seven bowl judgments become clear. With the rendering of each judgment, the satanic world-system will receive blow after blow as one continuous effort to break its grip that it has on the remnant of Israel. Again, we cannot help but recall similar judgments pronounced upon Egypt and Babylon in biblical history. Together, both become a composite type and embodiment of all the enemies of Israel, which Jehovah said to Christ, "Sit thou at my right hand, until I make thine enemies thy footstool." (Ps. 110:1). From the Old Testament viewpoint, we turn to the book of Isaiah, who describes this same Revelation event from another perspective:

> **Isa. 63:3-4:** "I have trodden the winepress alone [this is the second coming of Christ] and of the people there was none with me: for I will tread them in mine anger, and trample them in my fury, and their blood shall be sprinkled [or splattered] upon my garments and I will stain all my raiment. For the day of vengeance is in mine heart, *and the year of my redeemed is come* [emphasis added]."

In this passage, the Messiah comes for vengeance and deliverance, just like Jehovah delivered His people from Pharaoh and his army by the parting

---

[231] **Rev. 16:12:** And the sixth angel poured out his vial upon the great river Euphrates; and the water thereof was dried up, that the way of the kings of the east might be prepared.

of the Red Sea.[232] Both viewpoints from Revelation and Isaiah describe the beginning stages of the second coming of Christ. Isaiah tells it from the perspective of His wrath and judgment (vengeance) in the battle against the gathered armies of Antichrist,[233] as opposed to the Garden harvesting effort in Revelation. Isaiah also sees this event as the "year of redemption," just as the first Passover in Egypt represents.[234] From these observations, it becomes quite evident that there are many sides to this one major event, as far as Scripture is concerned.

In Matthew 24, Jesus calls Himself, "The Son of Man." Revelation also calls Him "The Lamb," who is the King of Kings and Lord of Lords (Rev. 17:14). So, not only do we see that the 7-year tribulation period is a time Jehovah is delivering a "newborn" nation, but again, we see it is also a universal outpouring of His wrath and judgment against all the enemies of God. From these associations, the words of Jesus ring true, "as it was in the days of Noah, so shall it be at the coming of 'The Son of Man.'" His second coming will be a global happening just as Noah's flood was, even though His focus is the city of Jerusalem and that portion promised to Israel.

In the heat of the battle, a "sharp sword" will come out of his mouth to strike down the nations. At that point, He will "tread the winepress of the fury of the wrath of God Almighty." On his robe and his thigh, there will be a name written, "King of Kings and Lord of Lords." (Rev. 19:15-17). From the Old Testament perspective, Zechariah describes this scene this way:

> **Zec. 14:1-4:** "Behold, the day of Jehovah comes, and your spoil shall be divided among you. For I will gather all the nations to battle against Jerusalem. And the city shall be captured, and the houses plundered, and the women ravished. And half the city shall go into exile, and *the rest of the people shall not be cut off from the city.* And Jehovah shall go out and fight against those nations, like the day He fought in the day of battle. And

[232] **Deut. 5:15:** And remember that thou wast a servant in the land of Egypt, and that the Lord thy God brought thee out thence through a mighty hand and by a stretched out arm: therefore the Lord thy God commanded thee to keep the sabbath day.

[233] See, the Song of Moses, Ex. 15.

[234] **Ex. 12:27:** That ye shall say, It is the sacrifice of the LORD'S passover, who passed over the houses of the children of Israel in Egypt, when he smote the Egyptians, and delivered our houses. And the people bowed the head and worshipped.

His feet shall stand in that day on the Mount of Olives,
which is before Jerusalem on the east; and the Mount of
Olives shall divide from its middle, from the east even
to the west, a very great valley. And half of the mountain
shall move toward the north, and half of it toward the
south [emphasis added]." (LITV).

In Revelation, we see Christ reaping the nations of the earth and de-
stroying them with the word of His mouth. However, Zechariah said the battle is the time Jehovah will fight against the nations and deliver the remnant
of Israel, which is described as "those not cut off from the city."

A Successful Deliverance Brings Victory

Chapter 14 of Zechariah reflects how the battle of Armageddon is won
by Christ's physical return on the Mount of Olives (vs. 4), which is confirmed by angels in Acts 1:9-13. He comes in full splendor and arrayed with
His armies of heaven, which includes the Christian Church[235] and the angels
(Rev. 19:11-21). Satan, as the dragon, supports the Antichrist armed with
his nations to "make war with the remnant,"[236] but is instantly defeated by
Christ's return.

All at once, the remnant of Israel is delivered from her oppressors.
With Babylon, the Great, and the evil powers defeated (Rev. 18,19:2-3),
the words of Micah come true, "And I [Jehovah] will make her that halted
a remnant, and her that was cast far off a strong nation: and the LORD
shall reign over them in mount Zion from henceforth, even for ever."
(Micah 4:7).

Zechariah also speaks how the face of Mount Olives will undergo dra-
matic changes as a result of these end-time events (vs. 4). A river will form,
which will flow from the Mediterranean through Jerusalem and out to the
Dead Sea. The Dead Sea will be made alive at this time and will be "dead"
no more. Zechariah continues:

Zec. 14:8-9: "And it shall be in that day, that living waters
shall go out from Jerusalem; half of them toward the
former sea [the Mediterranean], and half of them toward

---

[235] **Rev. 19:14:** And the armies *which were* in heaven followed him upon white horses, clothed in fine linen, white and clean.

[236] **Rev. 12:17:** And the dragon was wroth with the woman, and went to make war with the remnant of her seed, which keep the commandments of God, and have the testimony of Jesus Christ.

the hinder sea [the Dead Sea]; in summer and in winter shall it be. And the Lord shall be king over all the earth."

Notice how Zechariah's prophecy highlights Christ's earthly rule and conveniently skips the battle of Armageddon. From his viewpoint, the Messiah returns to the mount as king over all the earth, not heaven. From the Jewish standpoint, this is the time when the Nation of Israel will finally enjoy everything promised to Abraham in Genesis 15. At that time, Jerusalem will rule from the Mediterranean to the River Euphrates, and down to the Red Sea, and west to the River of Egypt, and back. That entire area will be the homeland of Israel, which begins at the Millennial Reign.

In verse 9, Zechariah confirms that "In that day, there shall be one LORD, and his name one." This agrees with Revelation 19:16, which describes Jesus as the "King of Kings and Lord of Lords," over a physical and literal earthly kingdom. Still, how is the remnant saved? The book of Isaiah helps with this detail:

> **Isa. 66:7-8:** "Before she travailed [speaking of delivery] she brought forth; before her pain came, she was delivered of a man child [the man child refers to Christ]. Who hath heard such a thing? who hath seen such things? Shall the earth be made to bring forth in one day? *or* shall a nation be born at once? for as soon as Zion travailed, she brought forth her children."

Here, Isaiah speaks of the born-again experience of Israel as one united body. Isaiah notably employs the deliverance theme, just as Christ did, to compare the deliverance of the man child (Christ) with the delivery of Israel. Again, we have another example of how Christ and Israel are two sides of the same firstborn coin.

However, in Israel's case, Isaiah then asks, "shall a nation be born at once?" The immediate answer is, "Just as soon as Zion travailed, she brought forth her children." This parable points to the newly born-again nation of Israel as it relates to Jehovah's marriage to the land of Jerusalem. In other words, when the remnant sees the physical return of Christ, they will be born-again,[237] like their younger brother, the Christian Church as one complete body.

The Remnant Reborn by "The Light" Like Paul

Paul regarded his salvation as a "pattern to them which should hereafter believe on Him" (1Tim. 1:16). When we apply this thought to Israel, their deliverance carries a striking likeness to Paul's own conversion experience on the road to Damascus (Acts 9). As a fellow Jew of the highest caliber (Phil. 3:5), he too was spiritually bankrupt and blind, yet he was instantly "reborn" by a "face to face" encounter in "The Light" of the risen Christ, just as Israel will be according to the prescribed set time.

Appropriately, Paul also viewed himself as "one born out of due time." (1 Cor. 15:8) and then spoke on the order of the resurrections (1 Cor. 15:23), which was discussed earlier in Chapter 9—*Rules for Harvesting Souls*. But in this chapter, it now becomes evident that Paul had a full grasp of his company and order in terms of the Divine plan. More specifically, Paul knew his lot was supposed to be among his kinsman, the remnant of Israel, which we now understand is set to be "reborn" at the end of the age.

Again, we are reminded that Paul's company and kinsman include "thy people" of Daniel (Dan. 9:24), and the Gospel Kingdom converts because they all looked forward to the first resurrection. (Job 14:13- 17; Jn. 11:24; Rev. 20:3-6). But Zechariah offers one more detail we need to discuss:

> **Zec. 12:10-11:** "And I will pour upon the house of David, and upon the inhabitants of Jerusalem, [Kingdom Saints] the spirit of grace and of supplications: *and they shall look upon me whom they have pierced,* and they shall mourn for him, as one mourneth for his only son, and shall be in bitterness for him, as one that is in bitterness for his firstborn. In that day shall there be a great mourning in Jerusalem, as the mourning of Hadadrimmon in the valley of Megiddon [emphasis added]."

---

[237] **Mt. 24:30-31:** And then shall appear the sign of the Son of man in heaven: and then shall all the tribes of the earth mourn, and they shall see the Son of man coming in the clouds of heaven with power and great glory. And he shall send his angels with a great sound of a trumpet, and they shall gather together his elect from the four winds, from one end of heaven to the other.

Zechariah curiously links the bitter mourning of the Remnant (those "who look upon Him whom they have pierced," which Revelation 1:7 flags as a separate focus group for the occasion) with the bitter morning caused by the apocalyptic holocaust that ended instantaneously by Christ's victorious appearance at the battle of Armageddon.

No doubt, Megiddo has another important role to play. This time in the Millennial Kingdom. In addition to its ancient battle associations, Megiddo was the central trade route of the Fertile Crescent. This connection assures, in type, that the memory of the apocalyptic bloodbath will become synonymous with the ruins left from the "great supper of God" where the birds will feast upon the massive carnage left in Christ's wake. (Rev. 19:17).

Later, Zechariah foretells how the Feast of Tabernacles will continue to be observed during Christ's Reign (Zec. 14:17-19). This means, for a thousand years, the families of the converted nations must travel to Jerusalem to meet this requirement annually. As they do, their travels on the main route to Jerusalem will serve as a stern reminder that destruction comes to all that oppose His iron-rod rule. This picture fits nicely since the battle of Armageddon is the day Christ returns as the literal Tabernacle of God exactly on the Feast of Tabernacles.

Thy Kingdom Come

In anticipation of Christ's physical return, Chapter 19 of Revelation erupts on the scene with a massive explosion of praise and worship in heaven. The central theme is "Hallelujah! the Salvation, and the glory, and the power of our God are come."[238] A voice later proceeds to announce, "the marriage of the Lamb is come, and his wife hath made herself ready. And to her was granted that she should be arrayed in fine linen, white and clean. For fine linen is the righteousness of the saints." (Rev. 19:7-8). Here, all of heaven celebrates the salvation of the remnant, which demands a righteous covering that prepares them for the marriage of the Lamb as Isaiah 54 foretells:

---

[238] Translation rendered by Bullinger. "This is the first occurrence of the word Hallelujah in the New Testament. The Greek spelling in the New Testament is (...) *allelouia*; and the word is left untranslated. In the Old Testament the word is always translated "praise ye the Lord." The first occurrence of the word Hallelujah in the Old Testament corresponds in a marked manner with its first occurrence in the New Testament...We first find it in . So here, in Rev. 19:1. The utterance begins and ends with the word "Hallelujah"; and Jah is praised for a similar reason, for at length is come the salvation and the glory and the power of God, manifested in the judgment of chap. 18 and in 19:11-16, when the sinners will be consumed out of the earth, and the wicked will be no more; and when God's people will be avenged." (Bullinger, *The Apocalypse or "The Day of the Lord,* p. 584).

Isa. 54:4-10: "Fear not; for thou shalt not be ashamed: neither be thou confounded; for thou shalt not be put to shame: for thou shalt forget the shame of thy youth, and shalt not remember the reproach of thy widowhood any more. For thy Maker *is* thine husband; the LORD of hosts *is* his name; and thy Redeemer the Holy One of Israel; The God of the whole earth shall he be called. For the LORD hath called thee as a woman forsaken and grieved in spirit, and a wife of youth, when thou wast refused[239] saith thy God. For a small moment have I forsaken thee; but with great mercies will I gather thee. *In a little wrath I hid my face from thee for a moment; but with everlasting kindness will I have mercy on thee, saith the LORD thy Redeemer. For this is as the waters of Noah unto me: for as I have sworn that the waters of Noah should no more go over the earth; so have I sworn that I would not be wroth with thee, nor rebuke thee.* For the mountains shall depart, and the hills be removed; but my kindness shall not depart from thee, neither shall the covenant of my peace[240] be removed, saith the LORD that hath mercy on thee [emphasis added]."

In the context of the "judgment waters of Noah," Jehovah's faithfulness to His elect nation by executing judgment, defeating all their enemies, and invoking His Everlasting Covenant with them is again reassured in Isaiah's passage. Paul's letter to the Romans also confirms this understanding:

Rom. 11:26-29: "And so all Israel shall be saved: as it is written, There shall come out of Sion the Deliverer, and shall turn away ungodliness from Jacob: For this *is* my covenant unto them, when I shall take away their sins. As concerning the gospel [Paul's gospel], *they* [blind Israel] *are* enemies for your sakes [the Christian Church]: but as

---

[239] Or "when *she* was rejected;" one who had been a wife of youth (Eze. 16:8, Eze. 16:22, Eze. 16:60; Jer. 2:2) at the time when (*thou,* or) she was rejected for infidelity [Maurer]. "A wife of youth *but afterwards* rejected" [Lowth]." (*JFB Commentary,* Isa. 54:6).

[240] Isa. 51:6; Ps. 89:33-34; Rom. 11:29. Re: Covenant of my peace (2 Sam. 23:5): "The covenant whereby I have made thee at peace with Me." (*JFB Commentary,* Isa. 54:10).

touching the election, *they* [blind Israel] *are* beloved for the fathers' sakes. For the gifts and calling of God *are* without repentance [emphasis added]."

Paul is quoting the Old Testament to confirm how Christ is the Deliverer from Zion (Sion). He is the only one who can turn away ungodliness from Israel, His elect nation, as represented by Jacob's troubles of "trust." But the prophets reassure us that Israel's severed relationship with the Father will come full circle. The firstborn line in that day will, once again, be considered "of God." Once Christ renders judgment at His second coming, He will pronounce an everlasting decree upon the land. In sheer joy and celebration, rest and peace will follow His elect as they lead a joyous Jubilee right into the Millennial Kingdom, just as the Cain-line summary statement foretells.

From there, the focus turns to the restoration of all things under the New Covenant format. The next chapter tracks the epic conclusion to *HIS-Story* as it relates to the last portion of Revelation, to "sum up" all things in Him.

CHAPTER 12
THE CONCLUSION
"The Regeneration and Restoration of All Things"

The Long and Short of It

With the epic saga still fresh in our minds, it has become abundantly clear that His bloodline has the power to bring new life to His Book. Remarkably, *HIS-Story* has been buried deep within one of the most ancient portions of the Bible all this time. Just as archeologists carefully search out the treasures of the past to find its applications for today, so it would seem this same process applies to His book and His bloodline.

Incredibly, our efforts have not been in vain. As we pieced together the skeletal remains of the Christ-line from the pages of Genesis, new life burst forth to speak of Christ and His mission to save the two lost lines of Adam. From that perspective, Christ's Prodigal Son Parable became the perfect companion to Cain and Abel as the two lost sons of the Father in type. Their lost lines, then, proceeded to represent all lost families of the earth who are apart from the Christ-line.

Without the discovery of the Christ-line's ability to form a summary statement, we would never have found our starting point to this epic story. There would be no reason to compare Cain with the Christ-line and no motive for this book. Once we did, it was like opening Pandora's Box.

The biggest surprise of all was when the two bloodline charts interconnected horizontally to produce a Prophetic Timeline of the Ages (Chart 8). From there, the Christ-line functioned as a global timeline of the ages showing the way of escape for the two lost lines of Adam, which turned out to be Israel (the firstborn line) and the Christian Church (the younger, spiritual line). In this chapter, the epic saga will conclude as we trace the final events in Revelation that sums up *all things* in Him.

The Sons of Zion

The extreme differences between the two lines of Adam exemplify the concept of "Thy kingdom come; Thy will be done on earth as it is in heaven."

159

It is only by and through Christ that these material and spiritual realms exist, as well as intersect. Both lines will ultimately conform to His image as one. This visual helps us to understand why Firstborn National Israel inherits the visible portion, as represented by the cleansed earth, and why the Christian Church inherits the invisible or heavenly regions of Zion.

Curiously, the two lost sons exhibit their opposing positions, just like the Old and New Testaments of the Bible. Under the Old Covenant, Israel followed Moses as their great dispenser of the Law, which can only bring judgment and death.[241] The new Law of the Spirit had to wait until after the "Blessed God" came down to complete His work, so He could send His Spirit on the Day of Pentecost as described in Acts 2.

With the new Law of the Spirit, came a new dispenser, Paul (Saul of Tarsus). He was appointed by the risen Lord from a personal encounter while traveling on the road to Damascus.[242] Even Peter and the early church council in Jerusalem confirmed Paul's ministry was to the Gentiles[243] and that his letters contained the wisdom given to him from the resurrected Messiah.[244]

Christ commissioned Paul to teach "his gospel" and the mysteries,[245] as opposed to the Law.[246] Due to Israel's blind and bankrupt condition, they rejected Paul's gospel,[247] and their journey to the promised rest was, once again, postponed.[248] From there, Paul turned to preach "his gospel" to the uncircumcised,[249] which forms the spiritual body of Christ (or the Christian Church) as the younger brother to Israel.

With different ministries came different blood signs. The Christian Church adopted the Lord's Supper (Communion) to partake of Christ's body. This was done in symbolic form by the internal consumption of wine

---

[241] **2 Cor. 3:7-9:** The Law of Moses brought only the promise of death, even though it was carved on stones and given in a wonderful way. Still the Law made Moses' face shine so brightly that the people of Israel could not look at it, even though it was a fading glory. So won't the agreement that the Spirit brings to us be even more wonderful? If something that brings the death sentence is glorious, won't something that makes us acceptable to God be even more glorious? (CEV).

[242] Acts 9:1-19, 22:3-13, 26:12-18; 1 Cor. 15:7-8.

[243] **Gal. 2:7-8:** But contrariwise, when they saw that the gospel of the uncircumcision was committed unto me, as the gospel of the circumcision *was* unto Peter; (For he that wrought effectually in Peter to the apostleship of the circumcision, the same was mighty in me toward the Gentiles).

[244] 2 Pet. 3:15-16; 1 Cor. 3:10; Gal. 2:7-9.

[245] **Rom. 16:25:** Now to him that is of power to stablish you according to my gospel, and the preaching of Jesus Christ, according to the revelation of the mystery, which was kept secret since the world began.

[246] **Acts 26:16–18:** [Christ speaking to Saul of Tarsus] But rise, and stand upon thy feet: for I have appeared unto thee for this purpose, to make thee a minister and a witness both of these things which thou hast seen, and of those things in the which I will appear unto thee; Delivering thee from the people, and from the Gentiles, unto whom now I send thee, To open their eyes, and to turn them from darkness to light, and from the power of Satan unto God, that they may receive forgiveness of sins, and inheritance among them which are sanctified by faith that is in me.

[247] Re: Paul's gospel, see Rom. 2:16, 16:25; 2 Tim. 2:8. Re: Paul's ministry rejected, see Acts 28:17-27; 2 Tim. 4:16.

[248] Mt. 23:3-38; Rom. 11:25-28.

[249] **Acts 28:28:** Be it known therefore unto you, that the salvation of God is sent unto the Gentiles, and *that* they will hear it.

(His blood shed for all) and bread (His body broken). Israel, however, continued to apply externally, both the blood and circumcision and is publicly called to repentance by the sign of the Spirit of Elijah.

With different ministries, so come different paths. The Christian Church walks by faith and not by sight,[250] and must pick up their cross[251] to become living sacrifices[252] to follow Christ. Yet, the older brother, Israel, is left to wander in the outer field stuck "working" under the Law. However, provisions were made for the firstborn, as the last chapter concluded.

Due to Lamech's 70 x 7 forgiveness extension plan, the remnant of Israel can complete their three-part pilgrimage journey and Provocation Trial in one harvest season as required. Then they can lead the nations in a joyous jubilee into the Millennial Kingdom.

The First Resurrection and the Regeneration

With different paths, came different resurrections (escape methods) in their specific order. (1 Cor. 15:23). We learned how Israel's harvest system was the Garden Program's model of the harvesting of faith found on the earth.

Firstfruits, in the spring, begin the harvest season, which Christ and those released from the graves represent.[253] Then the rapture, or the catching up of the Christian Church, completes the summer harvest as represented by Pentecost in Acts 2.[254]

Lastly, the Feast of Tabernacles concludes the fall harvest, when Israel and any Gentile believers who overcome will be gathered and gleaned from the four corners of the earth,[255] during the 7-year tribulation period. Jesus spoke to Peter and His disciples about this deliverance and their role in that future time:

---

[250] **2 Cor. 5:6-7:** Therefore we are always confident, knowing that, whilst we are at home in the body, we are absent from the Lord: For we walk by faith, not by sight.

[251] **Mt. 16:24:** Then said Jesus unto his disciples, If any man will come after me, let him deny himself, and take up his cross, and follow me. Also see, 1 Cor. 15:31; Phil 1:21.

[252] **Rom. 12:1:** I beseech you therefore, brethren, by the mercies of God, that ye present your bodies a living sacrifice, holy, acceptable unto God, which is your reasonable service.

[253] **Mt. 27:50-53:** Jesus, when he had cried again with a loud voice, yielded up the ghost. And, behold, the veil of the temple was rent in twain from the top to the bottom; and the earth did quake, and the rocks rent; And the graves were opened; and many bodies of the saints which slept arose, And came out of the graves after his resurrection, and went into the holy city, and appeared unto many.

[254] 1 Cor. 15:51-53; 1 Thes. 4:13-18.

[255] **Isa. 11:11-12:** And it shall come to pass in that day, that the Lord shall set his hand again the second time to recover the remnant of his people, which shall be left, from Assyria, and from Egypt, and from Pathros, and from Cush, and from Elam, and from Shinar, and from Hamath, and from the islands of the sea. And he shall set up an ensign for the nations, and shall assemble the outcasts of Israel, and gather together the dispersed of Judah from the four corners of the earth.

Mt. 19:27-28: "Then answered Peter and said unto him, 'Behold we have forsaken all, and followed thee; what shall we have therefore?' And Jesus said unto them, Verily I say unto you, That ye which have followed me, in the regeneration when the Son of man shall sit in the throne of his glory, ye also shall sit upon twelve thrones, judging the twelve tribes of Israel."

From this conversation recorded in Matthew's Gospel, we learn two details about the Millennium Kingdom. The primary aspect to keep in mind is that the disciples will be given thrones in the Kingdom to assume the position as judges in the form of kings and priests. The second detail is just as important. Jesus spoke of the Kingdom period as the *regeneration*. The Regeneration speaks of the process of the restoration of all things as they were before the fall. We see a preview of this process in the Millennial Kingdom, where the disciples will take their promised positions. However, the regeneration will not be complete until the installation of the new Jerusalem within the realm of the new heaven and new earth, as described in the last two chapters of Revelation.

Out of all the passages that concern the resurrection, the most striking is the sign of Jonah. Oddly, there are only two passages in the Bible that the Jews recognize as direct sources to Christ's claim to being "The Resurrection and Life,"[256] which rely upon Jonah 1:17 and Hosea 6:2. Jonah gives a personal account of his own near-death experience and miraculous deliverance from death. His message and experience caused the whole city of Nineveh to repent and ultimately avoid destruction. From that context, Jesus applied His death and resurrection to Jonah's three days in the great fish.[257]

Hosea, on the other hand, speaks of a three-day resurrection concerning Israel, not Jesus. He saw Israel's resurrection in the context of a future captivity and exodus from it. Such a mental picture becomes reminiscent of the Babylonian and Egyptian themes in Revelation, as we learned in the previous chapter. Hosea's prophecy uncomfortably casts a dark shadow of judgment upon Israel, which leaves them in dire need of deliverance and new life.[258] His prediction suddenly mirrors Christ's death and resurrection:

---

[256] **Jn. 11:25-26:** Jesus said unto her, I am the resurrection, and the life: he that believeth in me, though he were dead, yet shall he live: And whosoever liveth and believeth in me shall never die. Believest thou this?

[257] Mt. 12:40; Lk. 11:29-30, 32.

[258] Ten Tribes of Israel by means of the Assyrian exile (722 BC).

The Conclusion

Hos. 6:1-2: "Come and let us return to Jehovah. For He has torn, and He will heal us. He has stricken, and He will bind us up. After two days He will bring us to life. In the third day He will raise us up, and we shall live before Him." (LITV).

Here, we observe how resurrection is not a Christian invention. It is an ancient Jewish understanding of Hosea 6:1-2 in connection with Jonah 1:17 to strengthen dispersed Israel's hope of completing their pilgrimage to the homeland. Since we learned that the last half of the tribulation period is Israel's final Provocation Trial in the wilderness, this idea of dispersion as denoted in Hosea fits nicely.

The reason Jesus compares His own substitutionary death and resurrection with Israel is that both are physical and public figures. Once again, we see the two sides of the same firstborn coin. This firstborn connection is why Israel's salvation and resurrection must occur on a national platform. This public resurrection requirement is not for the Christian Church. They are an invisible body placed on a mysterious timeline. They are appointed not unto wrath, but to meet Christ in the air, in a blink of an eye—an event the world will never comprehend, much less see.[259]

Before the Millennial Reign begins, John's apocalyptic vision includes these crucial details about this global and public resurrection:

Rev. 20:4-6: "And I saw thrones, and they sat upon them, and judgment was given unto them, and I saw the souls of those who were beheaded for the witness of Jesus...and they lived and reigned with Christ a thousand years. But the rest of the dead lived not again until the thousand years were finished. This is the first resurrection. Blessed and holy is he that hath part in the first resurrection: on such the second death hath no power but they shall be priests of God and of Christ, and shall reign with him a thousand years."

From this account, we get a glimpse of what John calls the "first resurrection." For starters, because this event occurs after the battle of Armageddon,[260]

---

[259] **1 Thes. 4:17:** Then we which are alive and remain shall be caught up together with them in the clouds, to meet the Lord in the air: and so shall we ever be with the Lord.

[260] Rev. 16:14-16, 19:11-21.

the first resurrection is a result of a worldwide legal judgment proceeding rendered upon the nations, of which Israel is the firstborn. Likewise, Israel's transformation is also set to occur at this same end-time judgment due to the "First will be Last" Principle.[261] The first resurrection is so named because it occurs last.

Note carefully how the first resurrection has two separate stages that are one thousand years apart. The first stage is the resurrection unto life, while the last stage is the resurrection unto damnation. Many think the identity of those on the thrones and the souls that were beheaded a bit confusing. Fortunately, John also records Jesus' thoughts on the subject in his letter, which provides additional clarification to help us avoid this confusion:

> **Jn. 5:26-29:** "For as the Father hath life in himself; so hath he given to the Son to have life in himself; And hath given him authority to execute judgment also, because he is the Son of man. Marvel not at this: *for the hour is coming, in the which all that are in the graves shall hear his voice, And shall come forth; they that have done good, unto the resurrection of life; and they that have done evil, unto the resurrection of damnation* [emphasis added]."

In this account, Jesus was careful to stay consistent with the two stages of the first resurrection, as depicted in Revelation 20. To maintain a proper perspective in this review, we must also keep in mind the resurrection order as dictated by Israel's harvest system as another standard on the subject. So, when Jesus said, "all that are in the graves shall hear His voice," this does not include those saints who arose from the graves shortly after Jesus was resurrected (Mt. 27:51-53). Nor does it include the catching-up of the Christian Church (I Thes. 4:17).

We must also keep in mind that the two separate stages of the first resurrection will involve two different groups of people that are collected alive or have died in the past as it relates to Israel. The first stage, remember, is called the resurrection unto life, and the second is the resurrection unto damnation (Jn. 5:29). Jesus refers to the first stage as "the resurrection of the just" (Lk. 14:14), and John tells us that they are "those that sat on the thrones and given unto judgment." (Rev. 20:4a). Again, we see a ruling

---

[261] Mt. 19:30, 20:16; Mk. 9:35, 10:31; Lk. 13:30.

class. Instantly, we think of Christ's promise to His disciples that thrones will be given to them in the regeneration when "The Son of Man" sits in glory in His Kingdom (Mt. 19:27-28), which would supplement this scene in Revelation (Rev. 20:4a).

Besides the ruling class who sits in judgment, Revelation 20 also speaks of the souls who died in the 7-year tribulation period. Both groups, the ruling class, and the tribulation martyrs, even though they died, they "lived [came to life], and reign with Christ for a thousand years, the rest of the dead did not come to life until the thousand years have concluded." (Rev. 20:4b-5).

With respect to the first group who "sat upon the thrones in judgment" (Rev. 20:4a), Daniel and "his lot" fit this description. From that perspective, we immediately understand why the angel told Daniel to "go thou thy way till the end be: for thou shalt rest and stand in thy lot at the end of the days." (Dan. 12:13). Remember, Daniel and his lot include the Old Testament saints, and any convert under the Kingdom Gospel, not those who are saved by Paul's Gospel of Grace.

The Regeneration During the Millennium Reign

The Millennial Kingdom will begin the times of refreshing. The "refreshing" will come from the presence of the Lord.[262] That is because of the blotting out of sins, which will occur in the year of His redeemed.[263] Christ's Millennial Reign is the time when the earth is delivered from its bondage of decay and restored to its original beauty, balance, peace, and rest.[264]

Carnivorous beasts will be a thing of the past.[265] Deadly animals will cease to be poisonous and a threat to humanity.[266] Plant life will flourish and produce bountifully.[267] The land of Israel will transform. Visitors will proclaim in amazement, "This desolate land has become like the garden of Eden."[268] In this Millennial Reign, Christ "shall rule them with a rod of

---

[262] Isa. 28:12; Acts 3:19-21.

[263] **Isa. 63:4:** For the day of vengeance is in mine heart, and the year of my redeemed is come.

[264] Isa. 11:10; Rom. 8:18-23.

[265] **Isa. 11:6:** The wolf also shall dwell with the lamb, and the leopard shall lie down with the kid; and the calf and the young lion and the fatling together; and a little child shall lead them.

[266] **Isa. 11:8-9:** And the sucking child shall play on the hole of the asp, and the weaned child shall put his hand on the cockatrice' den. They shall not hurt nor destroy in all my holy mountain: for the earth shall be full of the knowledge of the LORD, as the waters cover the sea.

[267] Isa. 35; Eze. 34:25-31.

[268] **Eze. 36:35:** And they shall say, This land that was desolate is become like the garden of Eden; and the waste and desolate and ruined cities are become fenced, and are inhabited.

iron,"[269] to manifest His glory and His strict rule as foretold about his coming Kingdom.[270] He will rule the nations from Mount Zion in Jerusalem, as we learned in the last chapter on Noah.[271]

During the Millennial Reign, His Spirit will be upon His people,[272] and their numbers will expand in abundance along with their land.[273] He will make them the head nation of the world.[274] They will serve as an object lesson of God's grace, "And it will come about that just as you were a curse among the nations, O house of Judah and house of Israel, so I will save you that you may become a blessing." (Zec. 8:13; LITV).

Because the rebels of Israel will be gone,[275] blessings will abound in the Kingdom. It will be said, "ten men shall take hold out of all languages of the nations, even shall take hold of the skirt of him that is a Jew, saying, We will go with you: for we have heard that God is with you." (Zec. 8:23).

At this time, the Christian Church, who comes back with the Lord in their new glorified bodies[276] at His second coming, will serve as worldwide administrators, civil judges, and spiritual tutors to those who enter the Kingdom in the flesh[277] (the tribulation survivors) and their children born to them.[278] Israel's birthright destiny as a nation of Kings and Priests[279] will be established within the Kingdom.[280]

Peace, righteousness, justice, and holiness will rule the day by the Prince of Peace and King of Righteousness, and "the earth will be full of the knowledge of the Lord as the waters cover the sea." (Isa. 11:9). Even the "bells on the horses' bridles and the pots in the kitchens will bear the inscription 'Holiness unto the Lord.'" (Zec. 14:20, 21). Nations will "hammer their swords into plowshares, and their spears into pruning hooks," and "will not lift up a sword, neither shall they learn war any more." (Isa. 2:4).

---

[269] **Rev. 19:15:** And out of his mouth goeth a sharp sword, that with it he should smite the nations: and he shall rule them with a rod of iron: and he treadeth the winepress of the fierceness and wrath of Almighty God.

[270] Isa. 66:18-24; Zec. 14.

[271] Dan. 7:13-14; Isa. 2:2-4; Zec. 14:8-11.

[272] Isa. 32:15, 44:3-7.

[273] Eze. 36:10-11.

[274] Isa. 60-62.

[275] Zep. 3:11-20.

[276] 1 Cor. 6:2-3; 2 Tim. 2:12; Jud. 1:14-15.

[277] Zec. 8:6-8; Isa. 24:6, 13, 59:20-60:4; Rom. 9:27; Rev. 11:13.

[278] Isa. 59:21, 65:20, 66:18-24; Jer. 3:14-17; Eze. 37:26; Zec. 8:5-8, 10:6-9.

[279] Deut. 7:6; Ex. 19:6; 1 Pet. 2:9; Rev. 1:6, 5:10.

[280] Mt. 19:28; Lk. 22:30.

The Conclusion

The Regeneration After the Millennium Reign

As glorious as the Millennium Kingdom will be, it must come to an end to give way to an even more glorious day—eternity. This process does not come without a price. The beginning of the end, as before, starts with Satan:

> **Rev. 20:7-10:** "And when the thousand years are expired, Satan shall be loosed out of his prison, And shall go out to deceive the nations which are in the four quarters of the earth, Gog and Magog, to gather them together to battle: the number of whom is as the sand of the sea. And they went up on the breadth of the earth, and compassed the camp of the saints about, and the beloved city: and fire came down from God out of heaven, and devoured them. And the devil that deceived them was cast into the lake of fire and brimstone, where the beast and the false prophet are, and shall be tormented day and night for ever and ever."

Here, we learn Satan is allowed one last chance to rally the nations against Divine authority. This event in Revelation draws us back to the Garden of Eden, except now the satanic deception falls upon nations who should know better instead of two innocent individuals, like Adam and Eve, who did not. Just as soon as the rally begins, it will end abruptly and quickly by fire sent from heaven.

Finally, Satan will be thrown into the lake of fire to stay for good. Then "The Resurrection and the Life,"[281] Himself, will come to implement the second stage of the first resurrection, being the resurrection unto damnation, which is executed at the Great White Throne. As the wicked-dead stand before the Lord Jesus Christ in their resurrected bodies fit for the lake of fire, the books will be opened and read. John continues:

> **Rev. 20:11-15:** "And I saw a great white throne, and him that sat on it, from whose face the earth and the heaven fled away; and there was found no place for them. And I saw the dead, small and great, stand before God; and the books were opened: and another book was opened, which

---

[281] **Jn. 11:25-26:** Jesus said unto her, I am the resurrection, and the life: he that believeth in me, though he were dead, yet shall he live: And whosoever liveth and believeth in me shall never die. Believest thou this?

is the book of life: and the dead were judged out of those things which were written in the books, according to their works. And the sea gave up the dead which were in it; and death and hell delivered up the dead which were in them: and they were judged every man according to their works. And death and hell were cast into the lake of fire. This is the second death. And whosoever was not found written in the book of life was cast into the lake of fire."

On this occasion, everyone will account for their public works as examined under the light of the Law. Like Satan, "the judged" will also be thrown into the lake of fire, next is death itself, and then hell. This event, John indicates, is the second death. From our human experience, we instinctively know that the first death is *physical*, but here in this passage, we have a glimpse of a second and final death, which is known as *spiritual* death. This idea constitutes a complete and total separation from the Almighty for all eternity.

Again, we point out that the Great White Throne event represents the fulfillment of Jesus' two parables about the separation of the wheat and tares[282] and the sheep and the goats.[283] Both parables are concerned with a vital process needed to conclude the harvesting of the earth.[284] After the Great White Throne Judgment adjourns, the next scene in Revelation is not only a new chapter, but it is also a new beginning that is in the realm of eternity. (Rev. 21).

The Restoration of All Things

Once both stages of the first resurrection are complete, which again are (1) resurrection unto life and (2) resurrection unto damnation (Jh. 5:29), John begins describing the new heaven and a new earth:

> **Rev. 21:2-3:** "And I John saw the holy city, new Jerusalem, coming down from God out of heaven, prepared as a bride adorned for her husband. And I heard a great voice out of heaven saying, Behold, the tabernacle of God is with men,

---

[282] **Mt. 13:40:** As therefore the tares are gathered and burned in the fire; so shall it be in the end (Gk. *Sunteleia* means consummation) of this world (Gk. *aion* means unbroken age, universe).

[283] **Mt. 25:41, 46:** Then shall he say also unto them on the left hand, Depart from me, ye cursed, into everlasting fire, prepared for the devil and his angels... And these shall go away into everlasting punishment: but the righteous into life eternal.

[284] See Section, *The Timeline Reset* in Chapter 10.

> and he will dwell with them, and they shall be his people,
> and God himself shall be with them, and be their God."

The setting of Revelation 21 is within the realm of eternity and in the context of the Kingdom of Zion. Zion occupies both heaven and earth, where the holy matrimony and the bride takes center stage in the form of the New Jerusalem coming down from God out of heaven to the new earth. She is an organic blend of both the land and the living; instantly occupied with the children of promise (Rom. 9:6-8, 24) as the product of the Garden union.

Scripture uses the Zion-Nuptial imagery to reinforce our understanding that we cannot rightly divide that which cannot be divided, namely Christ and His Church. There is no division in the eternal Kingdom. All are one, just as Adam and Eve along with "her seed" in the Garden were one. The following verses reflect the eternal view of the Garden union that incorporates the land with its generations:

> **Isa. 62:4:** "Thou shalt no more be termed Forsaken; neither shall thy land any more be termed Desolate: but thou shalt be called Hephzi-bah, and thy land Beulah: for the LORD delighteth in thee, *and thy land shall be married* [emphasis added]."

> **Jer. 3:14:** "Turn, O backsliding children [apostate sons], saith the LORD; *for I am married unto you: and I will take you one of a city, and two of a family,* and I will bring you to Zion [emphasis added]."

It is important to know that the "bride" is referred to as the Lamb's wife in Revelation Chapters 19 and 21 to indicate marital status. As already noted, Chapter 21 describes the glorified wife from an eternal perspective (Vs. 9) where Christ is the literal Tabernacle of Zion (Vs. 3). But just two chapters earlier (Rev. 19), we see the wife in her unglorified standing from the perspective of Christ's second coming and judgment of the nations of the earth as the literal Tabernacle on the Feast of Tabernacles. Without His final verdict, the heavenly throne could not joyfully pronounce, "Let us be glad and rejoice, and give honour to him: for the marriage of the Lamb is come, and his wife hath made herself ready." (Rev. 19:7). Therefore, the instant the "physical" bride in her unglorified standing is judged "ready" is the instant the couple officially becomes "one body" in a physical sense, which is what a marriage ceremony depicts figuratively.

Thanks to Revelation 19, the glorified wife in Chapter 21 can now be understood in the light of the New Jerusalem who comes from heaven to join the spiritual body of Christ (the Christian Church) with the physical body of Christ (Remnant of Israel). She immediately occupies both heaven and earth in one married personality unto Christ, the Last Adam.

The marriage supper of the Lamb is the crowning achievement for the epic saga of *HIS-Story*. Together, the glorified couple of Revelation 21, instantly yield children innumerable in the Kingdom. It is a breath-taking event that testifies to the success of the Garden Program of old. So, when Isaiah wrote, "Who hath heard such a thing? who hath seen such things? Shall the earth be made to bring forth in one day? or shall a nation be born at once? For as soon as Zion travailed, she brought forth her children," (Isa. 66:8), we can now somewhat understand.

The description of the New Jerusalem is depicted to extend three-dimensionally and measure approximately 1,500 miles high by 1,500 miles wide and by 1,500 miles long.[285] By that description, the magnitude and the grandeur of this city will automatically require a new heaven and a new earth. Revelation[286] goes on to describe the glory of the city in detail, which descended from heaven to rest on earth. Here is where the book of Hebrews provides some more information about this scene:

> **Heb. 12:20-24:** "For they could not endure that which was commanded, And if so much as a beast touch the mountain, it shall be stoned, or thrust through with a dart. And so terrible was the sight, that Moses said, I exceedingly fear and quake. [This is speaking of the terrifying experience at Mt. Sinai, when the Law was given to the Israelites.] But ye are come unto mount Sion [Zion], and unto the city of the living God, the heavenly Jerusalem,

---

[285] **Rev. 21:15-17:** And he that talked with me had a golden reed to measure the city, and the gates thereof, and the wall thereof. And the city lieth foursquare, and the length is as large as the breadth: and he measured the city with the reed, twelve thousand furlongs. The length and the breadth and the height of it are equal. And he measured the wall thereof, an hundred and forty and four cubits, according to the measure of a man, that is, of the angel.

[286] Rev. 21:11-27.

and to an innumerable company of angels, To the general assembly and church of the firstborn, which are written in heaven, and to God the Judge of all, and to the spirits of just men made perfect, And to Jesus the mediator of the new covenant, and to the blood of sprinkling, that speaketh better things than that of Abel."

This account compares Israel's first Provocation Trial in the wilderness under the Law at the base of Mount Sinai (Ex. 19) to a new Holy Mount, Zion, under grace. As we have consistently seen, Revelation describes this future happening where Sinai and the Law will be replaced entirely by a new Mount (Zion) and a New Covenant. This location will still be at "the chosen place of meeting," which becomes the eternal Tabernacle, who is Christ as their King. He is also said to be their literal Temple with God Almighty.[287]

Because the Law and Mount Sinai associate with the terrors of the majesty of God, this automatically puts man at a distance. No one was to approach Jehovah or even touch His mountain because the consequence was death to both man and animal. Even Moses feared and trembled at the presence of Jehovah. However, under grace, Zion is where Jesus, the Mediator of the New Covenant, sits as King on His throne cleansed with "the blood of sprinkling which speaketh better things than that of Abel." (Heb. 12:24).

John Darby points out,[288] that Zion, in principle, is the intervention of sovereign grace (His free gift, which is His Life) in the person of the King as applied to His Kingdom. The extent of the earth is far from being the limits of "The Son of Man" and His inheritance. Zion on earth is Jehovah's promised rest, but it will not be the whole "city of the living God," nor the whole of that rest. There will be a portion reserved in the heavenly aspect of Zion.

By using the term Zion, the author of the book of Hebrews associates the New Jerusalem from above to link us to a glorified, eternal perspective, which finds itself with more people of God amidst a multitude of angels. In this heavenly assembly, we see "the Firstborn Church of Heaven" (Heb. 12:23a). In other words, Darby says they are not from heaven like the angels, but they are the object of the council of the Godhead, to reach

---

[287] **Rev. 21:22:** And I saw no temple therein: for the Lord God Almighty and the Lamb are the temple of it.

[288] Darby, *Synopsis of the Bible*, Heb. 12-1-29.

heaven as well as to become glorious occupants and joint-heirs with Christ as the Firstborn of Creation (Col. 1:15).

The Christian Church is called to be "in Christ," and belongs to heaven by grace. Unlike Israel, they desire to be citizens of heaven, not the earth.[289] Heavenly blessings are prepared for the Body of Christ by God Himself.[290] Theirs is an adoption in "the Name," and a life in Him at the highest point.

John Darby then points out that having reached the highest point, Jehovah takes another seat. The Hebrew writer calls Him, the judge of all (Heb. 12:23b), who looks down from on high to judge all that is below. Here, another class of people of His Kingdom takes center stage, who just arrived. This "just arrived and overcoming" language is reminiscent of the remnant finishing their legalistic pilgrimage journey. Amid His people in the New Jerusalem, Christ will become their tabernacle and the restoration of all things.

> **Rev. 21:3a, 4b, 5:** "And I heard a great voice out of heaven saying, Behold, the tabernacle of God is with men... for the former things are passed away.... And he that sat upon the throne said, Behold, I make all things new. And he said unto me, Write: for these words are true and faithful. And he said unto me, It is done. I am Alpha and Omega, the beginning and the end. I will give unto him that is athirst of the fountain of the water of life freely. He that overcometh shall inherit all things; and I will be his God, and he shall be my son."

From this account, we see Christ as the literal Tabernacle (place of meeting) sitting on the throne of His Holy Kingdom. This post-apocalyptic scene reflects total reconciliation and the restoration of all things at that time. All the former things will be gone, and all will become new. In this scene, Christ as King of Kings declares that all things have been renewed.

The last chapter of Revelation provides some interesting features about the realm of eternity, which revolves around the throne of God and the

---

[289] 1 Cor. 15:47-49; 2 Cor. 5:2; 1 Thes. 4:17; 2 Thes. 1:7; Phil. 3:20-21.

[290] **Eph. 1:3-5:** Blessed be the God and Father of our Lord Jesus Christ, who hath blessed us with all spiritual blessings in heavenly places in Christ: According as he hath chosen us in him before the foundation of the world, that we should be holy and without blame before him in love: Having predestinated us unto the adoption of children by Jesus Christ to himself, according to the good pleasure of his will.

Lamb. It concludes with Jesus' last words of promise and warnings. With Revelation's final scene fresh in our minds, we turn to review its sum effect in terms of Daniel's 70 x 7 prophecy as it relates to Israel's extended time-line in addition to the two bloodline statements:

FULFILLMENT OF DANIEL'S PROPHECY (DAN. 9:24-27)

"Seventy weeks are determined upon thy people (Firstborn National Israel derived from the 12 biological sons of Jacob);
and upon thy holy city (Jerusalem/Zion);
to finish the transgression (Firstborn Cain's sin and 7-year right, Gen. 4:15);
and to make an end of sins (Adam's sin, Gen. 2:17);
and to make for iniquity (Israel's last pilgrimage journey and Provocation Trial);
and to bring in everlasting righteousness (By the ministry of reconciliation, 1 Cor. 5:18-19);
and to seal up the vision and prophecy (Daniel's book as well the whole Bible);
and to anoint the most Holy (Christ as King of Kings and Lord of Lords, 1 Tim. 16:15; Rev. 19:16).

FULFILLMENT OF THE CAIN-LINE PROPHECY

Man (Firstborn Cain/Israel, the firstborn line);
Acquired (Redeemed/bought by Christ as the Passover Lamb/Firstborn Replacement Son);
Dedicated-witness, (Firstborn Cain/National Israel's firstborn 'marked' destiny);
Declined fugitives, smitten by God, who is of God, (Cain/Israel, both blind and bankrupt in faith and dispersed in outer field on a pilgrimage journey to find rest);
Powerfully humbled (To become a second group of the Despairing);
the Despairing, (Apart from the Christ-line's group of the Despairing);
Leads a joyous jubilee (In the Millennial Kingdom and beyond).

FULFILLMENT OF THE CHRIST-LINE PROPHECY

Man (The first family, who represents all families of the earth born of fallen Adam);
Appointed Mortal Sorrow (All are born to die);
The Blessed God Shall Come Down (Christ's First Advent);
Teaching (Faith by Grace, the free gift of Christ as the Lamb slain from the foundation of the world);
His Death (Christ's finished work on the cross as the Lamb of God that taketh away the sin of the world, Jn. 1:29);
Shall Bring [the] Despairing (The two lost lines of Adam: "Circumcised Israel and Uncircumcised Christian Church are taken two by a family to Zion, Jer. 3:14);
Rest (Eternal life and promised rest in the Lord of the Sabbath).

Chart 12 – Conclusion Chart

From the conclusion of Chart 12, we can see how the summary statements from the Cain and Christ-line align perfectly with Daniel's prophecy and Christ's Messianic mission to seek and to save that which was lost. Together, both lines in the pre-flood period testify that the two lost lines of Adam will not only be found, but they will also find rest in their own despairing way and time. The words of Jehovah through Jeremiah ring true; *I am married unto you: and I will take you one of a city, and two of a family, and I will bring you to Zion.* (Jer. 3:14).

As we bring John's apocalyptic vision to a close, Jesus' self-pro-claimed title as "Alpha and Omega, and the Beginning and the End," will forever remain. He will reflect all things because all things will reflect Him. As the Word, He completes the books. In that context, His words hold true, "Behold old things have passed away, behold all things have become new."[291] With that, Jubilee's times of refreshing[292] will continue into eternity.

[291] 2 Cor. 5:17; Rev. 21:5.

[292] **Acts 3:19-21:** Repent ye therefore, and be converted, that your sins may be blotted out, when the times of refreshing shall come from the presence of the Lord; And he shall send Jesus Christ, which before was preached unto you: Whom the heaven must receive until the times of restitution of all things, which God hath spoken by the mouth of all his holy prophets since the world began.

Bibliography

Abarim-Publications. 2011. *Meaning and Etymology of the Names.* Accessed June 22, 2020. https://www.abarim-publications.com/Meaning/index.html#.XvFhkkBFw2w.

Baker, et al. 1992. *The Complete Word Study Dictionary.* Chattanooga: AMG International.

Barnes, Albert. 1847-85. *Notes on the Bible.* Public Domain.

Brenton, Sir Lancelot Charles Lee. 1851, 2020. "eBible.org (dba) Wycliffe, Inc." *Brenton English Translation Septuagint.* Accessed June 24, 2020. https://ebible.org/eng-Brenton/.

Brown, Francis, Samuel Rolles Diver, and Charles Briggs. 1906. *A Hebrew and English Lexicon of the Old Testament (BDB Commentary).* Public Domain.

Bullinger, D.D., E. W. 1984. *Commentary on Revelation.* Grand Rapids: Kregal Publications.

—. 1967. *Numbers in Scripture.* Grand Rapids: Kregel Publications.

—. 1611, 1922. *The Companion Bible, The Authorized Version of 1611.* Grand Rapids: Kregal Publications.

—. 1897. *The Divine Names and Titles.* Public Domain.

Butler, Trent C. 1991. *The Holman Bible Dictionary.* Nashville: Broadman & Holman.

Clarke, Adam. 1810-26. *Commentary on the Bible.* Public Domain.

Darby, John. 1857-62. *Synopsis of the Bible.* Public Domain.

Elwell, Walter A., ed. 1996. *Baker's Evangelical Bible Dictionary of Biblical Theology.* Grand Rapids: Baker Books, a division of Baker Book House Company.

—. 1984, 2001. *Evangelical Dictionary of Biblical Theology.* Grand Rapids: Baker Publishing Group.

Gill, John. 1748-63. *Exposition of the Bible.* Public Domain.

Ginzberg, Louis. 2002-2011. *The Jewish Encyclopedia; The unedited full-text of the 1906 Jewish Encyclopedia.* Accessed June 24, 2020. http://www.jewishencyclopedia.com/articles/1377-ambrose.

—. 1901. *The Legends of the Jews Volume 1, Translated by Henrietta Szold*. Public Domain.

Harcourt, Houghton Mifflin, Publisher. 2005. "Dictionary.Com." *The New Dictionary of Cultural Literacy, 3rd Edition*. Accessed June 24, 2020. https://www.dictionary.com/browse/due-process-of-law?s=t.

Henry, Matthew. 1708-1710. *Exposition of the Old and New Testaments (Commentary of the Whole Bible)*. Public Domain.

J. Hampton Keathley III, Th.M. 2004. "Bible.org ." *The Doctrine of Rewards: The Judgment Seat (Bema) of Christ*. May 25. Accessed June 24, 2020. https://bible.org/article/doctrine-rewards-judgment-seat-bema-christ#P28_4737.

Jasher, Prophet. 1984. *Jasher (The Upright Record)*. Glendale: Dolores Press, Inc.

Jones, Alfred. 1990. *Jones' Dictionary of Old Testament Proper Names*. Grand Rapids: Kregel Academic & Professional; Subsequent edition.

Judaica, Encyclopedia. 2008 The Gale Group. *The Jewish Virtual Library, A Project of AICE: Firstborn*. Accessed June 24, 2020. https://www.jewishvirtuallibrary.org/firstborn.

NOBSE. 1960, 1990. *The New Open Bible Study Edition (NIV)*. Nashville: Thomas Nelson Publishers.

Oliver, Peter LL.D. 1797. *The Scripture Lexicon, or a Dictionary of Above Four Thousand Proper Names of Persons and Places, Mentioned in the Bible: Divided Into Syllables with Their Proper Accents; with the Description of the Greater Part of Them. Also The Explaination of Many Words and Things in the Bible, Which are Not Generally Understood*. 4th Ed. London. Printed for R. and C. Rivington No. 62, St. Paul's Church Yard. Public Domain.

Pink, A. W. 1886-52. *The Doctrine of Election: The Grand Original*. Public Domain.

—. 1886-1952. *The Prodigal Son*. Public Domain.

Robert Jamieson, A.R. Fausset, and David Brown. 1871. *Critical and Explanatory on the Whole Bible (JFB Commentary)*. Public Domain.

Ryrie, Charles C. 1986, 1999. *Basic Theology*. Chicago: Moody Publishing.

Strong, James. 1890. *The Exhausive Concordance of the Bible*. Cincinnatti: Jennings & Graham. Public Domain.

Thayer. 1886, 1889. *Thayer's Greek Definitions*. Public Domain.

Bibliography

Walter A. Elwell, Ph.D., and Philip W. Comfort, Ph.D., eds. 2008. *Tyndale Bible Dictionary*. Coral Stream: Tyndale House Publishers, Inc.

Willmington, H. L. 1987. *Book of Bible Lists*. Coral Stream: Tyndale House Publishers.